In Oceania

IN OCEANIA

Visions, Artifacts, Histories

Nicholas Thomas

Duke University Press   Durham and London 1997

© 1997 Duke University Press
All rights reserved
Printed in the United States of America on acid-free paper ∞
Typeset in Scala by Keystone Typesetting, Inc.
Library of Congress Cataloging-in-Publication Data appear
on the last printed page of this book.

for Margaret Jolly

CONTENTS

LIST OF FIGURES

ACKNOWLEDGMENTS

This set of essays arises from many conversations in and about Oceania. The diversity of their subject matter is reflected in my debts, ranging from support of all kinds during fieldwork to assistance from many archivists and librarians.

I owe a great deal to the Australian Research Council for a Queen Elizabeth II Research Fellowship and a Senior Research Fellowship. Without these appointments and the support of the Australian National University, where I have been affiliated, I would never have been able to sustain the range of projects reflected in the chapters of this book. Some of the essays were initially written while I was at King's College, Cambridge; I am most grateful to the college for the fellowship and for research grants that enabled me to conduct the research in Fiji that is drawn upon here. I must again thank the Government of Fiji and the people of Korolevu village for giving me an opportunity to understand something of the Fijian way of life.

Many more people than I can name here contributed in one way or another to the refinement of earlier versions of these essays. I cannot, however, pass over a few people who have been consistently important to my work. I am sure that these texts themselves reveal how much I owe to the writings of Greg Dening, Marshall Sahlins, Marilyn Strathern, and Bernard Smith. The late Roger Keesing was consistently generous and encouraging; I have gained a great deal from conversations with Bronwen Douglas, Klaus Neumann, and Matthew Spriggs, and with Robert Foster, to whom I am also indebted for two sets of comments on this book. The revision of these essays has been invigorated by conversations over the last few years with Maori and Polynesian artists in Aotearoa, New Zealand, particularly Brett Graham, John Pule, and Jim Vivieaere. I owe more than I can say to Margaret Jolly for her intellectual advice, partnership, and support; our daughter Anna's companionship has been no less important to me.

I must also thank Richard Eves and Jenny Newell for bibliographic and editorial assistance in the final stages of preparing this manuscript, and Ken Wissoker and Richard Morrison at Duke for their encouragement and assistance.

I am grateful to the publishers of previous versions of these essays for their permission to reproduce the texts, which in almost all cases have been revised or updated, though for reasons explained in the introduction, I have not attempted to homogenize the style or disguise the fact that their earlier intended audiences were diverse. Chapter 1 is based on an article published in the *Journal of Pacific History* 25 (1990): 139–58. Chapter 2 initially appeared as "Alejandro Mayta in Fiji: Narratives about Millenarianism, Colonialism, Postcolonial Politics, and Custom," in Aletta Biersack, ed., *Clio in Oceania: Toward a Historical Anthropology* (Washington: Smithsonian Institution Press, 1991); somewhat different versions of chapter 3 appear as "Liberty and License: The Forsters' Accounts of New Zealand Sociality," in Chloe Chard and Helen Langdon, eds., *Transports: Travel, Pleasure, and Imaginative Geographies, 1600–1830* (New Haven, N.J.: Yale University Press/Paul Mellon Center for Studies in British Art, 1996), and in Jonathan Lamb and Bridget Orr, eds., *Voyages and Beaches* (Honolulu: University of Hawaii Press, in press). Chapter 4 has not been previously published but incorporates material from "Licensed Curiosity: Cook's Pacific Voyages," in John Elsner and Roger Cardinal, eds., *The Cultures of Collecting* (London: Reaktion Books; Cambridge, Mass.: Harvard University Press; Melbourne: Melbourne University Press, 1994). Chapter 6 appeared in *Meanjin* 51, no. 2: 265–76; chapter 7 in the *Age Monthly Review* 8, no. 11: 15–8; chapter 8 in *American Ethnologist* 19, no. 2: 213–32; and chapter 9 in Margaret Jolly and Nicholas Thomas, eds., *The Politics of Tradition in the South Pacific,* a special issue of *Oceania* (vol. 62, no. 4: 317–29).

In Oceania

INTRODUCTION:
TUPAIA'S MAP

The Polynesian priest and chiefly advisor Tupaia comes across in the writings of James Cook, Joseph Banks, Johann Reinhold Forster, and others as a man in their own inquiring mode. From a family of navigators on Raiatea but resident on Tahiti, he was certainly enough of a voyager to want to join the *Endeavour* when the ship departed from Tahiti in July 1769. Cook "found him to be a very intelligent person and to know more of the Geography of the Islands situated in these seas, their produce and the religion laws and customs of their inhabitants then [*sic*] any one we had met with" (1955–74, 1:117). Banks anticipated his assistance as both a pilot and an interpreter in dealings with other Polynesians, but had more dilettantish reasons for wanting to "collect" the man. "Thank heaven," he wrote, "I have a sufficiency and I do not know why I may not keep him as a curiosity, as well as some of my neighbours do lions and tygers at a larger expence than he will probably ever put me to; the amusement I shall have in his future conversation and the benefit he shall be to this ship . . . will I think fully repay me" (1962, 1:312–3).

Johann Reinhold Forster never met Tupaia, who died in Batavia in December 1770, but saw him rather as an informant, or even a cointerpreter of Oceanic geography and linguistics. When Forster was writing his monumental series of reflections on the human species in the Pacific, he made much use of a map (fig. 1) that Tupaia had prepared on the *Endeavour,* and he "caused [it] to be engraved as a monument of the ingenuity and geographical knowledge of the people in the Society Isles, and Tupaya [Tupaia] in particular" (Forster 1996, 310–1).

Tupaya the most intelligent man that was ever met with by any European navigator in these isles . . . when on board the Endeavour, gave an account

A CHART

representing the

ISLES of the SOUTH-SEA,

according to

the NOTIONS of the INHABITANTS of

o-TAHEITEE

and the Neighbouring Isles, chiefly

collected from the accounts of

TUPAYA.

Opa-tooe-rou (North)

Meridian of 150° W. from Greenwich

I. of Danger or S. Bernardo

o-Ahouron 55

o-Rai-havai 53

o-Rima-tarra 52

o-Toomoo-papa 56

o-Karo-toa 54

o-Adeeha 49

Ururutu 48

Touteepa 57

o-Ahoua-hou 50

Navigators I.

o-Reeva-vai 58

o-Weeha 51

Woureeo 47

Mopeeha 44

Whennua-oora 45

o-Papatea 46

Tubai 20

Tereati Tootera (West)

Tainuna 59

o-Rotooma 61

Scilly I.⁹

Howo I.

Mourooa 11
Bowbora 19
o-Isha 18
Ulinehene 13
Raietea 17
Tedhu

Tahina-manua
I. Charles Saunders I.

o-Poppoa 62

Palmerstones I.

o-Rimatema 60

64 Te-Toopa-tupa-eahou

Hervey I.
Moe-no-tayo 63

o-Hittepotto 65

Savage I.⁹

o-Hitte-toutou-atu 66

Oheavai 78

o-Hittetoutounee 67

Te-Errepoo-opo-mattehea 77

o-Hitte-toutou-rera 68

Ooparroo 76

Wouwou 75

Ohiteroa 12

Te-Orooro-Mativatea 74

o-Tootoo-erre 73

o-Hitte-taiterre 69

Te-Amaroo-hitte 70

Te-Atou-hitte 71

Ouowhea 72

N. The
by u

Opa-toa   South

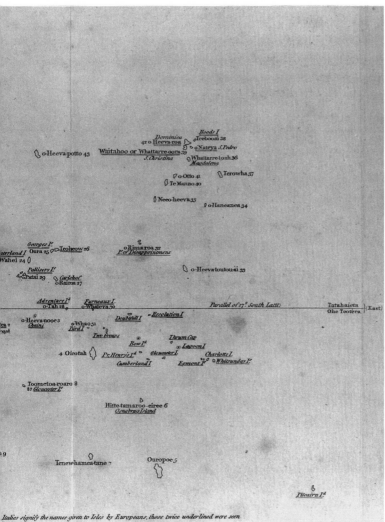

Italics signify the names given to Isles by Europeans, those twice underlined were seen
evolution, 1773 & 1774, those once were seen by other Navigators.

1. "A Chart Representing the Isles of the South Sea, according to the notions of the inhabitants of O-Taheitee and the neighbouring Isles, chiefly collected from the accounts of Tupaya." Published in Johann Reinhold Forster, *Observations Made during a Voyage round the World* (London: 1778), to face p. 513 (see also Forster 1996). Tupaia drew a map himself, but it is not extant; several copies were made of it, including one apparently by Cook that is now in the British Library. This engraving appears to have been executed after a different copy (see David 1988, 130–3; Cook 1955–74, 1:291–4 for further information).

of his navigations and mentioned the names of more than eighty isles which he knew, together with their size and situation, the greater part of which he had visited, and having soon perceived the meaning and use of charts, he gave directions for making one according to his account, and always pointed to that part of the heavens, where each isle was situated, mentioning at the same time that it was either larger or smaller than Taheitee, and likewise whether it was high or low, whether it was peopled or not, adding now and then some curious accounts relative to some of them (Forster 1996, 310).

Though Tupaia's map has figured as a key source for subsequent inquiries into the geographic knowledge of Polynesians, its extraordinary character as a graphic document that fuses an indigenous perception of the world with the moralizing cartography of the Enlightenment has been strangely unremarked upon. In Forster's work, among that of other Linnaean travelers, the recruitment of native informants was at once a gesture of scientific imperialism and an insistence upon their shared humanity and their common stake in beneficial knowledges. If natural history typically imposed Linnaean universals over indigenous classificatory schemes, this chart is surely a singular exception: though it was not suggested that Tupaia's understanding of Oceania was as valid as a scientific mapping, his vision was presented in its integrity. In the two centuries subsequent to this foundational moment of intellectual contact, Polynesian and European understandings of place would very rarely be drawn together in this way again. The map could be seen as the exception that proves the rule. In general, European and indigenous imaginings—of history and place—have intersected, not merged.

I thought of Tupaia's map when I read a recent essay by the eminent Tongan scholar and writer of fiction Epeli Hau'ofa. In "Our Sea of Islands," he argues that expatriate academics have generally represented the Pacific as a region of tiny islands, mutually isolated in a huge ocean, too small to escape a cycle of economic dependency. He suggests that it is time to adopt a more affirmative understanding of the region, one that emerges from the travel and exchange that were endemic precolonially:

The difference between the two perspectives is reflected in the two terms used for our region: Pacific Islands and Oceania. The first term, "Pacific Islands," is the prevailing one used everywhere; it connotes small areas of land surfaces sitting atop submerged reefs or seamounts. Hardly any anglophone economist, consultancy expert, government planner or development banker in the region uses the term "Oceania," perhaps because it sounds grand and somewhat romantic . . . "Oceania" connotes a sea of islands with their inhabitants. The world of our ancestors was a large sea full of places to explore, to make their homes in, to breed generations of seafarers like themselves. People raised in this environment were at home in the sea . . . They developed great skills for navigating their waters, and the spirit to traverse even the few large gaps that separated their island groups (1993, 8).

This contemporary vision is not that of Hau'ofa alone but is shared by a remarkable group of Pacific people, mariners who have established voyaging societies in Hawaii, the Cook Islands, Micronesia, and elsewhere and who have reconstructed traditional canoes, resurrected indigenous navigational knowledge, and made extraordinary journeys from one end of settled Oceania to the other. These projects are akin to many other efforts to recover tradition, but they are special because they do not affirm particular peoples in a nationalist mode as much as they celebrate the connections between peoples. The history of contact and exchange is foregrounded in particular in *Vaka*, a novel by Tom Davis (1992) that reconstructs the histories of famous canoes and their movements between Samoa, Rarotonga, Tonga, the Marquesas, and elsewhere. Davis, a former prime minister of the Cook Islands, wrote the book over the same period as the first of the Cook Islands Voyaging Society's vessels, the *Takitumu,* was built; he then proceeded to navigate that vessel. As a focus of cultural expression, the canoe is not limited to a particular genre or a particular region: witness the tee-shirt (fig. 2) again from the Cook Islands, and the remarkable sandstone canoe by contemporary Maori sculptor Brett Graham (fig. 3). But canoes also remain objects of quotidian and ceremonial use, in rivers as well as seas and lagoons, for the Gogodala of the Papuan Gulf, among other Oceanic peoples (fig. 4).

Inspired by these artifacts and visions, this book is called *In Oceania.* It evokes not a cartographic abstraction of scattered islands but a sea full of places that were intimately connected by relations of traffic and colonization, that moreover were theaters for imagining. My emphasis is perhaps less on romantic imaginings of place and identity in Oceania than on the full range of outsiders' and insiders' constructions—some pessimistic or cynical, others seemingly detached and ethnological; some committed to the way of tradition, others to indigenous versions of modernity—but I engage with these representations as they have been played out in the region. Tupaia's map is a constitutive beginning for this exercise because it is also a European document, but one that prompts us to ask questions about European culture from an Oceanic vantage point. These are essays in what some scholars insist on calling "Pacific studies," but

Pacific studies, as I understand it, includes not only the extensions of European culture and government in the Pacific, but also, in a sense, Europe itself.

These essays are not about "images of" Pacific islanders; instead, they deal with constructions of indigenous culture that have been fashioned both by a variety of outsiders and by islanders themselves. These constructions are not inventions or mystifications, but they are artifacts of rhetoric and imagination. They are not static stereotypes but often narratives that can be seen as historical or metahistorical in the sense that they evoke pasts and futures, trajectories of progress or decline, and moral comparisons between old lives and new, between

2. Tee shirt produced by the Cook Islands Voyaging Society, 1996.

3. Brett Graham, *Te Hekenganui*, stone and wood. 130 × 96 × 33 cm. Courtesy Artis Gallery, Auckland, and Brett Graham. Photo: Mark Adams.

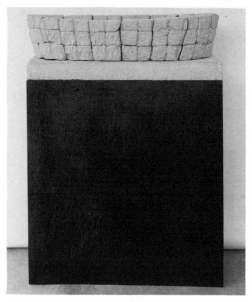

4. Two Gogodala racing canoes, shown after a race held on Papua New Guinea Independence Day celebration, September 16, 1995. The canoe in the foreground is from a red
clan, Gasinapa, and is called Kanaba. The second canoe is from a white clan,
Lalamana, and is called Bainale. This race was held at Balimo, Western Province, and
celebrated the twentieth year of Papua New Guinea's Independence. The male paddlers
have already departed to join the women in dancing and feasting at the Balimo football
field. Photo: Alison Dundon.

the ways of natives and those of whites. This storytelling has been engaged in by
Enlightenment explorers, evangelical missionaries, other colonists, fiction and
travel writers, historians, anthropologists, and of course Pacific islanders—as
political actors in the rapidly changing situations of early contact, as villagers
under the colonial order, as Christians practicing a Pacific rather than a British
or a European religion, as contemporary writers and painters. Some of these
narratives have been structured by indigenous plots (the enhancement of a
warrior-chief's reach and *mana*) and others might be seen as "Western" in
origin (progress toward civility, conversion to Christianity, modernization, self-
government, and—in a more negative register—"fatal impact," deculturation,
and decay). In most cases they have been shaped by both the singularity of the
place and by intrusive European forms: they are products of cultural exchange
and appropriation.

This inquiry into representations of Oceania embraces both scholarly accounts of Pacific cultures and histories and a range of other colonial and indigenous discourses concerning the same objects. I respect the specificity and
distinctiveness of academic knowledge but assume that it relates to other perceptions and ideas in a complex way—sometimes unreflectively adopting wider
preoccupations and prejudices; sometimes critically engaging them. Since the
eighteenth century, natural historians, scientific travelers, and anthropologists

have often been at pains to differentiate their interests from those of common or commercial travelers and from tourists, just as the latter have equally often sought to elevate trafficking in artifacts, pornographic photography, and morbid curiosity about cannibalism to the level of ethnography. I am concerned both with artifacts in the literal sense and in the rhetorical artifacts of discourse that have also been collected and burdened with new meanings in new contexts.

As I have already signalled, this book is also about the ways in which Oceanic identities and histories *should* be represented. It engages critically with historical and anthropological ways of knowing the Pacific and argues for certain reorientations. I also discriminate among representations of island societies in exhibitions, travel books, and novels and suggest that some of these representations stigmatize the present as a scene of derivative inauthenticity, while others effectively acknowledge and negotiate Pacific varieties of modernity and cultural hybridization. But I do not assume that there is any simple sense in which certain ways of representing cultural differences and cultural conjunctures are more adequate or—however this might be measured—politically desirable than others. I have been motivated both by a critique of anthropology and by a sense of the strength of localized anthropological knowledge, relative to the textual style of criticism characteristic of much postcolonial theory and the distanced perspective on Oceanic culture and history found in disciplines such as political science and international relations.

If anthropologists long neglected and disparaged creolized cultural forms, the pendulum has now definitely swung the other way: hybridity is widely celebrated. The concept may be more apt to the range of identities that are expressed today, but it also perhaps detracts from the capacity of Pacific indigenous peoples to mobilize and represent themselves. As Simon During has written,

> the thrust of postcolonial theory does not always serve the interests of the communities most damaged by colonialism . . . postcolonial theory argues, first, that there is no simple continuity between pre- and post-contact eras, and secondly, that after contact each group can only articulate its identity in relation to the other. Thus, to take two examples close to home, by its logic there is no authentic and long-lasting "Aboriginality" to which Kooris can now attach except mythically; and the concept of the "sacred," which is so important to the protection of certain Koori spaces from economic exploitation, is a Western one that transforms the Koori life-practices it is used to describe and defend (1992, 350).

In the Pacific, this was made evident not long ago by the controversy surrounding Allan Hanson's interpretation of "the making of the Maori."[1] His essay on that theme appeared in the *American Anthropologist* and was extensively reported and excerpted in New Zealand newspapers; it also received some press in the United States and Australia. Hanson began by noting that it had become widely understood that "cultures" and "traditions" were not stable realities but inventions "designed to serve contemporary purposes"; his specific concern was with the role of anthropologists in the process of invention, which he attempted to illuminate through reference to legendary accounts of the Maori migration to New Zealand and the notion that Maori religion possessed a supreme deity, Io. Hanson found that the myth of a "Great Fleet" migration had been advocated by white scholars such as Percy Smith in the late nineteenth and early twentieth centuries. While the Maori certainly arrived in New Zealand by canoe from central Polynesia, "the notion of an organized expedition . . . in about 1350" was one of a number of "fabrications" derived from an amalgam of Maori myths that were not taken to be historically factual by nineteenth-century Maori themselves (however, Hanson did not discuss what notions of factuality were salient or suggest what attitude Maori did have to the myths, if they did not regard them as true) (Hanson 1989, 891–2).

Hanson proceeded to point out that a number of recent Maori writers took the traditions to be historically precise and seemed unaware of the white role in their creation; the traditions moreover figured in the renaissance of Maori culture associated with the term Maoritanga. In his conclusion, Hanson insisted that "the analytical task is not to strip away the invented portions of culture as inauthentic, but to understand the process through which they acquire authenticity" (1989, 898). But while the anthropological deconstructionist here sought to distance himself from any critical debunking of Maori culture, he was reported as having identified calculated invention, rather than a more diffuse process of cultural reformulation and recreation. According to the *Australian,* a right-wing newspaper (though not one always opposed to indigenous claims in Australia), Maoritanga "has been deliberately designed to contrast with the most unattractive aspects of pakeha (white) culture" (26 February 1990). Unsurprisingly, Hanson's arguments met with an angry response from many Maori, such as the prominent academic, journalist, and activist Ranginui Walker. Walker complained about the level of foreign anthropological interest in the Maori, and he rejected Hanson's arguments: "Normal cultural change has occurred in response to new circumstances but there was no question of invention" (*New Zealand Herald,* 1 March 1990).

One reading of the debate would be that the article was interpreted in terms of the logic of authenticity and inauthenticity that it sought to question. Criticism became inevitable when the effort to describe a process of invention was reduced to one that discriminated between the genuine and the invented. This might be apt if Hanson's general claims reflected the style of the whole essay, but there was evidently a tension within his text; the discussion of the Great Fleet and related episodes did, in fact, carry the aura of an exposé. Perhaps more significantly, there was, between the lines, a sense of resentment over the power being acquired by Maori reinterpreters of Maori tradition: "Many Maoris . . . insist that they, not Pakehas, be the proper custodians and managers of knowledge about the Maori heritage . . . some advocates of Maoritanga have invited Pakeha scholars out of Maori studies . . . " (Hanson 1989, 894).

Hanson noted that some Pakeha scholars had supported "the present invention of Maori culture" by "according special authority to Maoris in matters pertaining to Maori culture," that "steps have been taken to avoid offending Maori sensibilities," and that "Maoris insisted that art objects produced by their ancestors are tribal treasures . . . [so that] tribal proprietary rights became an important issue in the mounting of 'Te Maori' [the major exhibition of Maori artifacts of the early eighties]" (1989, 895–6). He insinuated that these stances are self-evidently unreasonable and that the cultural renaissance as a whole is politically tarnished: "The present image has been invented for the purpose of enhancing the power of Maoris in New Zealand society" (897). We are invited to visualize a handful of power-hungry Maori activists sitting around a table in a smoke-filled room, flipping through the pages of discredited texts of colonial ethnology and cynically figuring out what it might be most convenient to invent next.

On a more charitable reading, Hanson's article seems a somewhat confused attempt to develop a deconstructionist perspective on cultural change in the Pacific. It put forward the credible claim that culture needs to be seen as a continually reinvented array of meanings, yet it valorized "invention" as a calculated and interested act rather than as a broader and partly unself-conscious process that responded to novel governmental and institutional circumstances, new practical and ideological resources, and political imperatives. It found Maori culture to be politicized, yet failed to acknowledge that American anthropologists might have their own stakes in the situation, stakes that directly conflict with the assertion of Maori control over Maori studies. I too might object to the exclusivist position that only Maori should be permitted to conduct research into Maori history and culture, but this is in fact enunciated far more rarely than the view that researchers must be accountable in ways that are defined through practical, case-by-case negotiation. In lieu of an array of difficult questions concerning conduct that any prospective ethnographer or historian must now address, Hanson evokes the spectre of a rigid identity politics that he refrains from explicitly criticizing.

While the article aspired to deconstruct the logic of authenticity, that logic was preserved in critical language that stressed the "fabricated" and "invented" character of the representations at issue and that could only subvert Maori claims in New Zealand political argument. At best, the article was innocent of the significance of traditionalism and cultural authenticity in the broader political context, despite the fact that this was part of its subject matter. At worst, the paper could be seen as a disingenuous attempt to regain authority in a contest over who can legitimately represent Maori culture. Hanson later expressed his support for the Maori aspiration to make New Zealand into a "truly bicultural" society (*New Zealand Herald,* 24 February 1990), a sentiment that may further attest to the difficulties experienced by postmodern anthropologists in reconciling liberal political commitments they are unable to disavow, professional territorialism they are unable to avow, and theoretical fashions they are unable to see beyond.

As During noted, this kind of conflict between deconstructionist and postcolonial theory and indigenous communities cannot be resolved in a theoretical or general way. The issues may, however, be better negotiated if "postcolonial" cultural conjunctures can be described differently, in ways that do not equate hybridity with a lack of authenticity or that chart the senses in which the uses of the "sacred" (to go back to During's example of Aboriginal culture) draw upon both indigenous and Western (or European settler) cultural realities. If postcolonial theory generates arguments that have problematic or positively pernicious political implications for indigenous political actors, this may be so because there is a clash between credible knowledge and sound politics, but it may also be the case because the postcolonial arguments are simply *wrong.* It would hardly be surprising, after all, if theorists primarily concerned with the critical rereading of European texts remained caught within metropolitan categories and overestimated the efficacy and reach of colonial discourses.

While the tenet of postcolonial theory that During refers to—"that after contact each group can only articulate its identity in relation to the other"—provides a useful corrective to any more simple notion that identities are somehow self-subsistent, it must be appreciated that identities are contextual and that the relation between colonizer and colonized does not exhaust or specify the whole range of indigenous identity or self-consciousness: in some cases an indigenous group may be concerned primarily to articulate its distinctiveness, not in relation to white colonizers but in relation to other indigenous groups. "Contact" is not an all-or-nothing, one-shot event that transforms the world: it is a process, and some phases of that process have far more limited ramifications than others.

This problem can be contextualized in the wider field of anthropological thought in the following way. It may be suggested crudely that anthropology, always a discipline that aspired to range globally, has embraced four forms of cross-cultural comparison. One of these has entailed adopting various universalisms and citing material from a range of societies in an effort to demonstrate underlying commonalities in human culture, cognition, or society. Lévi-Strauss's structuralism has been the most influential of recent anthropological universalisms. Secondly, evolutionism places diverse cultures into a single frame by ranking them on such grounds as scale and technical advancement. Although this hierarchical ordering is associated above all with nineteenth-century thought, in which claims for the growth of civilization were advanced less hesitantly than either before or subsequently, it has retained eloquent proponents such as Ernest Gellner. Many theories of modernity and postmodernity either unwittingly lapse back into "great divide" accounts that radically juxtapose the west and the rest, or reformulate those contrasts in more sophisticated and perhaps defensible terms.

Evolutionism has long been contradicted by anthropological relativism, which refused hierarchies of cultures and races and insisted on the equivalent worth and interest of all cultures. Associated especially strongly with Boas and Mead, relativism remains foundational to much anthropological comparison. Many anthologies concerned with particular topics such as sexuality, mortuary ritual, kingship, and so on lay a range of cases side by side, each taken from one "culture" or another, and they are treated as equivalent entities, each an island of data. There is, therefore, a methodological relativism, basic to much anthropology, that need not embrace relativism in an ethical or philosophical sense.

Much has been said, of course, about the ethical conundra that this relativism confronts when dealing with issues such as clitoridectomy and about its inadequacy in grasping cognitive universals, among other problems. I am not concerned to pursue these issues here. Historical anthropology has been built out of a kind of comparative method that is neither universalist, evolutionist, nor relativist. A body of recent scholarship sees Western and non-Western societies neither in terms of the relativists' abstract difference nor the ranked space-time of evolutionism, but rather in the context of relations in history. Ethnographic phenomena such as caste in India and exchange in Melanesia are seen not simply as purely different social forms to those of the West, but as historically shaped social and cultural phenomena. Colonialism is seen to have loomed large in the historical shaping of these practices, not in a direct and monocausal sense that would make caste or "the gift" an artifact of European discourse or European intervention, but perhaps rather because it has given those institutions the particular forms that ironically strike Europeans as most unfamiliar and exotic. Europeans and non-Europeans, in other words, are mutually entangled.

This point is made in part toward an autocritique. In some publications (e.g., Thomas 1992b) I now see that I overemphasized—in contradiction to the ahistorical comparisons of relativism—the entanglement of cultures and the local effects of colonialism. It was not or should not have been my intention to suggest that entanglement was efficacious *in principle*. It is not defensible to propose that local cultures' constituent structures, dispositions, values, and so forth were generally and pervasively influenced by contact with colonial discourses and institutions. The stance I adopted, which prescribed that neotraditional or postcontact cultures were organized reactively—that is, in opposition to those of the colonizing order—was in effect too similar to what During noted was the postcolonial tenet—that identities are articulated relationally. This must be true as a universal proposition, but it is evidently not true that indigenous peoples, or any others, need constantly express their identities in relation to colonizers rather than to each other, or in relation to other indigenous peoples or nonindigenous peoples other than the colonizers (e.g., nondominant migrants). Nor, obviously, is an articulated identity to be equated with culture in general: practices associated with the birth of a child, for example, may certainly become vehicles of cultural affirmation, but they also have a whole range of more specific meanings that are perhaps never subsumed by ethnic politics.

Hence, while it is vital that cultural inquiries are situated in wider cross-cultural histories, entanglement should not be elevated as a comparative principle. The effects of colonialism need to be traced, as do the ramifications of contact with indigenous cultures for metropolitan societies, but it cannot be presumed, as Sahlins (1993) pointed out with respect to my earlier discussion of the Fijian practice of *kerekere* (1992b), that indigenous institutions have been pervasively altered or shaped by an oppositional logic simply because contact has taken place.

The point to grasp about entanglement is that histories may be linked but not shared. This is surely attested to by the European representations of the Pacific that I discuss in the middle part of this book. The narratives and images I explore were prompted in many of these cases by practical encounters, but what is striking is that European accounts and arguments, though marked by exchange in the Pacific, in the end speak from cultural ground that is fundamentally distant from the perceptions of the peoples with whom the writers and artists I discuss came into contact. Conversely, though Maori, Fijians, and others have been influenced in many ways by intrusive discourses and institutions, their socialities remain intractably different from those colonizers sought to impose. Historical anthropology must be concerned both with the limits as well as the effects of cultural exchange.

Jean-François Lyotard has argued that one of the distinctive features of the postmodern epoch is a "decline of grand narratives," meaning particularly that the growth in consumerism and the decline of the nation-state as a container for people's biographies and an object of loyalty undermined various patriotic, progressive, and emancipationist projects (1984, 37–8). Given the extent to which grand self-imaginings and projected futures rely upon binary worlds of darkness and light, tyranny and freedom, tradition and advancement, this may be more true now than when Lyotard first put the claim forward: in the interim we have witnessed the end of Eastern European socialism and the concomitant disorientation of the conservative politics that were largely defined against it. It is at these moments that we realize, in Cavafy's unforgettable figure, that the barbarians were a kind of solution. The crisis of narratives produced or compounded by a breakdown of "us and them" juxtapositions is not peculiar to the postmodern epoch: Linda Colley has argued persuasively that eighteenth-century British national identity was above all a Protestant identity forged through a condition of hostility and often through actual wars against Catholic enemies within and without (Jacobite and French); the political loyalties thereby fashioned were thrown into disarray after 1774, when the enemy was not Catholic and continental or Irish, but the Protestant United States (1992, 137–43).

In the Pacific, the grand narrative that has conspicuously been diminished is that of decolonization. If colonialism enforced an array of binary distinctions and value judgments, it also enabled emancipatory inversions and shifts of those judgments that provided nationalists with obvious strategies and targets. Oppositional politics was no doubt valid and necessary, but it could only lose its salience once a formal colonial relationship, an opposition between natives and *mastas*, whites and indigenous peoples, was displaced by a plethora of neo-colonial hegemonies. Decolonization, in the sense of the transfer of state power, of course does not necessarily produce more equitable relationships—no more than women's suffrage marks an end to sexual inequality—but it does produce a more complex set of power relations and forms of dominance that often do not readily admit a narrative of progress or emancipation. The figure of the hybrid may be peculiarly important to such a shift. Just as the "half-caste" produced a variety of problems for colonial hierarchies and legislative classifications, the person who is a native but a bureaucrat, or a native but "Westernized" and wealthy, or a Polynesian but an artist who works with "Western" media, may be difficult to conceive of as a legitimate and authentic cultural actor from perspectives that emphasize the importance of sustaining, representing, and living one's culture. In the next chapter, I consider examples that are still more difficult, such as the man who is "in fact" a half-caste (as if the issue concerned facts rather than representations), who is also both a big-man in the Papua New Guinea highlands and a white plantation-owner. His history has been told, but it is, I suggest, almost an illegible history because Joe Leahy cannot represent a place or collectivity, or exemplify any progressive change that can be rejected or endorsed. The films that largely concern Leahy attest to the divided character of his own location and subjectivity and to equally deep and consequential divisions among his Ganiga neighbors. The stories do not enable any clear moral adjudications but attest rather to the near impossibility of arriving at a political or moral attitude.

The themes of the essays in this book intersect at a number of points, but I have divided it into three parts in order to draw out distinct emphases. The first two chapters, which together comprise the first part, are concerned particularly with issues of overall disciplinary orientation. Chapter 1, "Partial Texts," (here much expanded and revised) began as a review of the state of play in the writing of Pacific islands history and addressed questions of authority in history writing, the representation of colonialism, and the representation of agency. What I suggest is that while certain stances on these issues were once clear and adequate, changed circumstances in Oceania draw attention to issues that were marginalized in the past that concern especially the cultural complexity of colonialism and the burden of historical narration. A better approach to these questions requires a historiographic attitude that acknowledges not only the plurality of histories but also the politics of different versions, and that interrogates the larger stories through which colonial encounters and their ramifications have been imagined. In "Partial Texts" I resist the notion that history writing is problematic because it is incomplete and can somehow be rectified through the addition of other forms of knowledge (such as anthropology). In chapter 2, "Alejandro Mayta," I present a correlate of this argument, suggesting that history and anthropology might be synthesized without the disciplinary blindnesses of either field being ameliorated. In this case, my argument is not general or theoretical but proceeds rather through case materials of the kind of culturally hybrid action, or cross-cultural appropriation, that might be transposed from the margins to the centre of anthropological inquiry.

The second part of this book is about the way in which Pacific Islanders have been represented, and partly also about the way in which scholars have approached the problem of the "representations of the other," a topic that has produced a voluminous, and perhaps now an exhausted, literature. Again, I am less concerned to elaborate a general critique (though there is something of this in chapter 1) than to exemplify a distinct approach. In chapters 3 and 4, I focus upon Cook voyage descriptions of certain encounters with the Maori people of Te Wai Pounamu (southern New Zealand) and an odd class of engravings of ethnographic artifacts from the same period. I argue that what the latter mediate is less a concern to understand indigenous peoples ("the Other") in some spe-

cific way than an effort to present the work of natural history, travel, and exploration in morally unambiguous terms; yet the construction of these interests and
endeavors in the late eighteenth century made a collapse of legitimacy, a slip-
page from the noble practice of science in the public interest into a private
licentious curiosity, peculiarly difficult to avoid. What I insist on in this context
is a proposition that should be unexceptional: neither the stories of violence in
New Zealand nor the images of artifacts can be accounted for simply through
reference to enduring "colonial discourses."

Instead, they need to be related to debates and preoccupations of their own
time, and this contextualization may show, as it does in this case, that the
authority of Western knowers, of colonial ethnology, did not possess the kind of
epistemic mastery that is sometimes presumed. At the time, these projects seem
constantly to have been prone to be confused with, or actually to lapse into,
pursuits that were considered inconsequential if not immoral. The key term for
this inquiry is "curiosity": this cannot be seen as a transhistorical propensity or
form of desire that could somehow be more freely exercised during the Enlightenment than it was at other times; it was rather a category with particular and
problematic connotations that entangled science, and especially natural history,
with other forms of impassioned desire captivated by novel and particular
things.

I turn from artifacts back to geographical imaginings, to the divisions imposed by Europeans on Tupaia's sea of islands. This is to reveal, in a different
way, that colonial representations are not productively taken to be unitary or
enduring stereotypes. I focus not on an image of a particular people, nor on a
trope employed widely, but on a distinction: the geographic-cum-ethnological
division of Pacific islanders into "Melanesians" and "Polynesians." What is
remarkable about this is that the juxtaposition is very much alive in current
scholarship, despite long being discredited on archaeological and linguistic
grounds (mainly because Polynesia is if anything a subclass of Melanesia, not an
opposed category of the same level, and because Melanesia combines unrelated
languages and peoples and is not made up of groups possessing any shared
ancestral history). The continuities between earlier ethnological typifications
and current anthropological usage were explored in an earlier polemical article
(Thomas 1989) that inevitably overstressed the conformity between colonial
and recent anthropological criteria for determining cultural boundaries. Here I
work through some of the same material but attempt to redeem what was
distinctive to the successive articulations of the Melanesia/Polynesia contrast.
In its larger implications, this essay aims to sustain Bernard Smith's judgment
on Edward Said's *Orientalism* (1978)—that however valid the book is as a commentary specifically on representations of Islam and the Middle East, the notion

that colonial discourse is an enduring and self-authorizing set of ideas is not helpful for the Pacific. (This overly homogenized notion of "Western" representation is, in any case, much qualified in Said's more recent texts, such as *Culture and Imperialism* [1993].) What is striking for this region is the extent to which constructions of indigenous peoples shifted and were at the time questioned; the repetitive character of the discourse emerges more at the superficial level of the type—the cannibal or dusky maiden—than at the more complex level of the narratives and classifications in which these types figure.

Chapter 5, "Melanesians and Polynesians," concludes with a brief discussion of some of the ways in which these regional identities recently have been represented by Pacific islanders. While there are points at which modern indigenous constructions recapitulate or invert those of ethnologists, explorers, and others, what is striking, on the whole, is the irrelevance of the earlier representations for contemporary identities. This material is of some salience to the argument that dominant ideologies in decolonized societies are "derivative discourses," and that indigenous elites reproduce the classificatory schemes and codifications of custom that were generated by colonial ideologies. Of course, the fact that the terms "Melanesia" and "Polynesia" are employed at all attests to the influence that colonial ethnic categories have had; but the criteria of demarcation that were important before (and that remain important for some comparative anthropology), and the particular force of the Melanesia-Polynesia juxtaposition, are simply not significant in contemporary discourse.

My discussions of European representations are here biased toward eighteenth- and early-nineteenth-century sources, and the essays in this book might be seen in conjunction with other publications on late-nineteenth-century official representations of Fijians, some pessimistic fiction from the same period, and early-twentieth-century missionary discourses and popular exploratory writing (Thomas 1990c, 1991, 1992a, 1994). I do, however, bring the coverage of these themes in this book up to the present through discussion, in chapter 6, of representations of the Pacific in popular fiction. The distinctly negative construction of Pacific modernity in a thriller of Peter Corris's and in the travel writing of Paul Theroux, among others, underlines the complexities of representing the region in the epoch of decolonization that I have already referred to.

The third part of the book focuses on the politics of tradition in the Pacific. Like the Hanson essay on Maori culture mentioned earlier, it draws on the literature on the "invention of tradition" but takes this in a different direction to that pursued by some recent writers, such as the political scientist Stephanie Lawson (1996). While Lawson is primarily concerned to demonstrate that fabricated traditions serve the purposes of indigenous elites, I have adopted an ethnographic perspective and am concerned with what values tradition actually bears and how it is mobilized rhetorically in various situations at the local level.

Chapter 7, "Tin and Thatch," addresses the question of differences between Fijian and European ways of recognizing what is traditional, but it is something of a hybrid text in the sense that it blurs ethnographic and travel writing; because it was written while I was living in Fiji in 1988 I have chosen not to revise it at all for republication here (though I should say that it was written more as a story than as an essay and is accordingly a partly fictionalized account). Questions concerning the construction of indigenous identities are reviewed more conventionally and extensively in chapter 8, which draws upon, and departs from, a considerable literature in Pacific studies on inventions, reinventions, and codifications of tradition.

On the basis of a range of examples from early contact, colonial, and more recent histories, I stress that identity construction is a relational process: representations of the "Fijian way," the custom of the place, and so on are reformulated over time and through particular encounters. The customs that are taken to be emblematic of these collective identities shift according to what is at issue in relationships with other populations, and those customs are themselves articulated and objectified in novel ways as they are rendered emblematic. A further point that I emphasize is that while much of the literature on this theme takes it for granted that traditions and identities are affirmed, objectification also makes it possible for them to be rejected or inverted: these cultural dynamics thus create scope not only for anticolonial traditionalism, but also for modernist antitraditionalism. The late Roger Keesing reminded me that tradition tends to be affirmed even by its advocates only in certain contexts, and that for every advocate of tradition or custom, there are many advocates of development, tourism, commerce, and so forth. These arguments are elaborated upon in what is essentially a case study, in chapter 9.

Some of these essays appeared previously in journals or books aimed mainly at anthropologists and others in publications aimed mainly at historians; but in one case the historians were Pacific historians and in another they were cultural and art historians more or less within British eighteenth-century studies. Two chapters, also, were initially published in literary magazines rather than academic texts of any sort. I am not making this clear by way of an excuse for the essays' heterogeneity; nearly all have been at least slightly revised, but I have not made a great effort to smooth over differences of style or orientation that result from the differing audiences for whom they were initially composed.

I suggest rather that these differences reflect the range of positions that the field that I have loosely called "historical anthropology" needs to adopt. Historical anthropology cannot be ethnography that is gesturally contextualized through archival sources. Neither should it entail abandoning fieldwork and local conversation in favor of a critique of colonialism based exclusively in library research. If anthropologists have habitually celebrated the complexity of the indigenous societies they have studied and disparaged the prejudices of colonizers without investigating their cultures with comparable sensitivity, this long-standing lopsidedness should neither be perpetuated nor simply inverted. Research concerned with the histories and multiple cultural burdens of a region such as Oceania must embrace anthropological inquiries into the artifacts of both locals and visitors, both indigenous peoples and colonizers; at present we run the risk of unreflectively stereotyping and essentializing the Europeans who we imagine unreflectively stereotyped others. Hence I am no less concerned to engage with the "native point of view" on the decks of Cook's *Resolution* than in western Fiji. Though research conducted in that area in 1988 informs several chapters here, the book is somewhat imbalanced toward the narratives produced by Europeans; but I hope that readers will appreciate that these essays complement other books of mine that either focused exclusively on indigenous cultural expressions and dynamics (e.g., Thomas 1990a, 1995) or addressed both indigenous and European cultures and the processes of interaction between them (1991).

As I noted earlier, an interest in cultural exchange cannot presume that exchange always takes place, or that it has significant and equivalent ramifications for both sides. Accordingly, the stark difference between the subject matter of chapter 3 (the anthropological ideas of certain eighteenth-century Europeans) and that of chapter 9 (contemporary Fijians' perceptions of themselves, Fiji Indians, and Europeans) is intended in itself to make the point that imaginings that are historically connected may nevertheless remain not only distinct but distant.

I am also concerned to engage with the specificity of the region's history while avoiding a framework of regional or area studies. Though rarely subjected to reflection or scrutiny, the paradigm of "area studies" has been enormously important in intellectual life, especially since the Second World War, as institutes and centres of Asian, African, Middle Eastern, European, and occasionally Pacific studies have proliferated within and around universities. The worst aspect of this trend is that noted by Edward Said with respect to American research on the Middle East; area studies institutes are frequently funded or partially funded by foreign affairs or defence departments rather than through higher education budgets, and therefore often foreground government concerns, even if they do not toe the government line in a direct way. When this is not the case, area studies research is frequently disengaged from wider intellec-

tual concerns in the humanities and instead tends to address specialist preoccupations in a somewhat introverted way.

There are, however, also positive elements in regional studies, not only because they obviously generate necessary resources such as specialized archives,
bibliographies, and contexts for discussion. Area studies may at least implicitly
contradict the globalizing tendency of grand theorizing in the new discourses of
cultural studies, as well as the universalism and Eurocentrism characteristic of
the older humanities disciplines, by generating analytical languages and problems that emerge from the cultural formations of regions and their distinctive
colonial histories. In Oceania, it makes sense to generate a body of theorizing
and argument concerning the nature of both indigenous and European voyaging and the early traffic between indigenous people and Europeans, and it
makes sense to foreground the question of the politics of tradition in debates
around contemporary culture and social change. It also makes sense to foreground indigenous paradigms such as the "sea of islands" that can only slip into
obscurity in global disciplinary discourses, even those in fields such as anthropology that are ideally highly sensitive to local perceptions. Tupaia's map, as
published by Forster, is both an appreciative "monument" to indigenous knowledge and something of an appropriation. It remains foundational not only
because it imaged the "sea of islands," but because it revealed the imagining of
that sea as both a European and an indigenous romance. If the simple cartographic unity of the map obscures the great distances between the Polynesian
and European perceptions of Oceania, it at least shows that both Polynesians
and Europeans could, occasionally, be drawn into the other's ways of imagining
the place. I hope that those occasions have a future and that this book helps
foster them.

PART I
VISIONS OF HISTORY
AND
ANTHROPOLOGY

I

Partial Texts:
Representation,
Colonialism,
and Agency
in Pacific History

Findings

In his *History of the World in Ten and a Half Chapters*, Julian Barnes writes, "There's one thing I'll say for history. It's very good at finding things" (1989, 242). If history might be a kind of collecting that excites an undisciplined curiosity through its documentation of resonances and oddities, through its retellings of extravagant tales, it has predominantly been understood as something more serious, and by some as something more seriously and deeply culpable. It is difficult to tell a story without evoking at the same time a moral topography, if not also a larger projection of somebody or something's growth and maturity or decline, that might exemplify a principle or chart an appropriate future. Collecting might be merely playful if it did not lead to classification and display; history displayed might be harmless if it was evidently less persuasive.

One of history's recent findings is Joe Leahy. His history is one that I suggest is emblematic, not merely of changes under way in the independent Pacific islands nations, but of problems that arise in the representation and narration of such changes, in Oceania and elsewhere. If the term "postcolonial" can really be employed at all at present, it might refer here, not to some transcendence of colonial relationships that can be welcomed, but to an evaporation of the moral certainties that colonialism has simultaneously enforced and enabled.[1]

Joe Leahy's historians, Bob Connolly and Robin Anderson, are filmmakers rather than teachers or writers of academic history. *Joe Leahy's Neighbours*, released in 1989, deals with conflict around the profitable Mount Hagen coffee plantation of Joe Leahy, the mixed-race son of one of the prospectors whose early visits to the Papua New Guinea highlands were documented in the previous Connolly/Anderson film *First Contact* (1983).[2] While the earlier film turned

5. Bob Connolly with Ganiga men preparing to film a meeting.
Photo courtesy Ronin Films and Bob Connolly.

upon the familiar dichotomization of white and indigenous perspectives, *Joe Leahy's Neighbours* (figs. 5, 6) is something quite removed from another tale of colonial villainy, though there are harsh contrasts between the modest thatch huts of the villagers and Joe's luxury car and concrete bungalow, in which his wife—a Melanesian woman, but a Papuan from the coast, rather than a local—reads Australian women's magazines. One clan leader strongly supports Leahy's use of communal land; another is initially bitter and resentful about unfulfilled promises but becomes tired and seeks Joe's patronage again; younger men are strongly opposed to the inequitable distribution of profits but lack the resources to mobilize opposition. The distinct interests of men and women are apparent, and big-men are seen enhancing their personal prestige by driving around in trucks and presenting cash as well as traditional valuables at marriages and funerals. The burden of women's agricultural labor seems increased rather than ameliorated by cash cropping and "modernization": old and new inequalities are thus visibly complicit.

Though rejecting any romanticized view of Ganiga society, *Joe Leahy's Neighbours* raised the prospect of some form of locally owned development and on my reading, was residually optimistic: the closing frames showed local men bringing a clapped-out truck to life, its engine belching and struggling up a muddy

6. Still from the film *Joe Leahy's Neighbours,* directed by Robin Anderson
and Bob Connolly. Photo courtesy Ronin Films and Bob Connolly.

road. The vehicle, a gift from Joe, was inadequate reciprocity, and seemed to
demonstrate the scope, the limited scope, for the local appropriation of the
products of development. All these ambiguities are intensified in a third film,
Black Harvest (1992), that tells the story of the joint venture that emerged, a story
that excludes any optimism: not only does progress toward any kind of indigenized or equitable development seem impossible, but highlands societies
seem locked into a spiral of killings and payback.

The film opens with a powerful instance of Joe's insider status: he is walking
down a path, weeping, toward a group of men mourning a dead big-man; in the
speeches that follow, the leader, Popina Mai, proposes that Joe now be recognized as their premier big-man, at least so far as business is concerned. He and
Joe are then seen discussing the jointly owned plantation, and Joe tells Popina
Mai that he will be up to his neck in money, that everyone will be rich. This
typifies the ambivalence with which Joe is presented all the way through; he is
hectoring and manipulative, and even after the coffee prices fall, he encourages
the Ganiga to believe that they will be much better off than could ever have been
likely; yet he is also portrayed as someone emotionally caught up with other
Ganiga men, expressing unmistakable grief, and seeing himself as their helper
and partner. The way the handheld camera walks beside Joe toward the place of

the funeral in the opening scene prompts and abets the viewer's awkward sympathy, which is reinforced and strained as Joe is portrayed alternately as a victim of circumstances and as an exploiter who is more white than "mixed race."

The film's action is concentrated over the period when the coffee plantation has matured and should be harvested for the first time. The news comes through that prices have fallen, and the local pickers are asked to accept drastically reduced wages. Long standing grievances over Joe's wealth resurface, and Popina Mai, his closest supporter, is devastated by the realization that "we'll never be millionaires now." Simultaneously, Ganiga men are drawn into a tribal fight and seem disinclined either to end hostilities or resume picking; Joe is furious and says, "You can go primitive again for all I care." The coffee, meanwhile, begins to rot on the trees.

In one of the film's most remarkable sequences, Joe wraps up a bundle of rotten coffee beans and suspends them between poles in the manner of traditional mortuary practices. The Ganiga, who are bemused and take the edifice at first as some strange trick of the enemy neighbors, are appalled when Joe reveals that he is responsible. "That's Ganiga Kaugum and Ganiga Kilima up there," he says, referring to the plantations. "They've been killed . . . killed under your noses while you fought . . . Custom demands that you weep for them now. So weep . . . and then go and pick coffee. You've lost your two big-men." It's difficult to know what response Joe anticipated; several speakers immediately turn on him and describe the act as a blasphemous outrage and a mockery of their traditions; the meeting degenerates into acrimonious argument about money and the running of the plantation.

The distinctiveness of cultural politics in Papua New Guinea in the 1990s is illustrated by the gulf between this scene and another famous instance of cultural hybridity, one that provided the title for an equally memorable film. *Trobriand Cricket* dealt with a very funny indigenous adaptation of the missionary-introduced game and showed how a variety of outside products and people, such as chewing gum, cameras, tourists, and so on, were parodied through performance. For critics such as James Clifford, the Trobriand example has typified what is going on in the postcolonial world: new cultural scenes are being composed through fertile and exciting appropriations that transgress authentic traditions and bounded cultures (1988, 148). Joe's performance reminds us that these conjunctures are political in a sense that goes beyond gentle subversion of tourist behavior or missionary imposition: hybrid performances project specific and contentious arguments about who we are, where we're going, and how we regard our past that can be injurious as well as amusing.[3] Traditional ritual may no longer be a compelling topic for postmodern anthropologists, but it evidently retains authenticity and sanctity for some highlands big-men, who reject not only Joe's theatrical gesture but the project of modernization he personifies. "Popina flaps his cock about, but he'll die poor too," says one of the critics. But if this resistance is an affirmation of tradition, it is not readily endorsed or romanticized; if anthropologists and others have often almost instinctively supported indigenous cultures against development, "indigenous culture" cannot constitute a unity here: women seen later on the fringes of an evangelist's meeting have a different attitude to Joe's display. "When we heard about your 'coffee funeral,'" they tell him, "we urged all our people to come and pick. That really moved us. You bared your heart . . . Fighting's a rubbish thing. We all want to pick coffee." Not that women's perceptions should be privileged—or taken as homogeneous either; but fighting indeed seems a rubbish thing, the way Connolly and Anderson present it, through remarkable footage that is more typical of frontline journalism than ethnographic film, through painful sequences in which attempts are made to extract arrows, through moments of dying and mourning and burying.

There's little sense here of why the men feel compelled to fight or why they value it, insofar as they do, and it's easy to fill the ethnographic gap by giving old stereotypes new life (they really are savages) or by attributing inappropriate weight to the "payback" idea, as though men were not able to apply this selectively or receive compensation in cash, pigs, or valuables instead of killing again. What is compelling about the film as a visual experience could thus be seen as a fault, if it is regarded as a document: the viewer is bewildered by a succession of events that seem to arise from mere belligerence, that might have somehow been accounted for if a warrior had spoken more extensively for himself. Ironically, given that *Joe Leahy's Neighbours* was accused of neglecting the perspectives of Ganiga women, *Black Harvest* presents warriors as women see them rather than as they see themselves.

If Ganiga warriors are not treated as "informants" who might explicate the cultural meanings of warfare, Joe does talk to the camera a good deal, and his perception of fighting as unambiguously regressive passes largely unquestioned and unchallenged. It seems to be Popina Mai's view, and that of the women, too; the sheer pain and loss that this warfare produces would perhaps make most viewers agree with them. But are we also agreeing that fighting is the past and business the future? Even if we believe that development should take place, we need also to assume that it can; if not, we are imagining only a negation of precolonial activities, rather than some transformation from an undesirable condition to a desirable one. This is the point at which the film's moral landscape is most fraught. By showing customary practice as violent and patriarchal, and by invalidating commercial progress, *Black Harvest* does something more radical than displace an optimistic account of decolonization with a pessimistic account of the postcolonial present: it excludes both anticolonial celebrations of traditional culture and antitraditional celebrations of modernity.

Histories

Nicholas Dirks has written recently that "history has played a key role in the modern production of the nation-state and of the various constituent bases of modernity, at the same time that the nation has played a critical historical role in defining what a modern conception of history should be" (1990, 25). Canonical forms of historical writing have thus centered upon processes of nation-building, political evolution, and the exemplary biographies of great leaders. While various kinds of populist, socialist, and oppositional history have displaced monarchs, generals, and prime ministers with union leaders, peasants, and "ordinary" women and men, the histories from beyond Europe, which might have been expected to challenge the narrative forms of European historiography still more radically, instead appear deeply caught within its logic: "whereas social historians and feminists had to attack the assumptions that great men and great events made history, nationalist historians in India had to start with a more basic point; they had to replace British great men and great events with Indian ones . . . For the colonized, the new history necessarily reproduces many of the fundamental assumptions of the old" (Dirks 1990, 26).

If a history is as necessary to a modern nation as a currency, a flag, a census, a novel, and a museum, it does not follow that historical practice is, or ever really has been, encompassed by the imperatives of nation-ness; even some official histories may be sufficiently manifold, capacious, or even incoherent to encompass more than one class of privileged actors, more than one construction of progress, and anticipations of more than one public or audience. It is evident, however, that the same kinds of considerations and choices that shape national emblems, that order exhibitions, that define certain questions and preclude others, enter into history writing, whether historians explicitly acknowledge their choices and strategies or not. Which actors, and what aspects of their lives, are rendered central? Where are they situated? What kind of belonging characterizes their relations with places and landscapes? What differences among them energize conflict and change? What moral or political value is that change accorded, and what future does it lead toward?

It is ironic that Dirks's short essay begins by pointing to the failure of Indian nationalist historians to transcend the categories and narratives of the colonial historiography they contested, yet ends by reiterating the need to "decolonize" all our histories and anthropologies (1990, 31). What exactly is being advocated? If Dirks means that a range of hegemonic structures and discourses should be contested, there is little to argue about at a general level, but the risk is that the idea of "decolonization" may prove to be as circumscribed by the logic of the nation-state as the process has been in fact. It conveys the idea that a certain terrain or heritage has been unjustly possessed, and implies a redistributive justice: not only nations (Indians, Fijians, Papua New Guineans) but also subaltern classes and minorities of various kinds should have their histories, and presumably they should also narrate them and control them themselves. The problems of a commoditized concept of history and its evident ethnocentrism are too obvious to require detailed comment; one of the ramifications must, as Dirks's example of Indian nationalism suggests, be the substitution of one set of privileged subjects, or narrators, of a history for another. While a concentration on the actions and perspectives of subalterns may be more appealing in principle than one upon the activities of elite nationalists, historians and anthropologists must be wary of romanticizing or normalizing resistance. This impulse of oppositional history presupposes that a militant stance is generally the most worthy or the most historically consequential; it withholds historic significance from those who were not engaged in some kind of resistance; it may obscure quite crucial questions concerning the reasons why particular regimes were actively supported or complied with by people who were not members of an elite. On the issue of authorship, it may indeed be a good thing if Bengali history is written by Bengalis rather than Americans or Australians, but it is certainly a bad thing if the identity of a writer is reduced to his or her membership of a national, minority, or subaltern group and taken to be more important than what is actually written.

Given that the question of how history really might be decolonized seems peculiarly intransigent and that it is not even obvious that "decolonization" aptly glosses the range of shifts in historical practice that might be desirable, there is something to be said for focusing on questions that are at once more specific and less tied to the problem of the ownership of the past (though I return to reconsider that issue in a later section of this chapter). These notes are concerned with what historical writing on and in the Pacific privileges or avoids; how historians' narratives, among others, construct the agency of various islanders; and how the process that is so central for this as for most other non-Western histories—that is, colonialism—can be described without either diminishing or overstating its ramifications.

Emphasizing the ways in which larger questions of orientation and substantive problems are entangled, I review epistemological, theoretical, and interpretative questions. This is inevitably a selective exercise; claims about conventional styles and approaches in a discipline or subdiscipline can only suppress the field's actual diversity. The aim is not to set out an approach that might claim to be radically original, but rather to see enduring issues, altered political circumstances, and available intellectual innovations as providing new and distinctive possibilities—or necessities—for the writing of cross-cultural history in Oceania. My sense is that the present moment is an intellectually challenging one for the humanities, and not merely because there is much scope for experimentation. The circumstances of postcolonial hybridity do demand new approaches to ethnography, historical research, and cultural studies; but the present must also be seen, I suggest, as a threatening moment, simply because such histories as the biography of Joe Leahy may disable both liberal and radical understandings of colonialism and emancipation to the same extent that the end of empire threw imperialist narratives of history and progress into uncertainty and confusion.

My key reference point for the liberal scholarly understanding of Pacific history is a charter for the field set out as long ago as 1955 by J. W. Davidson, who was founding professor in the subdiscipline at the Australian National University. His prescriptions have been remarkably influential, as they continue to be among senior scholars who were his colleagues and students, though interest has also developed in forms of cultural and ethnographic history associated particularly with Greg Dening's work, which I discuss below. Davidson's central point seems remarkably uncontentious today: he contested a then prevailing blindness to actual developments in the colonies on the part of imperial historians, who instead concerned themselves with Colonial Office debates and policies: "Imperial history must give way," he insisted, "to the history of European expansion" (1966, 8–9). Davidson also emphasized the importance of avoiding ethnocentrism; while the concepts of feudalism, nationality, sovereignty, and capitalism were inevitably carried over from the study of modern European history into that "of European contacts with the remainder of the world . . . that contact has been two-sided."

> The reaction to it of non-European peoples has been in terms of the values and institutions of their own cultures. As is well shown by the modern history of Japan, their attitudes, as well as those of the Europeans, have determined the character both of the changes in the non-European world and of European policies towards it. For a full understanding of the phenomena with which we are concerned, the historian must analyse situations from both points of view (9–10).

Davidson's language may be dated, but this kind of point has remained foundational for ethnohistorical research in the Pacific and in other regions. In the 1980s a book on "the other side of the frontier" (Reynolds 1981) was a pioneering work on settler-Aboriginal conflict in Australian history; as recently as 1991,

Anne Salmond's *Two Worlds* was acclaimed as a pathbreaking reinterpretation of early Maori-European contacts. The guiding principle of her book was consistent with that set out by Davidson: "For the sake of accuracy as well as fairness, the story . . . has to be rethought. In this experimental account I have tried to respect the perspectives of both sides, while taking the narratives of neither side for granted" (1991, 12). Salmond's history indeed provides, as far as the sources permit, an account that balances European and Maori perspectives, and that for example explains instances of indigenous violence, such as the massacre of Marion du Fresne and members of his crew in 1772, through reference to Maori expectations and most importantly the violation of *tapu*:

> From a local point of view, from the moment that Te Kauri's tapu was attacked the responses of his people were inevitable, and the French were given many warnings of the danger that they were in—from sentry cries and signal fires at night to direct verbal cautions. For some extraordinary reason, however, they chose to take no notice of these signals, and walked calmly to their deaths (429).

Two Worlds evidently makes a constructive contribution to the mutual understanding between Maori and Pakeha (white settlers) in contemporary New Zealand. It accomplishes the kind of historical decolonization that Dirks refers to by placing a Maori history on a par with the European histories for the period that is covered; and this is something that Salmond does in a culturally and ethnographically sensitive manner. The premise of the project is, of course, that the field of differences is readily divided into two "worlds" or "sides." If we know that in the past one side of his history but not the other was told, it goes without saying that the imbalance should be redressed. However, the instinctive, persuasive character of the juxtaposition may possess its own historical contingency, and its seeming logic may even be ephemeral. In chapter 6 of this book I turn to a history of another massacre, one in the Solomon Islands early this century. In this case, a book by Roger Keesing and Peter Corris that attempted to redress imbalances in existing accounts was not well received; it was not clear which collectivity possessed a history that should be told and restored, and not clear that a newly independent nation wanted to own the history that it was offered. For the nations of the South Pacific, a narrative organized around "two sides" may have lost its coherence and legibility.

Politics

Pacific historians in the late twentieth century work in a very different political and intellectual context from that in which Davidson set out his agenda for a new history of islands, islanders, and European expansion. The prevalent style of historical writing was then empiricist and technically rigorous; what was novel was the subject matter rather than the methods or theoretical orientations. There was an emphasis on the documentation of archival resources, the publication of well-annotated texts, and the writing of precise general narratives, rather than on such projects as theorizing colonial states, economic imperialism, or experimentation with discipline crossing.[4] This approach was clearly fertile, in the sense that a considerable number of dense scholarly accounts of Pacific missions, administrations, trading endeavors, and contact histories were produced. In most cases earlier general accounts either did not exist, or were unsatisfactory (because, in the case of missions for instance, virtually the only accounts were official histories by the societies themselves). However, the fact that the frame of reference was "the Pacific islands," rather than historical processes or cultural issues of a more general kind, meant that these products tended to be isolated from broader discussions that had an analytical and interpretative, as opposed to a documentary, emphasis—a shortcoming conspicuous in "area studies" more generally. As Dening noted nearly twenty years ago:

> Research is dominated by a narrow geographic area, an institution, a period. History is what happens or what the sources let know what happens within those limitations. No problem, no theory, no methodology takes the researcher outside those confines. Missionaries as intruders carry their cultures and perceptions across the beaches with them . . . Even if one raised the Marxist issues of exploitation and hegemony only to pour scorn on them, the issues would have raised questions about the mission support systems, about the institutional church, about public image and propaganda. But more than that, the critical advantage of cross-cultural history is that the cultures in their exposure to one another lay bare their structures of law, of morality, their rationalizations in myth, their expressions in symbolism and ritual (Dening 1978, 82).[5]

More will be said below about the limitations referred to here and the potential alternatives. Setting aside the question of the extent to which the discipline suffered from intellectual isolation, there was manifestly no comparable disengagement in the political and practical field.

In the 1950s and 1960s the political environment in the islands was one of progression toward independence, and from a liberal perspective it was generally clear that formal colonialism was a paternalistic system that had to give way to indigenous self-management. Davidson participated in advisory processes in several states, and other scholars were also involved or were writing about "political advancement" (Davidson 1967; West 1961).[6] The context for this type of engagement has virtually evaporated. Although independence is still a political issue in such places as New Caledonia and west Papua, as cultural autonomy is for the Maori and the Hawaiians, most South Pacific countries are now "postcolonial" states—even if the persistence of economic colonialism and informal metropolitan political influence is hardly to be disputed. A consequence of independence has been that political differences within indigenous populations have become much more conspicuous, and the liberal attitude of support for local nationalism now confronts an array of much more difficult local divisions, such as the factional struggles of Vanuatu politics and the war over the secession of Bougainville from Papua New Guinea. At a more local level, the problem is illustrated by *Joe Leahy's Neighbours* and *Black Harvest:* the conflicts are not reducible to struggles between two general and clearly recognizable camps (colonists and natives, right and left, not even between national and local interests).

A link might be made between the novel political problems associated with conflict and theoretical developments in anthropology. In the 1960s and 1970s most approaches other than Marxism, or some forms of Marxism, treated social structures and culture as coherent and unitary systems. These orientations have been displaced by interests in practice—which, as an analytic object, is clearly more susceptible to historical and political mutability—and perspectival difference in meanings and discourses (Bourdieu 1977; Ortner 1984; Keesing 1987). But I shall argue below that while many historians are interested in drawing anthropological concepts into a cultural or "ethnographic" history, most have drawn upon theorists who resist the notion that culture is fractured and politicized. These issues about forms of interpretation can be placed in the context of larger perceptions of the status of historical accounts.

Interpretations

For those with critical inclinations, the authority of singular "History" may now be displaced by histories and be manifested equally in scholarly monographs, verbal anecdotes, and personal letters (Dening 1988a). The narrated and contrived character of various source materials has been explored, as have the narrative forms of historical genres and discourses; the consequent blurring of the line between history and fiction has enabled self-conscious inventions such as Simon Schama's "unwarranted speculations" (Davis 1987; White 1973; Bann 1984; Schama 1992). I cannot attempt to review all these developments here (see Hunt 1989; de Bolla 1986) but focus instead on the exciting style of cultural history exemplified by Greg Dening's work in the Pacific, which is also manifest in studies of other colonial histories—Virginia and New York (Isaac 1983; Merwick 1990)—and of the Spanish encounter with Mayans and Aztecs (Clendinnen 1987, 1991). Like some of the Princeton cultural historians (Darnton 1984) and the "new historicists" in literary studies (Greenblatt 1992), these writers are influenced particularly by the work of Clifford Geertz, and also to some degree by the ideas of other anthropologists such as Mary Douglas and Victor Turner concerning boundaries, ritual action, and symbolism. They do not aim to fashion a poststructural or postcolonial history, but rather to open historical analysis in a gentle way to anthropology, and, perhaps more radically, treat history as anthropology, as an exploration of otherness and a pursuit that requires an ethnography of itself. Though Geertz himself (1990) has dubbed this group the "Melbourne school," I do not wish to attribute a homogeneous approach to Isaac, Clendinnen, Dening, or others, and I focus on Dening's writing because he has made an epistemology explicit; this makes it possible to link his assumptions about histories with his approach to cultural analysis. I would acknowledge that these stances are advances on earlier understandings—certainly upon the constrained and largely antitheoretical objectivism that has prevailed in Pacific islands history—and ones that enlarge the scope for historical reading and writing; but I do suggest also that they are no longer adequate to the circumstances around us.

Dening's relativist stance toward the texted past is structured in opposition to a conventional objectivism in which multivocality is recognized in source materials rather than in the products of historical knowledge. A good historical narrative is conventionally seen to encompass the differing perspectives of historical actors, the caprice of their partial and interested accounts, and the incompleteness of their understanding. The product is thus seen to derive not so much from a particular perspective on the past as from the reading of diverse and scattered sources. The apprehension of this totality is taken to be the basis of historical authority. The tautologies entailed in regarding the factual as "really real," or independent of social acts of observation and notation, have been sufficiently discussed. If it can be recognized that histories are cultural projects, embodying interests and narrative styles, the preoccupation with a transcendent reality of archives and documents should give way to dispute about forms of argument and interpretation. Thus far this has been rendered secondary by another consequence of the objectification of factuality: the corresponding subjectification of interpretation. Where flawed, a perspective is reduced to "bias"; where adequate, it reflects sound judgment. In either case, the permutation of interpretation with its attendant moral and political judgments is thus seen as a personal vision rather than as an expression or permutation of any broader cultural structure, as an individual rather than as a discursive product.

Dening has eloquently expressed the relativist reaction to authoritative history: "Our sense of History is embedded in our different usage. Our different usage is what History is, not what I or you say History should be. We have different histories for different occasions" (1988a: 99). While there is much in both *Islands and Beaches* (1980) and in Dening's more recent studies (1988a, 1988b, 1992) that stimulates wider reflection, the mere displacement of authority through the assertion of a multiplicity of histories that each have particular contextual value seems insufficient. The fact that the practices of expressing historical narrative through writing and speech are inevitably diverse does not mean that there should be no argument over the force and effect of interpretations. Dening's tenets do not exclude critique, but in his writing judgment and discrimination are consistently resisted and evaded, just as they are in the story he tells of the death of a minor officer in Hawaii in 1792:

> So William Gooch was dead. Who killed him? His going to Cambridge? His utilitarian spirit and his false sense of confidence in easily controlling his life? The intrusion of empire on native peoples? The greed for profit in the purchase of "artificial curiosities"? The ambivalent symbols of a ship part-navy, part-trade? The personal history of an erratic Hergest? . . . The politics of chiefs? The accidents of misconstrued signs? (1988a: 94).

In the face of orthodox authoritative history, it may be liberating to sustain a sense of possibilities, of alternate readings, of uncertainty. But if it were elaborated as a model for historical practice, the refusal to commit oneself to certain accounts and regard others as misguided or wrong would entail impractical disengagement. If nobody would refrain from making adjudications about different meals, different medicines, or different tables, what separates the practical activity of history making from cooking, medicine, and carpentry, such that permissiveness is appropriate in one domain but not all? Ironically, through his deflection of argument, Dening would marginalize and undercut the critical process of reinterpretation, which was also rendered secondary to the construction of factual narrative in the more conventional paradigm: "Perhaps for you History is what really happened—the poor exploited, the colonized degraded, hegemony extended. Let us not argue over what History ought to be. Let us flourish our commitments later" (1988a: 2).

A historical poetics of this kind, which delights in the diversity and contrivances of texted pasts, must underspecify the cultural sense of particular texts unless these are situated in their historical and political motivations. Histories do not merely differ and enrich knowledge through complementary diversity. Rather they reflect interests in practical projects, in legitimizing or destabilizing; they entertain, and perhaps they perform some symbolic violence with respect to those who are spoken about but whose own voices are absent. Stories are told, and should be told, simply because storytelling is a good thing to do—

but particular stories are never innocent of wider agendas. Our texts are partial because they are plural, as Dening suggests; the point that history has its rituals of authorizing and circulating is well taken. But histories are also partial in the sense of being culturally and politically interested, and thus must be exposed to commentary and debate. Perhaps, then, History is what didn't really happen— the hero apotheosized, the other exoticized, the native victimized, an ideology demystified. There is no need for us to flourish our commitments—they're there to be read between the lines anyway. Let us argue now, not about what History ought to be, but about the sense and salience of particular accounts.

Colonialisms

The question of what kind of larger narrative subsumes particular events is of specific importance in Pacific history because the subdiscipline was established through the professional claim to discover history *in* the islands, a history distinct from that of metropolitan imperialism, as Davidson emphasized (1966). Though the focus was initially on European expansion, a close connection developed between the relocation of analysis and the recovery of the indigenous perspective, and particularly of indigenous agency. Insofar as any single story has provided a context for the various particular histories, it has been the refutation of the fatal impact of colonialism upon passive Pacific peoples. The argument counterposed islanders' interests and strategies with stereotypes of exploitation by foreigners. This debunking was effected for various episodes in contact history, was especially central to "revising" work on the labor trade (which was shown to involve the active collaboration of islanders, rather than the kidnapping described in popular accounts of "blackbirding"), and has been the central theme of several textbooks (particularly Howe 1984; see also Howe 1977, Scarr 1990, and Campbell 1989). This trend resonates not only with the work of historians and ethnohistorians in many other parts of the world, but also with Marshall Sahlins's structuralist history, which is less concerned to affirm individual subjectivity than the persisting importance of prior symbolic categories for indigenous perceptions of contact and consequent responses. Despite the considerable theoretical differences, the orientation may be said to have been anticipated in Davidson's emphasis on the determining effect of "the values and institutions" of local cultures.

While obviously an advance upon earlier approaches, the historians' emphasis upon local agency had a number of shortcomings: the lack of a framework for cultural analysis meant that indigenous perceptions tended to be seen in narrow and pragmatic terms; the interest in dismissing both popular horror stories and abstract theories of colonial exploitation meant that any discussion of power asymmetries was marginalized; there was a tendency to regard "the" indigenous perception of history as unitary; and there was a failure to reflect upon why the West should postulate a "fatal impact" in the first place. If the project of structural history redressed the lack of interest in the cultural dimensions of contact, it was hardly more adequate than that of conventional history in addressing power relations, indigenous diversity, and metahistorical imaginings. These points can be expanded upon seriatim.

Socioeconomic and political accounts of contact history tended to pass over the question of how indigenous peoples perceived foreigners, or took those perceptions to be self-evident and relatively unimportant. The study that has made the most suggestive and provocative claims for the shaping by a prior cultural order of the events of contact and their consequences is *Historical Metaphors and Mythical Realities* (Sahlins 1981). Irrespective of whether Sahlins's particular arguments concerning the indigenous assimilation of Captain Cook to the Hawaiian deity Lono can be sustained (see Friedman 1985; Bergendorff, Hasager, and Henriques 1988; Obeyesekere 1992a; Sahlins 1989, 1995), the implications of this effort to contextualize events of contact history in local cultural structures (however provisionally these might be understood) are not limited to such spectacular identifications between gods and chiefly foreigners. Early "traffic" between islanders and European vessels, and the later, more regularized trade in such things as axes, tobacco, and muskets for sandalwood and bêche-de-mer, constitute significant phases in the economic history of the region, but for too long it has been assumed that the interest in manufactured articles derived from simple technological superiority or from local fancy, inaccessible to analysis.[7] The analysis of what is reported about attitudes to the objects exchanged displaces the idea that we already know what such things as axes, red fabric, and guns are by an attempt to understand or partially understand what they, and foreigners themselves, *became* in indigenous perceptions and uses (Thomas 1991). The simple point that the meanings of trade articles, the process of "barter," white attempts to assert authority, cross-cultural sexual relations, and so on were not stable but locally singular provides scope for a range of attempts to displace the fixed categories of contact history with unavoidably elusive local cultural constructions. Such projects might be taken further, to consider not only the significance of novel European articles and intrusions but the meanings attached to new groups of islanders—those encountered through journeys on European ships, or because of the indigenous role in evangelism, or because of the labor trade. For such people as Tolai or Roviana speakers, who were the Fijian, Samoan, and Tongan missionaries? Does talking about "mission teachers" really tell us anything about how these nonwhite, non-European foreigners were imagined and dealt with?

The strategy of insisting upon the localized character of responses and perceptions should not, however, be converted into a dogmatic principle. Structural history has generally proceeded by identifying an event in terms of precedents, novelties in terms of prior categories, and foreigners in terms of the local counterparts or types to whom the former are assimilated; this may be sound if a stranger actually is identified with some prior figure, but it neglects the learning process inherent in sustained contact: sooner or later an object such as a flag will not be treated as a special form of an indigenous feather girdle but will be given a distinct value that must draw upon both an indigenous perception and some understanding of how flags are used by the people who introduce them (cf. Binney 1986). Another way of expressing this is to say that structural history has yet to effectively characterize creolized cultural forms: instead, it postulates actors imprisoned within the nativist space of enduring traditional categories, capable only of assimilating novel content to preexisting forms (cf. During 1992, 346). If creolization, or some profound change in indigenous culture, cannot be seen to have taken place to a significant degree in the case of the contact between participants in Cook's third voyage and the Hawaiians, this is not true of later colonial relations around labor migration, pacification, and formal administration; a paradigm more attuned to hybridized and morally ambiguous power relations is certainly demanded when we reach the postcolonial space of *Black Harvest*.

If the anthropologically informed project of interpreting indigenous perceptions of history and historical change thus ought to be extended in this qualified way, shorn of the "nativist" bias of historical structural interpretation, cultural analysis should not restrict itself to islanders as though ethnography was a science only of the other. It has often been said that conventional anthropology postulated natives with no history, but it might be added that both historians and anthropologists have written as though colonizers had no culture. Some of the former have suffered such immersion in administrative sources as to emerge with an indistinguishable voice, while the latter have often overstressed the racism of missionaries and others (Jolly and Macintyre 1989). An overgeneralized notion that all Europeans in the Pacific were racist invaders hardly enables one to determine the present-day ramifications of the colonial experience in specific island nations. Imperial discourses and practices are belatedly receiving a better ethnography that exposes their peculiarities and efforts to frame an order—not just their transformative effects, but also their failures in the face of indigenous resistance and parody (Cohn 1985, 1987; Comaroff and Comaroff 1991; Dirks 1992; Jolly 1991; Stoler 1989a, 1989b; Thomas 1990c, 1992a, 1994).

If the desirability of a cultural approach to colonialism is now well established, it is by no means clear what kind of cultural analysis is most appropriate or adequate. In Oceania as elsewhere, much cultural history has referred to the writings of Clifford Geertz. In fact, while Geertz's earlier style of cultural interpretation[8] has ceased to be a coherent reference point within anthropology, and Geertz's own work has clearly encompassed several distinct perspectives, there is a genre of cultural history that has more coherence than its anthropological point of origin.[9] Many writers have drawn upon Geertz in a relatively loose way, to provide justification for an interest in cultural values and the symbolic context, but a more generalized adoption of the Geertzian perspective is apparent in Dening's work. In a discussion of "The Culture of Cultural History," Dening suggested that the general theme common to historians' formulations was that cultures "were wholes possessed of discernible integration. The wholeness was observable to outsiders in patterns and foci, was determining of insiders' behaviour and perceptions . . . " (1988b, 103). He proceeded to refer to Geertz's emphasis upon the "essentially public nature" of culture and its multiplicity: "Every cultural act stands as a text multiply read, not stripped of its meanings until it is revealed in essence but standing always manifold" (106).

This might appear to be an encompassing approach, one dedicated to decoding the richness and multiplicity of culture, past events, and the inventiveness of their representation. It is not apparent that it systematically excludes any of the questions one might want to raise about meanings, happenings, or their depiction. But it is useful to recall that Geertz's perspective on culture emerged within the terms of a Parsonian sociology that rigorously separated social and cultural systems, thus sundering the meaningful and the political. The distinction was quite fundamental in some of Geertz's most celebrated essays, such as "Ritual and Social Change: A Javanese Example" (among others republished in *The Interpretation of Cultures* [1973]), in which he argued that a ceremony became a context for political conflict because the culture and social position of the actors were out of phase. The detachment of meaning is also manifest in more recent studies, such as *Negara* (Geertz 1980), in which the general issue of the social and political dynamics of the Balinese states is simply displaced by (rather than integrated with) a cultural analysis; this is not merely theoretically unsatisfactory, but partial and inadequate as a treatment of these particular polities (Tambiah 1985, 321; Schulte Nordholt 1986, 8–9; 1994). It is not surprising, then, that political questions have no particular or theoretically necessary status in Dening's history, just as the political process of adjudicating a conflict of interpretations is excluded at a more epistemological level.

The emphasis on cultural totalities exemplifies a more general difficulty of interdisciplinary conversation—concepts taken from another field of discussion are appropriated in a highly selective manner and are often unfortunately precisely the ideas that have become or are becoming discredited. The notion of an integrated cultural system has a problematic relation to agency and enactment—as Dening himself notes (1988b, 107)—but tends particularly to exaggerate the meaningful coherence of particular cultures and to suppress both the nuances of practice and perspectival difference. Too often, the codified culture of the chiefly perspective, or that of some senior male informant, has been taken to represent everybody's culture; too often, elaborate symbolic models with uncertain foundations in experience are displayed as coherent structures of meaning. In an exploration of conflict in New Caledonia, Bronwen Douglas argued that:

> the explanatory process must partly be couched in cultural and institutional terms, especially when it involves interaction between members of very different cultural and social systems, but this approach is inadequate if it ignores internal differentiation within each of the main sociocultural blocs (1980, 49).

If the qualification is extended to an insistence upon the divided perceptions and interests of both indigenous populations and Europeans, this is crucial both for the analysis of contemporary political divisions and their precursors.

Feminist history and anthropology have played a pivotal role in establishing that unitary notions of culture and authoritative histories suppress the differing and sometimes contradictory perspectives of women and men. But this is not the only reason why gender has become central in cultural histories of colonialism. The imagination of colonial places and relations with them has long been profoundly gendered and sexualized. It has often been pointed out, for example, that in Western representations, the femininity of Asia was constantly evoked through various images of physique, dress, scent, emotional caprice, languor, and passivity (see, for example, Guest 1989 on William Hodges's paintings of India and Tahiti). Such constructions were by no means unitary, and in the cases of tribal "savages" such as the Maori, were often displaced by masculine constructs of wild and aggressive warriors who had to be tamed and domesticated. Variations relate both to regional differences and to genres of colonial representation. Missionaries tended to employ familial language rather than (or in addition to) a simple gendered code: the benighted heathens were children in the dark, mission "boys" and "girls" ready to learn, not just about Jesus, but also about "social and domestic habits," as if they were growing up for the first time (Thomas 1992a). Images of adult islanders as children and specifically the children of missionaries are extraordinarily pervasive in mission texts and in photographs that imply a familial order and hierarchy. The patronizing character of these ideas is now striking, but it should be recalled that in contrast to the ideas of other classes of colonizers, the missionaries did at least emphasize shared humanity and "siblingship": in Australia, missionary and philanthropic opinion provided a sustained critique of settler racism and violence during the nineteenth century (Reynolds 1987).

Gender is pivotal in *Joe Leahy's Neighbours* and *Black Harvest* because the manifestly different consequences of modernization for men and women, and their manifestly different attitudes toward warfare, make a straightforward celebration of indigenous society, and straightforward judgments about a variety of events and developments, impossible. This is a divisive perception—in an innocent sense that a unitary entity is differentiated, but also in the usual politically culpable one, in that the voice and self-representation of a collectivity might be subverted. While Connolly and Anderson could have chosen to present "the" indigenous attitude toward development, they instead reveal a plethora of attitudes and arguments. I have taken this perception, which denies that indigenous people constitute anything like a unitary bloc, to be symptomatic of postcolonial historiography, but it is not of course peculiar to postcolonial *history*. With the benefit of hindsight, earlier colonial encounters can be understood in a divided fashion, a fashion that may also be precariously divisive. It should have been apparent all along that the different interests of people in different regions, of different ages and sexes, could frequently cut across the larger opposition between "Europeans" and "Marquesans" or "Maori"; and this should have been all the more apparent because, at least in early meetings between islanders and European ships, the whites were conscious of divisions between officers and common men, sailors and scientists, even when and if they understood themselves collectively as Europeans. Still less, in early phases of contact, did islanders think of themselves as Maori or Marquesans rather than people of particular *hapu* and *iwi* or *henua* (descent groups or lands). This empirical complexity was always visible enough, but tended to be overwhelmed by the larger rhetorical juxtaposition between "two worlds," which is more vital to the scene of reading and writing than to the moments we read and write about.

Anne Salmond is too good a historian to pass over the fact that different tribal groups had quite different relations to visiting Europeans: one of the crucial determinants of the 1772 massacre of Marion and his men seems to have been that different descent groups or factions capitalized upon the unwitting *tapu* violation of the French to challenge the *mana* of the leader Te Kauri (1991, 387–8). However, her preoccupation with the essentially separate character of Maori and European narratives and perspectives leads her to neglect the way in which sexual relations between sailors and Maori women marked divisions among both groups, and entailed collaboration between indigenous men, or some indigenous men, and the white men who bartered iron nails and baubles for sexual services. During Cook's second voyage (which Salmond does not discuss), the men at Queen Charlotte's Sound liberally and coercively prostituted their women; this behavior enabled the naturalists Johann Reinhold Forster and George Forster to understand Maori society in particular terms, as a degenerate form of the happier tropical Polynesian order in which women were more favorably treated, and at the same time to castigate the common sailors who debased themselves by making the women vehicles for their animal gratification (see chapter 3).

A scholar today is hardly likely to concur with the Forsters' larger reading of Maori gender relations, but there is no particular reason to question the particular observation that the women were compelled by their menfolk to supply sexual services and hence that these experiences of contact were no doubt radically divided: the men, presumably, were delighted to obtain iron tools and other such articles, while some women formed casual relationships voluntarily (as typically took place elsewhere in Polynesia—at Tahiti, for example) but others were raped. A scholar today might similarly want to contextualize the Forsters' condemnation of the common sailors in the struggle that ran on throughout the voyage between scientists and others—the latter never accorded the privileges the former felt themselves entitled to—but again there is no denying that participants in the voyage were not simply "European," but products of different national and class backgrounds and bearers of sharply divergent interests. The point, then, is not simply that the use of the category of gender in historical analysis shows that men and women have different experiences and concerns—though that is hardly unimportant. It also establishes that divisions among men may be most starkly expressed in relation to women; that gender relations—or "the treatment of women"—were crucial to the ways in which members of one society responded to another, and especially to the ways in which eighteenth- and nineteenth-century Britons pathologized various primitive and Oriental socialities. An essentialism of cultural identity that speaks of undivided "natives" or "colonizers" is no more plausible or helpful analytically than one based on sex, which pretends that women or men globally have shared interests, oppressions, or psychologies.

Perspectival differences need not be marginalized in cultural histories, even though they tend to have been. Cultural interpretations of cross-cultural contact have mainly been attempted, as I've already noted, for the early stages of the process, or for Captain Cook rather than Dole Pineapple (cf. Carrier 1992, 140)—that is, in contexts where colonial expansion is manifest in less intrusive and exploitative forms than subsequently. Structural historians have thus been able to avoid more exploitative phases of the history, which may require more compromised styles of narration and analysis. Sahlins and his followers (Hooper and Huntsman 1985) have ranged across Hawaiian, Fijian, Maori, and other Polynesian cases but have had little to say about events in the latter part of the nineteenth century or subsequently—nor about plantation experiences or the representations of colonial states and external dominance in the Pacific. The exotic theater of nineteenth-century chiefly politics has displaced the more immediate processes that have had profound ramifications for the societies that Pacific islanders now inhabit.

A parallel might be made with the lack of attention given to such topics as wage work and the nature of formal colonial dominance by Pacific historians (but see, on Papua New Guinea, Gammage 1975 and Nelson 1976). The assertion of agency axiomatic among Davidson's followers entailed a reaction against stereotypic constructs of colonial villainy, to such an extent that the power dimension of the colonial encounter was almost effaced.[10] For example, Peter Worsley's view (1957) that the well-known Fijian *Tuka* movement could be seen, like other so-called cargo cults, as a reaction to colonialism was rejected by Deryck Scarr, who stressed that *Tuka* predated formal colonial rule and probably even European contact: "Any purely reactive explanation of *Tuka* in terms of dispossession or decay does injustice to the Fijian imagination, its fertility and its capacity to play with, interpret and integrate an alien cosmology" (1984, 93). It may have been legitimate and important to emphasize that indigenous practice was not a reflex of colonial impositions, but the issue of whether or not some form of this cult existed in precontact times has little bearing on how its later manifestations are interpreted: the movement (like similar forms of religious insurgency) clearly did become a kind of political theater that parodied colonial relationships and protested against such impositions as the native taxation system.[11] These innovative subversions of the colonial order were not, however, explored by Scarr; here the affirmation of indigenous agency seems little more than a means to dismiss an approximately Marxist view and preclude more searching discussion of the relations of domination and resistance in colonial history. Scholarship around colonialism tends to lapse in this way into binary contrasts and reactive positions: it makes of *either* local continuity, culture, and agency *or* global intrusions, politics, and dominance a sufficient and independent frame of analysis. Against the mutual exclusiveness of these frames of analysis, a zone of appropriations and cultural strategies can be imagined in which local and extralocal determinations are significant according to the nature of the encounter. It is not enlightening to argue that local agency and autonomy are significant *in principle;* what are important rather are the ways in which local efforts to encompass colonizers' activities and offerings may be efficacious in some circumstances and limited and unsuccessful in others. In *Black Harvest,* commercial modernization certainly takes a local form, and it is represented in various ways that are certainly distinctively indigenous; but this is not to say that the process has somehow been successfully accommodated.

I've already noted that much of the work produced by Davidson's associates from the 1960s through the 1980s amounted to a critique of the "fatal impact" view of contact between Pacific islanders and Europeans. Breaking from the popular view of contact as destructive and exploitative was obviously necessary, but opposing what was clearly a larger moral narrative, a way of imagining the historical trend, with particular facts and an insistence upon complexity, entailed overlooking the difference in levels between these concerns.

The more basic question should perhaps have been: why is there an interest in a tragic history, in rendering islanders as victims? Permutations of this moral account are found in the earliest commentaries upon contact—witness Quiros's lament over the violence occasioned by misunderstanding in the Marquesas (1904–1905, 26, 29) and Forster's misgivings about the effects of trade goods in Tahiti (1996, 201)—and persist both in popular and scholarly histories in the present (Cameron 1987; Withey 1987, 11; Bayly 1989, 191). Beyond Oceania, we see the victimization of natives playing a variable but often morally pivotal role in films ranging from John Huston's *Key Largo* (1948) to Kevin Costner's *Dances with Wolves* (1992). Interests in representing contact as corrosive and destructive have obviously varied: for instance, the missionary construction of the labor trade as kidnapping, or "blackbirding"—in which the active interest or complicity of islanders is completely denied—emerged from an attempt to monopolize responsibility for the positive work of civilizing. Government interventions were ignored, and traders were represented merely as criminal exploiters; only the missionaries themselves were shown to act against heathen and savage practices, encourage industry, and create a social order. The interests of the numerous readers since 1966 of Alan Moorhead's *The Fatal Impact* (which remains in print, much to the irritation of those Pacific historians who see its interpretations as misguided and wholly superseded) have presumably been different; general associations with the internal critique of industrial civilization are obvious. Just as urbanization and the complexities of mechanical modern life may be seen to have dehumanized social relations and created widespread alienation and psychological trauma, industrial society from the time of its birth was seen to move outward to disrupt, consume, and destroy those who still lived in harmonious kinship-structured natural societies. The general relevance of the fatal impact narrative thus emerges from both countermodernist and progressivist imaginations, since it was also drawn upon by planters who saw native races dying out in the face of a more vigorous stock.

The lack of deeper inquiry into the misleading presentation of Pacific islanders and other indigenous peoples as victims manifests a more general neglect of the larger discursive frames of European historical metaphors. Although Bernard Smith's brilliant *European Vision and the South Pacific* was first published over thirty years ago, the topic of European representation and its relation to colonial practice in the Pacific has not been much pursued. In the wake of Edward Said's work, there has been a recent explosion of literature on "representations of the Other" and related topics, but much of this has proved less sophisticated than either Said or Smith, and it has been constrained, in particular, by a preoccupation with European stereotypes, which are seen to vary or conflict in the sense that one succeeds another rather than because such images might be actively and consciously debated at particular times (e.g., Nicolson 1988). Certainly, colonial texts and visual representations brought forward a plethora of "noble savages," "cannibals," and "dusky maidens," but an emphasis on these *as types* can only pass over more complex questions of their articulations in narrative—in something like *Black Harvest* or the thriller and historical novel I discuss in chapter 6—and neglect other issues, such as the ways in which visitors' or settlers' associations with prospectively colonized places were presented and inflected. The question also arises of the extent to which more scholarly narratives are encompassed by these discourses, by preoccupations with certain ways of incorporating or distancing the other.

Authors

Reference has often been made to the colonial character of history writing itself, and to the desirability of creating a new history by islanders (and other colonized peoples) rather than about them. While apparently laudable, such efforts tend to postulate a unitary "islander" perspective and to universalize an interest in certain modes of historical narrative; the authorship of European styles of narrative history is displaced from its metropolitan origins onto those who have generally been written about, a step taken in the name of democratizing history that curiously affirms the generalized authority of certain ways of establishing a command of the past. As Dirks suggests, the "new" histories are likely in many ways to reproduce the assumptions and hierarchizing devices of the old. More simply, some writing on this topic also presumes that the colonial framework through which history has been produced can be transcended in a straightforward and unproblematic manner. Without denigrating the considerable volume of history already published by Pacific islanders, the question of how this corpus relates to any decolonization of historical knowledge should be raised, as it has been in South Asia through the critiques of nationalist history on the part of the Subaltern Studies group (Guha 1983–87).

In debate about what Pacific history should be, certain historians (and ironically, mostly expatriates) have insisted that history must be not merely islands-oriented, as Davidson proposed, but written from an islander point of view. As

David Routledge has claimed: "Whole societies . . . must be studied, and studied, moreover, according to the worldview of the people themselves" (1985b, 93). The implication that the indigenous worldview can be grasped in some ready and unproblematic manner displays the author's innocence of the invariably difficult and occasionally intransigent work of cultural and ethnographic interpretation, but the more worrying notion is perhaps that one can speak of "the" worldview, as one can claim to write a history with an "orientation . . . from the Fijian point of view" (Routledge 1985a, 6). This is to ignore and suppress discontinuity among indigenous perceptions, to pass over contradiction and dissent within the indigenous social form as well as the divergent interests and histories consequent upon the differing entanglements with colonialism and neocolonial development. Routledge's history "seen"—how and by whom?— "from the Pacific Islands" has thus all too frequently been made in a complicit relationship with a local elite, with people who had their own reasons for constructing an authoritative history, a history that conveyed authority. This is also, of course, written from within a binarism that takes the separation between "colonizers" and "islanders" for granted and assumes that it is easy to say which is which. Where does this two-worlds vision place Joe Leahy? Is he any more hybrid than the big-men engaged in business? Even if we could, would we want to write their history from their "point of view"?

The quantity and range of work by islands writers is now considerable, and much of what has been published, for example, through the Institute of Pacific Studies in Suva has been valuable, but it would be merely patronizing to refrain from scrutinizing or criticizing such works on the basis of the same questions that have been raised about expatriate writing. In this context, debate about the Australian bicentenary and the history industry that emerged with it is relevant, especially to a number of official or semiofficial islands volumes (see, for example, Macintyre and Janson 1988). To what extent did works such as the trilingual book *Vanuatu* (Lini et al. 1980), partly written by the independent nation's first prime minister, legitimize not just the independent state but the dominance at the time of the Vanuaaku Pati in particular? To what extent are the histories of certain regions, of men, of Christians (as opposed to pagan *kastom* people), of dominant denominations, presented as "the" history of Vanuatu? Of course, it would only be surprising if these were not to some degree elite national histories like those produced elsewhere, but particular motifs and blindnesses reveal much about complicit colonial and postcolonial inequalities and the ways in which traditions and events are re-created as points of origin for an independent present (for a discussion of related issues in Africa see Neale 1985).

It must also be said that far from decolonizing history, these texts often merely relocate Western-style scholarship, or a more popular and accessible variant of it, and the inequality between a privileged writer and those whose stories are told, or not told, within a larger history. Like a variety of earlier accounts, independent history has thus often ignored and suppressed the inequalities and divergent perspectives within particular islands. Such questions are inadmissible if the politics of islands history are understood entirely in terms of the opposition between white colonizers or former colonizers and black islanders: it is clear that the burden of historical guilt lies with the former and that this must be expiated by repatriating history and refraining from criticizing versions that represent themselves as nationalist. But this construction of the politics of knowledge is reminiscent of the privileging of class in certain forms of socialism and Marxism, which argued that questions of "race," nationality, or sex were always secondary to class interest and would be automatically resolved through class struggle, even though there was generally no serious theory of the ways in which these forms of difference and inequality were imbricated. In the same way, any perspective that explicitly or implicitly disallows Pakeha, *palangi,* or *haole* (that is, white) commentary upon indigenous debate or difference effectively asserts that ethnicity or "race" is everything and that differences arising from gender, regional interests, rank, and class are inconsequential. While the fiction of an undivided ethnic identity opposed to the ways of foreigners may be a necessary one for ruling nationalists, it is not clear that such mystifications are especially useful to other islanders (whether politicians or ordinary citizens) or historians; yet the advertisement of Tongan or Fijian history by Tongan or Fijian writers depended upon precisely such a reduction of a plethora of salient social and cultural differences to the distinction between outsiders and insiders (Brady 1985). The important thing is not what the history says, but that it is a Fijian history; one could say, also, that the important thing about the Fiji dollar is that it is Fijian.

The preoccupation with encouraging indigenous authorship left aside the question of how far it should be expected that the historical imagination of Pacific islanders could be reproduced by organizing narratives in books. The extent to which such a model belonged to distinctively Western constructions of history and knowledge has not been much discussed (but see Borofsky 1987), and the interest of expatriate academics has seemed not so much to be in exploring indigenous historical perceptions as in encouraging islanders to write the same kind of history as themselves. That could be seen, ultimately, as just another strategy for normalizing and encompassing the other.

This is to place in another context the old question of "who owns the past?" One view would assert ownership of the Samoan past or the Tolai past on the part of Samoans and Tolai. There would be something improper in claiming to write "their" history as there is sometimes claimed to be in writing the ethnography of the other. It is true, of course, that the past is politicized; it is obviously available for use for or against particular present interests, and it can be rendered in a hegemonic manner. But the past differs from certain other cultural resources in the sense that if it is a scarce, it is not a unitary commodity (cf. Appadurai 1981). One either has the Elgin marbles or one does not, but scarcely any story exists in the absence of competing variants or alternate claims about what really transpired. One telling does not, in itself, preclude, marginalize, or even influence others. It is the institutional practices and modes of circulating written and oral histories that create dominant views and render dissent, or the views of the various actors themselves, peripheral. To suppose that foreign scholarly works that often have very limited circulation would actually displace other histories of the same place seems to entail an enormously inflated view of the practical effects of most academic research. The rhetorical force of the question Who owns the past? thus seems to imply a judgment of history written by whites about Oceania that might be at once excessively harsh and overly gentle. Posing the question at all suggests that what is largely controlled by white metropolitan scholars should instead belong to the people whose past it is; such a claim neglects the sense in which colonial history and its contexts are part of the past of Europeans and especially those who live in places of white settlement such as Australia and Hawaii (cf. Jolly and Macintyre 1989, 17). Not only do such people have a legitimate interest in matters such as the emergence of the colonial imaginings that continue to be manifest in tourist culture and museum exhibitions, it is imperative that they do, if superficially appreciative romantic or paternalistic attitudes are not to be perpetuated. On the other hand, the notion that the histories of certain Pacific islanders have merely been appropriated by those who should now repatriate them restricts and underspecifies the sense in which academic history might be regarded as embodying colonial values. It would thus seem important to displace the emphasis of debate from the "facts" of ownership (or theft) of a substantialized past to the content of particular renderings.

This might also cloud the judgment that representing others or producing narratives about them is *in itself* reprehensible. Islanders—and people everywhere—have always constructed cultural stereotypes of others, parodies of foreigners, and stories of the misunderstandings of contact.[12] Europeans' academic efforts to itemize and specify the real otherness of others are only one species of these more widespread efforts. The problem concerns not the fact of such representations, but their particular character and effect. Nationalist histories cannot immediately extricate themselves from the contradictions of colonialism, and the nature of neocolonial elites is such that there is rarely an interest in them doing so. This draws our attention to the motivations of narrative and, as Klaus Neumann has stressed, the displacement of hegemonic by counterhegemonic histories; here, the pluralization of authority demanded by Dening serves a tangible political need. In a farewell speech at the end of one of Neumann's periods of fieldwork, a Tolai man said, "What we need now is a *debate* about the past" (Neumann 1992a, 256). That is a simple point, but one that has eluded the discipline of Pacific history for too long.

Writing about the colonial encounter thus cannot be immediately "decolonized" but must rather deal with the persistence of colonialism and the consolidation of quasi-colonial relationships within the independent Pacific states. In this conjuncture indigenous as well as metropolitan histories should be considered as partial and interested products, but this suggestion does not diminish the value of indigenous accounts or consign them again to the margins of scholarly history. To the contrary, the discovery of diverse local perspectives upon contact and colonialism not only makes possible a critique of official versions, but also questions the general salience of Western and specifically scholarly notions of event and narrative. While it has surely been important to understand that a succession of encounters had two—or many—sides, it may be still more vital to acknowledge that the chronological history constituted by that succession does not order either indigenous memories or indigenous histories. We—both expatriate and indigenous scholars—have been so concerned to provide histories where they seemed lacking, and to do justice to indigenous constructions of the past, that we may have excluded the possibility that history was, anyway, less important than a canoe or a piece of barkcloth.

2

Alejandro Mayta in Fiji:

Narratives about

Millenarianism, Colonialism,

Postcolonial Politics,

and Custom

Nothing seemed more pathetic than the sight of an individual Seventh-day Adventist sitting with a glass of water on the periphery of a kava circle. This struck me not long after I began fieldwork in the western interior of Fiji's big island of Viti Levu: a man appeared to be excluded from a customary ceremony because Adventist taboos on alcohol were extended to the indigenous narcotic beverage. That personal reflection would however be justified by almost the whole corpus of anthropological literature on Fiji, rather than my own work. Kava drinking is visibly and manifestly a cultural practice, a ritual that is bound up with traditions, values, and social relations: in Fiji, as in Samoa and Tonga, it typically consists in a kind of sacrifice to the chief; the formal seating arrangements manifest a hierarchical order subsuming rank, age, gender, and contextual distinctions related to affinity and particular ceremonial events (see, for example, Toren 1990). In the formulae that are used daily, kava is "the water of the land" and "the chiefly kava"; the expression of pious religious (Methodist) sentiments in the context of these ritual utterances reinforces the explicit identifications between Fijian custom, a respect-structured kinship order, the way of the church, and the kava ceremony. Hence, although I was already aware that some Fijians abstained from drinking because of denominational laws, this visible marginalization seemed remarkable. How was it possible for people to take foreign religious prohibitions so seriously and eschew these crucial cultural values?

The extent to which Adventists set themselves off from village society in other respects is very variable, but there is no doubt that a great deal is at stake: a senior man who might otherwise have been a contender for a chiefly title was deemed ineligible because he could not "take the cup," while changes in religious affiliation on the part of individuals frequently lead to acrimonious disputes. In one instance, a chief excluded from his village several women who had switched to Adventism while working in town. Any denominational change is likely to be socially problematic, but the particular feature of the Adventist "sect" that has created tension in Fiji is the observance of the Sabbath on Saturdays, a correlate of which is taken to be an obligation to work on Sundays. This practice clashes with strict Fijian Sabbatarianism[1] and the rhythm of villages that are organized as much around church occasions as other major communal feasts and ceremonies. The issue has also frequently been politicized: since chiefs were and are predominantly Methodist, a change of church membership has usually entailed a challenge of some kind to the hegemony of the traditional hierarchy and what was in effect the "official" church (Catholicism provided a channel for dissent in the early days, but subsequently became almost as establishment as the Methodist Church). Exclusion, or self-exclusion, from a ceremony may thus reflect some wider differences.

Without denying tensions internal to contemporary Fijian society, which are also expressed in the spread of newer denominations such as the Assemblies of God, it must be recognized that there is also a problem of recognition that is internal to anthropology. The essentialist pursuit of cultural structures that are distinctly Fijian can only entangle itself with codifications of hierarchy, chieftainship, and the customary order and will exclude, in a more or less categorical fashion, notions and practices destabilizing that ensemble. There is no sense in which the ritual speech of old men exchanging whales' teeth in mortuary feasts or at traditional marriages and the ritual speech of old women in the Jehovah's Witnesses' hall can be equally Fijian from an anthropological perspective. And the issue is hardly restricted to Fiji. Ethnographers in Tonga, Papua New Guinea, and especially the Solomons have remarked (mostly privately) upon the "difficulty" of Adventist people and communities, their hostility toward custom (that is, toward what we might take to be their cultural milieux), their taste for money, and their lack of openness toward ethnographers.[2] Whereas in the eighteenth and nineteenth centuries, the "real savages" were those most hostile to inquisitive white outsiders, it ironically seems that now those who have sacrificed and destroyed most of their own culture resist inspection and refuse the supreme gift of intercultural dialogue, while authentically traditional (if mainstream Christian) people are generally both hospitable and interested in being anthropologists' hosts.

How can cultural interpretation interpret this dissociation from culture? If the problem arises from a pursuit of the *correct names* for, or the *original meanings* of, other people's meaningful practices, then perhaps I can construct something else by beginning from the objectification and distortion of customs and names:

we could thus regard historical anthropology as an inquiry into the inventive appropriation and recontextualization of culture, as a science of misnomers.

The particular investigation here is biographical, but the lives are those of narratives rather than the individuals whose practices have been caught up and ultimately effaced by a number of competing renderings. The accounts discussed arose from a sequence of prominent politico-religious movements of the period between Fiji's cession to Britain in 1874 and the First World War.[3] Although the British regime in Fiji has been widely regarded as a protectionist system in which traditional authority and indigenous rights to land were enshrined, the colonial state in fact embarked on an extraordinarily thorough and systematic program of social regulation and taxation that was resented and opposed by many commoner Fijians. The administration and indirect rule system was generally supported by the chiefly hierarchy, but chiefs in marginal areas, such as the interior provinces of Viti Levu, or those out of favor with the administration, were sometimes involved with commoners in protest and dissent— notably in Apolosi R. Nawai's broadly based Viti Kabani (Fiji Company), a politicized agricultural cooperative movement. Crosscutting loyalties, official repression, and a variety of other factors restricted the effectiveness of most of these movements, so that rural society has been characterized by suppressed but enduring tensions rather than open conflict (Thomas 1990b, 1990c).

Although I am partially concerned with how a number of important politicoreligious leaders of the early colonial period are represented now, my focus is upon one of least consequence, a man named Sailosi (this being the Fijianization of Silas and still a common name), who was an inspirational priest of some kind from the Tavua area on Viti Levu's north coast. In 1918 he announced a set of political prophesies and advocated reorganization of village society: wide interest was aroused in his area and in neighboring interior provinces, but the movement was rapidly suppressed by the administration. My concern here is thus with an ephemeral outbreak, a trivial matter that might be considered beyond the margins of serious history. However, the present work has been rendered substantially more feasible by a prior reflection upon the investigation of such topics.

An extremely marginal and ineffective historical character also figures in a recent treatise on the methodology of history and biography, which has been cunningly disguised as a novel, by the right-wing Peruvian politician Mario Vargas Llosa. *The Real Life of Alejandro Mayta* (1986) amounts to an analogous attempt to fabricate the life of an unimportant dissident, his character being a Trotskyist militant who tries to escape from years of sterile political discussion in tiny, marginal groups through direct action. He cooperates with an enthusiastic but inexperienced soldier in an attempt to launch a Peruvian revolution from the Andes. The insurrection was of course always doomed to failure, and based on total detachment from wider political realities. At the risk of introducing epistemological confusion, I may point out that the story is based on a real attempt initiated by someone with approximately the same name as the invented figure, although this basis in the factual is disclosed in critical commentary on the work rather than in the book itself (Dunkerley 1987, 119–20).[4] Vargas Llosa's fabrication proceeds, rather like *Citizen Kane,* through a tight interpenetration of his reconstruction of the events leading up to the insurrection and the conversations in the present through which these are known. The dialectic of disclosure and suppression is thus constituted through a stylistically dazzling paragraph-by-paragraph and even sentence-by-sentence transposition of then and now, of the history and the dialogue. The reflexivity of the project is insisted upon, and many of those interviewed by the author-character question *him* about why he is engaged in the inquiry.

> "What is it about Mayta that interests you so much?" Moisés asks me, as he uses the tip of his tongue to check the temperature of the coffee. "Of all the revolutionaries of those years, he is the most obscure."
>
> I don't know how to go on. If I could, I would tell him, but at this moment I only know that I want to know, even invent, Mayta's story, and as lifelike as possible. I could give him moral, social, and ideological reasons, and show him that Mayta's story is the most important, the one that most urgently needs to be told. But it would all be a lie. I truthfully do not know why Mayta's story intrigues and disturbs me.
>
> "Perhaps I know why," Moisés says. "Because his story was the first, before the triumph of the Cuban Revolution. Before that event which split the left in two."
>
> He may be right, it may well be because of the precursory character of the adventure. It's true that it inaugurated a new era in Peru, something neither Mayta nor Vallejos could guess at the time. But it's also possible that the whole historical context has no more importance than as decor and that the obscurely suggestive element I see in it consists of the truculence, marginality, rebellion, delirium, and excess which all came together in that episode . . . (1986, 44).

Vargas Llosa acknowledges to his informants that he intends deliberately and consciously to rework the past into "a faint, remote, and if you like, false version" (1986, 66; cf. 81). Here I cannot recapitulate the course of inquiry and the history that was its object, but instead privilege the interested contrivance of representation and intersperse two kinds of renaming that equally efface the historical fact of Sailosi's own motivation and action. I refer to the "distortions" of various perceptions of his movement and the constituted character of my own analysis. The claim behind this denial of any history outside recontextualization is not the relativist proposition that "we have different histories for different occasions" (Dening 1988a:99) but that both the hands of others and one's own hand ought to be disclosed. The cultural differences between different narratives emerge from political situations, from interests in particular constructions of the past. What confronts us is not merely a plurality of accounts, but a contested field. I do not put forward another history merely to add to those already in circulation or to succeed those that have been forgotten, but to intervene in debate about the Fijian past. I would not write if I did not have an argument.

It would be impossible, anyway, to resort to any claim about the historical primacy of Sailosi's action—unlike Alejandro Mayta, he was certainly not the first Fijian to call for a revolutionary transformation of social relations—but I will argue later that aspects of contemporary Fijian culture and politics amount to a generalization of the political imagination of characters such as Sailosi and Apolosi R. Nawai. But I must proceed to situate the unoriginality of his protest in the history of opposition to the chiefly establishment based on the small island of Bau and the British colonial administration with which, from the time of cession in 1874, the high chiefs were generally closely associated. Discontent was in fact something that distinguished his district, and those of the adjacent upland interior. Drauniivi Village on the Rakiraki coast had been the center of the Tuka activities, which were most conspicuous in the 1880s but had both antecedents and many later manifestations.[5] Sailosi had some involvement in these activities and at some stage kept a notebook of ritual formulae, inexplicable hieroglyphics, and prophesies; in 1896 he was among those who made requests through provincial councils that those who had been deported from their villages to outlying islands be permitted to return, which in fact did not happen for almost twenty years.[6] But that is not what got him into trouble.

The distinctive feature of the British colonial regime in Fiji was the indirect rule structure, which ostensibly provided for government through the chiefs— "in the Fijian manner," as the officials imagined—although the neat administrative hierarchy of appointed village, district, and provincial heads[7] was of course essentially foreign. The problem with creating and circulating names is, of course, that the uses to which these are put cannot be easily controlled. Hence, it became necessary to ask the *buli boubuco*, the official district chief, whether he had any complaints against his *ovisa*, his native constable.

Sailosi had apparently got into the habit of using the *buli*'s office, opening his mail, signing his name, "summoning the District Council on his own authority," and "doing a variety of other things in contravention of [the *buli*'s] office and dignity"—including, it seems, wearing his spectacles. On this occasion the *buli* defended his subordinate and said that the allegations, which had been set out in a letter from his own son and from an appointed village chief, were merely reactions to Sailosi's vigorous prosecution of his duty. The signatories were in fact tried for slander and each sentenced to three months' hard labor. However, less than a year later, A. B. Joske, the resident commissioner, found himself compelled to recommend Sailosi's dismissal.[8] He was not immediately convicted of any charge, but there was further trouble, and he was incarcerated, first in the Colonial Hospital and then in the Lunatic Asylum, after he had allegedly been so indiscreet as to inform his nurse that, if so instructed by his guardian spirit, he would kill her, the chief medical officer, or anyone else.[9]

These occurrences echo something more elusive than an individual case of madness. As with Mayta, the excess and marginality are "obscurely suggestive" because they are emblematic of historical tropes, of a cultural structure of colonialism. Sailosi's acts seemed necessarily irrational; this kind of resistance typified the unmanageability of Fijians that haunted the British quest for orderly representation and control: I thus take the appropriation of official chiefly spectacles to epitomize the subversion of these hierarchical colonial relationships through the abuse of their own status markers and mechanisms for rendering texts and colonized places visible.[10] White officials generally reacted by writing off such political mimicry as the result of mental derangement or emotional instability. Joske, who seems to have had some sympathy for Sailosi, could only say that "he has by bad temper got himself into a false position in his own village."[11] The notion that there were "false positions" had wide application, but Joske also noted uneasily with regard to quite separate "disturbances" that the "turbulent" young chiefs of Nagonenicolo were "very intelligent & have an extraordinary knowledge of law & of parliamentary Govt."[12]

This was a rare admission that dissent did not always originate in misinformation. False assertions were certainly conspicuous when Sailosi, evidently discharged from the asylum, addressed a crowded meeting in the town of Tavua in March 1918. He informed those present that he had been on a mountaintop in Europe and seen the king present a Fijian customary *soro*, or gift of submission, together with an indemnity, to the kaiser; this meant that the government in Fiji was finished, there would be no more taxes, and all the officials from the governor down to the village chiefs would be replaced by appointees from Apolosi R. Nawai's Viti Kabani (Fiji Company).[13] This was a powerful movement with an unmistakably political and antichiefly agenda: in songs connected with raising money,[14] Apolosi is sometimes referred to as "na jivu ni bula ni Viji"[15] (chief of Fiji's life or health). The odd use of the loan word *jivu* in lieu of the usual Fijian terms for chief typifies the name stealing characteristic of mille-narian practice. In the case of Sailosi's new order, this centered upon the cre-ation of a new church, the *lotu naba walu*, or Number 8 Religion, which rather resembled the Number 7 Religion, or Adventist Church (*lotu ka vitu*).[16] The key shift was that Saturday was to be observed as the Sabbath and work engaged in on Sunday.[17] These proposals were adopted immediately but unevenly in parts of the generally disaffected interior provinces of Colo East, Colo West, and Colo North—"On Easter Sunday there was actually housebuilding and weeding in towns—which is indeed strange for Fijians," noted a district official.[18] A series of witnesses' statements confirmed that, in this story, Britain had been beaten on 25 March, the government was abolished, and "the Wesleyan church & its sunday done away with—also the work in connection with it." One native minis-ter was more specific:

> This is the time that Fiji is to be at rest. There is no Government, no Governor, Roko, Buli, Turaga ni Koro, everything appertaining to the Gov-ernment. The people who take their place are the Turaga ni Koros of the Fiji Company . . . No taxes. No one is to pay his taxes . . . Concerning the Church. No missionary meetings, or quarterly collections, or food for min-isters . . . Sunday is to be observed on Saturday. The present Sunday to be done away with. All these things have been told to me [i.e., Sailosi] by God. Know this also that Apolosi is like John the Baptist, I like Jesus, God has spoken to me & told me to free Fiji.[19]

Another witness reported that after the news had been announced,

> we were asked if any of us wished to enter the Freedom of Fiji—& if so to sign on the right side of the paper—& if we refused to sign on the left side. The touching the pen was done—Rapuama wrote the names—he had one pen to write with—Onisimo took another pen which was touched by the people. They did not touch the pen which was used to write with as is the custom.[20]

I am not quite sure what "the custom" refers to, but the subversion of official practice evidently gave ritualized nominal rolls some force in other registers of dissent. In 1902, for instance, many Fijians signed petitions saying that they wanted to be part of New Zealand and have no local administration.[21]

Even at the time, Sailosi's narrative was consequential in locally modified forms. In the Noikoro area, the main proponent of the Number 8 Religion was a chief of secondary rank who had been engaged in a long-running struggle with the titleholder, Ratu Simione Durutalo, who was literate and a staunch Methodist, had been employed in various capacities by the government, and also had written the traditional history of the "tribe" for A. B. Joske. This compilation of definite histories of chiefly families of course displaced the claims of certain lines. Sailosi's prophesies were absorbed into a more general litany of complaints concerning the local hegemony of this particular progovernment chief, his group, and the manner in which this dominance had been established at the expense of other chiefs and clans in the area not long after cession to Britain. To some extent these conflicts are difficult to discuss because they are recapitulated in quite a specific manner by the descendants of protagonists on both sides and now have some connections with national political disputes. The general point is merely that adherence to the movement had different meanings and uses in different places, even at the time.

It is not surprising that the administration and white establishment found it necessary to contain Sailosi's transgression. They did this not merely by arresting him, but also by writing about him in a particular manner. With respect to generalized rumors concerning British defeat by Germany, the *Fiji Times* speculated that these emanated "from natives who can read English in a parrot-like fashion and do not quite understand its purport."[22] Almost immediately, though, this explanation of falsity in terms of the misreading of a clear text by anomalously literate Fijians was displaced by quite a different story. Predictably enough, these reports got Sailosi muddled up with one Sakuisa or Sakusia and further deconstructed him as the author of the trouble. The Rakiraki "Fijian prophet" was "but the mouthpiece of a German white Fijian" who had been successfully persuading "the gullible kai Viti [that] Kaiser Bill is omnipotent and the Germans unconquerable."[23] The few sentences of these Fiji-English reports are replete with disputed and confounded identities.[24] The "prophet" was said to have been not a liar or a political criminal but "deposed as an imposter"—in some sense because it had been revealed that he had been "tutored up to his assertions" by a German named Soderberg, who lived *vakaviti,* "in the Fijian manner," "in the same district as the alleged prophet."[25] Just as there was much disquiet about half-castes and partially assimilated natives who appeared to be "bad imitations" of Europeans, the European who adopted a Fijian village life to such an extent that he would be described as a "white Fijian" could hardly represent anything other than an origin of disorder.

The head of the Methodist Church also vigorously condemned Sailosi, and specifically denounced the new religion as "political"—the objection thus being that the correct meaning of religion had been abused by the agenda of the Number 8 Church. An editorial also expressed concern that "the native is becoming educated to the fact that it is possible to use religion as a cloak to hide a multitude of sins and ulterior motives."[26] The threat of disorder was thus closely connected to the circulation of language, and the power that Fijians were thought to be just then acquiring over introduced signs.

Sadly, that imagined control could not save Sailosi, who was regarded as fit to plead guilty to being a lunatic at large: he was thus permitted a moment of reason in which he could acknowledge his own madness. And there was no paradox since, as was noted above, resistance could only occupy "false positions" in the colonial British imagination of the time. Our hero was dispatched to the Lunatic Asylum, where he ceases to be named but presumably persisted in being documented through the statistical reports of the *Blue Books*. These fully record the number of occasions upon which it proved necessary to physically restrain inmates and specify in each case what form of restraint was employed.

Outside official discourse, Sailosi's name was attached to the adjective "mad" and circulated in a few texts.[27] With enviably balanced judgment, the historian Timothy Macnaught qualified this to "half-mad" (1979, 99). Setting aside this reiteration of official classification, Macnaught must, however, be credited with having mentioned Sailosi at all, since it seems that all the other historians of Fiji share the view of the Lunatic Asylum itself: that those who circulate misnomers should have their own names suppressed.

However, this connivance in the policing of madness represents bad historical practice in quite simple terms; as Macnaught noted, Sailosi's movement did have enduring ramifications for subsequent patterns of religious affiliation, and these, I will suggest, are of broader significance still.

The Number 8 Religion had caused substantial defections from the Methodist Church in parts of the eastern interior. The missionary Harold Chambers, who went up the Wainibuka Valley less than a month after Sailosi's arrest, found that some of those wavering had not broken with the church because of government action, but that in the villages higher up the valley, there were few who remained loyal. "Last year the people in crowds awaited me with smiling faces, warm was their welcome and joyous the services. This time a furtive sullen faced people slunk away at my approach or passed me with either none or but the scantiest response to my usual greeting."[28]

Of course, by this time legal action was being taken to suppress the movement and punish those who had been involved. In Colo West, twenty-nine cases were considered and sentences of hard labor or fines imposed; those who had been village chiefs or other appointees were also of course dismissed.[29] Under these circumstances the Number 8 Religion could hardly be overtly adhered to, but the government's sense that it simply could not suppress religious choice permitted a transposition of the "original" theft of meaning: what had initially been the referent for subversive imitation became reconstituted and politically valorized as an extension of its own parody. This was already taking place as Chambers visited the Wainibuka villages, where a former Methodist teacher, Pauliasi Bunoa, had been holding meetings.

> Of late days the position has been complicated by the pushing in of Pauliasi the 7th-day Adventist bummer. The wily Sailosites saw their chance and thinking to throw dust in the eyes of the Government professedly accepted the cloak offered them by the 7th day Adventists while they hold the doctrine of Sailosi secretly and await for his statements to be justified . . . Pauliasi wrote . . . that he had won 330 converts in his district. I think the number fairly correct but they are no more Lotu ni kavitu than I am. To the marrow of their bones their leaders are No 8 and the rank and file are "veimurimuriga" [followers].[30]

Pauliasi's speeches had allegedly consisted of diatribes against extractive Methodist fundraising and praise for Sailosi's knowledge and energy ("Au sa dokai Sailosi vakalevu" [I respect Sailosi very much], and so on). The consequences were permanent: these settlements have been Adventist ever since.[31] In Colo West, essentially the same swift defection occurred, but the bitter opposition of the chief and prompt action on the part of a district officer made it possible to expose the "political" motivations beneath the religious cloak. Intervention thus resorted to a distinction between "genuine" and "false" conversion, and one Noikoro man was considered a "sincere" Adventist. Again, there is a curious sense of displacement of the authorship of dissent: a figure identified at one point as the source of trouble is shown to have been put up to it by others who predictably occupy "false positions." The unruly character of one of those blamed, a dismissed "native stipendiary magistrate," was manifest in his detachment from his own home village: he had arrived in Noikoro after having been ejected from another district "for causing trouble there." In colonial discourse, the legibility of Fiji depended very much on its partitioning and proper ordering: wandering individuals and attempts to establish new or outlying settlements constituted "irregularities" to be regarded with extreme suspicion (cf. Thomas 1990c).

In 1918 the chiefly Methodist hegemony in Noikoro was reasserted, and those who had attempted to install the Viti Kabani and a competing chiefly clan were obliged to make customary apologies. Though the district official recognized that the people were in "a very sensitive state," he appeared confident that their promises never again to "have anything to do with the S. D. Adventist religion" would be kept. However, the families of most of those listed as party to the defection are now Adventists and on the basis of oral information seem to have gone over in about 1930. Some later and distinct disputes also seem manifested in the patterns of contemporary affiliation, and of course some of the older conflicts have become irrelevant. As the *Fiji Times* feared, the "cloak" of religion would inevitably be exploited.

There are some things I know about Sailosi that I have not included here. There are other things that I will never know and perhaps should have mentioned. I could have conveyed something more about the man, about the look of his village, about his own physique, about the eloquence or magnetism that made his heresy persuasive. That "fleshing out" would have enabled an understanding of the causes of the events that I have described in an individual's actions: there might have been a counterpart to the rebellious delirium of extravagant prophesies in a figure composed of personal idiosyncrasies. In fabricating such a historical character, I could even have suggested that Sailosi's sexuality manifested the same transgression and deviance as his cultural mischief: I could have taken some of the cases that came before provincial courts concerning sexual irregularities and placed Sailosi's name amongst those of the accused. And it was in fact the case that the colonial state policed the "false positions" of both bodies and religions.

But what if, at some point in these inquiries, I had met the man, or one of his relatives or descendants, and felt drawn into some dialogue of confession and concealment about what I had done—what I am doing—with these narratives? Would I have felt as awkward as Vargas Llosa did when he finally encountered Mayta and half discussed the events and his version of them with him?

> "The character in my novel is queer," I tell him after a bit.
> He raises his head as if he's been stung by a wasp. Disgust twists his face. He's sitting in a low armchair, with a wide back, and now he seems to be sixty or more. I see him stretch his legs and rub his hands, tense.
> "But why?" he finally asks.
> He takes me by surprise. Do I know why? But I improvise an explanation. "To accentuate his marginality, his being a man full of contradictions. Also to show the prejudices that exist with regard to this subject among those who supposedly want to liberate society from its defects. Well, I don't really know exactly why he is." (Vargas Llosa 1986, 301).

My account parallels Vargas Llosa's in the sense that a farcical rebellion unworthy of serious historical notice is made resonant of a conflict-ridden history. But unlike Vargas Llosa, I have refrained from imagining a character who personifies political irrationality, perversity, marginality, and excess. It may seem inconsistent to emphasize (in opposition to conventional history) the multiplicity of inventions and the creativity of history making while refraining myself from inventing a history: these stories have detoured around the absent space of their character. I hesitate to adumbrate Sailosi because he can only be imagined as a character through sources that reflect the official perspectives of both colonial and indigenous hierarchies, sources that necessarily distance him from rationality and emphasize his false positions. For this reason, I have imagined a succession of narratives rather than the creations of actors. Sailosi's understanding of his own actions remains beyond the vision of this account, just as it has always remained beyond the logic of the colonial schemes that sought to legislate and discipline indigenous dissent.

Let me now make a long temporal jump to consider a story, or rather a set of observations implying a story, that has some currency in Noikoro. I do not claim that all Fijians, even there, see things as described; if the military coups of 1987 had a single positive consequence, perhaps it was that it made it impossible to refer to "the Fijian view" in such a unitary and politically decided manner.

Noikoro people do not, so far as I have established, tell stories about Sailosi and the Number 8 event particularly. It must be recalled that this was merely one of a long sequence of "disturbances" and revivals of proscribed ritual activities, and it was among those that were most rapidly suppressed. Proscribed "heathen practices" are now understood to belong essentially to one class, while the individuals referred to are mainly much more prominent leaders such as Navosavakadua, the Tuka priest, and Apolosi, the leader of the Viti Kabani mentioned above.

The political and anticolonial aspect of their practices scarcely features in most accounts—which is not surprising, because the colonial presence itself is scarcely present in any local historical understanding. Although these facts of Fijian history are well known, through school education as well as other contexts, neither Fiji's cession to Britain in 1874 nor independence in 1970 are often alluded to. So far as the latter is concerned, this is understandable, because the postcolonial state has only sustained the inequities of resource distribution and representation that developed earlier: there is a sense of continuity over the whole postwar period rather than any great change around 1970. On the other hand, the earlier social transformation from pagan warrior society is represented exclusively as a consequence of "taking the *sulu*"—that is, conversion to Christianity—which as the phrase and certain narratives indicate, is seen to have been an uncompelled voluntary act. Associated changes over the same period— such as the concentration of settlements—are represented as outcomes of positive local choice rather than external imposition.

The elements of a story adduced here arose from a number of conversations in Korolevu, in the Noikoro district, but I have particular reason to recall a very long discussion that took place on the cement verandah of one of the village's few concrete block houses. This was a male group, and as usual we were drinking kava. I think it went on until 4 a.m., and normally that sort of thing numbed my brain to such an extent that I could hardly listen to what was said in a language in which I was in fact semifluent. But on this occasion I was so intrigued by the renderings of a ritual system that had supposedly been displaced 113 years earlier, and some other matters, that I felt alert and scarcely tired at all.

We had begun by discussing religious practices among Malays and Australian Aborigines. The Noikoro men were interested in the latter because I had given people some picture books featuring the Australian *taukei* (indigenous owners of the land);[32] knowledge of the former arose from some men's experience in the campaign against the communists in the 1950s. One man had in fact seen a few Aborigines while briefly at an airbase in Queensland en route to Malaya, as it then was, but he claimed that the Aborigines had been so terrified of the Fijian soldiers that they ran away. A direct analogy was made between the situations of ethnic Fijians and indigenous Malays: the latter also have a strong hold on custom but are weak in the path of money. These comparisons depend upon a perception of a proportionate relationship between customary strength and inability in commerce, which carries a heavy political burden in Fiji.

The stories that emerged concerning Navosavakadua, Apolosi, and certain more local prophets were variations upon those widely told in Fiji, or at least on Viti Levu, and dealt with miraculous acts, some of which had close Christian parallels. The fish bones Navosavakadua left over turned into whole fish; his taro leavings turned into whole tubers. There were many attempts to kill him. At Rotuma the king heard that attempts to get rid of him had been unsuccessful, so he called Navosavakadua to his house. As Navosavakadua stepped across the threshold, the king fired a pistol directly at his chest. When the smoke cleared, Navosavakadua, unhurt, said, "Yes? What did you want to see me about?" The sense of some of these stories turns purely on the miraculous. At Nukuilau, Apolosi once took a machete and cut a cat in half; the head was here and the back legs and tail there. Then he put it back together and it ran off, alive as before. He could also kick over a full kava bowl and it would be full again when it was placed upright. The power of these men was such that the possibility of their still being alive is widely entertained. Navosavakadua is said to have gone to rest. He was dressed and wrapped up in mats and placed in a coffin, and the house was then sealed for three days. When it was opened for his burial, the people found the coffin broken open and the mats scattered; the priest had vanished. Of Apolosi it is also said, "si cola tu e kia," he lives still.

It would be surprising, of course, if names like these were not drawn into stories about singular power, but the motivation of these narratives seems somewhat more specific. The fact that the capacities that are alluded to are distinctly mystical and indigenous becomes explicit in comparative statements concerning ritual activities at *nanaga* sites:

> White people could fly with machines, but up at that place the old people [*na tuqwaqwa*] flew without machines. That was where the priest gave the warriors the *mana*. If you were sitting by the river and there was a mango right up there in the tree, your arm would detach itself, fly up and pick it, and then be joined back to your body.[33]

A similar contrast between powers is sometimes manifest in statements concerning healing: prayers said over kava in the spirit house[34] had the same efficacy as the technical medicine of white people and are represented as a direct indigenous equivalent to it. Now, however, because the church is strong, these activities, and undesirable counterparts such as sorcery, cannot persist: "now everyone respects machines."

These people thus portray themselves as having moved from a condition of former parity with whites, based on qualitatively different kinds of power, to a situation of asymmetry. The transformation has both positive and negative features: the mutual implication of the church, kinship, sentiment, and hierarchy is—for the majority—unambiguously good, and in fact such institutions are central to Fijian ethnic pride and the conviction that their customary sociality embodies more mutual care and practical Christianity than the way of life of white foreigners. On the other hand, the people of Viti Levu's interior have a strong sense of their own poverty with respect to foreigners, Indians, and certain other Fijians. Whenever one is engaged in repetitive kinds of work connected with cash crops, people remark upon the laboriousness of weeding or planting by hand—"Overseas you have machines to do this. Here our machines are our hands!"

This may appear to take us some way from the question of the representation of figures such as Sailosi and Apolosi and the movements with which they were associated, and I have in fact argued that there are disconnections in contemporary historical consciousness. But just as stories about *mana* are recontextualized specifically as expressions of endogenous Fijian vitalizations of divine power, the political movements need not be conspicuous in contemporary views because their force has been transposed to another domain. I noted above that the commitment to custom—which is paradigmatically expressed in very costly ceremonial feasts and presentations connected with marriage, death, and so on—is understood to be directly related to weakness in the field of commerce. On one occasion in the midst of a ceremony a man remarked to me on the splendid abundance of exchange valuables—pots, mats, and so on—and in the next breath said, "In Fiji for us it is difficult. We are poor." The point is also established, so to speak, by the stereotypical perception of Fiji-Indians as individualists without real kinship but efficacious in business. The political resonance of the polarity however also emerges in disputes between Fijians; at a cultural level, it clearly makes possible a reversal of values and a rejection of what is selectively identified as custom.

The most extreme example of this was the Bula Tale (Live Again) Movement of the early 1960s, led by Apimeleki Ramatau Mataka, a former medical clerk. This was represented as a "Communist" movement, although its striking feature was a precise reversal of all of the key symbols of the Fijian customary system. The use of kava and presentations of whales' teeth in marriages and mortuary ceremonies were abolished; large-scale marriages and betrothals, which are now elsewhere absolutely central to the perception of the way of the land, were replaced by a strictly private exchange of vows—"there should be no feasting." Even the internal domestic hierarchy in eating—which, as Toren (1989) among other anthropologists has pointed out, is central to the daily spatial and experiential recreation of hierarchy—was rejected: "everyone eats together in a common dining house . . . everyone eats the same sort of food."[35] And while village people in 1988 were conspicuously reluctant to use clinics and hospitals in the absence of a real emergency, Apimeleki said that "when a member is ill, we don't tinker with Fijian cures but send him or her to hospital for treatment."[36]

This can be understood as a manifestation of the broader process of objectification and codification of culture in the form of kastom (custom, in Solomons pijin, Vanuatu bislama, and New Guinea tok pisin) in the Solomons and Vanuatu, and the local variants of the "Pacific way" in Tonga, Samoa, and elsewhere. "Customs," "traditional culture," and related labels do not refer merely to a set of beliefs and practices that happens to have persisted over a long period, but to a selective construct defined partly in opposition to foreign ways or intrusions.[37] The practices or attitudes that become significant may obviously not be "traditional" at all in the sense of historical continuity, but their authenticity from this perspective (which may or may not be salient locally) is less important than what people make of them. Objectifications of this kind have frequently been central to affirmations of national or local identity, but it is not necessarily the case that objectified cultures are positively upheld as resources to be preserved and employed. Once a set of practices and institutions has been named, the name can be displaced or rejected.

The Nadroga movement was not a bizarre exception but merely a strong expression of something inevitably generated within neotraditional Fijian culture, which is manifested all the time in more or less conspicuous and significant forms. For instance, an Assemblies of God woman whom I met on a bus attributed the fact that her marriage had broken up to its traditional "arranged" character (as she put it in English). It hardly needs to be reiterated that such an observation depends upon the naming of customs that did not formerly signify totalities of any kind, let alone a restrictive communal order.

It is rather surprising that one review of *The Real Life of Alejandro Mayta* saw the book as "strip[ping] bare self-indulgent insurrection and show[ing] its descent into squalid criminality" (Pickering 1986, 30). Although the essentially self-parodying character of Trotskyist sects can hardly pass undisclosed, there is rather an insistence upon the point that Mayta's action has undergone a historic if not a moral vindication. That is, the transformation of circumstances reveals in what was essentially marginal and politically unrealistic the germination of political reactions and disputes that now surround us. Vargas Llosa constantly refers to the fact that Mayta was trying to act as if the world then was the way it has become: then "the things that are happening now would seem impossible," "Mayta was twenty-five years too early with his plans," and so on (1986, 152, 169, chaps. 6 and 7 passim). In the same sense, before 1987, this essay would have lacked the truth it now possesses. How could I have imagined when I first began to research this that someone actually would change the name of the governor, that all political definitions would be contested, that Fiji, or at least urban Fiji, would become one of those tense places where soldiers are constantly seen but where violence ceases to be policed, where it has instead become an undefinable fact of daily life? There is an unknowable incidence of overt political harassment and assault that is perhaps relatively small, but also a marked increase of violence that is merely criminal in one sense but entirely enabled by new political circumstances and categories in another. The climate in Fiji is quite revolutionary in that many poorer men simply no longer accept the constituted distinctions that restrained them from seizing property in the past. This is not to suggest that the present wave of urban violence and sexual violence is in any sense politically productive or progressive, but merely to point out that order, hierarchy, and class privilege are contested to an unprecedented degree.

One claim about the historic significance of movements such as the Tuka and the Viti Kabani, as well as later cases like Apimeleki's Bula Tale, has been made by sociologists supportive of the Fiji Labour Party, which was formed in 1985, elected in a coalition with the Indian National Federation party in April 1987, and overturned in a military coup on 14 May that same year. The argument concerning the past and future basis for its support has been that there is a tradition of dissent from the conjuncture of chiefly and colonial rule and from the transformation of that conjuncture into the Alliance government, which was dominated by chiefs and marked by a strong probusiness orientation. In this view, various earlier movements stand as the precursors to a class-based multi-racial protest that comes to fruition in the formation of the Fiji Labour Party and its political triumph: the coup represents essentially a reaction on the part of an embattled elite that refused to surrender power.[38]

There is clearly much truth in this as a history for the present; but it is important to recall that the reasons why the coup was perpetrated by a certain group cannot be identified with the reasons why it was generally supported. This permits disclosure of another way in which the present is prefigured in the millenarian narratives.

The early-twentieth-century movements certainly did entail commoner protest, but this often took a nationalist form. One of Sailosi's prophesies was that both Europeans and Indians would be expelled from Fiji;[39] this is echoed in much more recent marginal charismatic churches such as the Congregation of the Poor (Rokotuiviwa 1985, 182) and rather disables any link with a politically sophisticated struggle based on a common front. The recontextualization offered here stresses that some people were positive about both Colonel (now General) Rabuka and the deposed Prime Minister Bavadra; they saw positive elements in Labour and in the coup that was seen to displace both the Alliance and Labour. And at certain times, such as around the second coup, it actually was the case that the old Alliance leadership was completely marginalized by a coalition between the military and (nationalist) Taukei Movement people who had either never been part of, or were alienated from, the Alliance and the old government.

This reaction is explicable if the significance of dissent from tradition is appreciated. "Tradition" represents a social order that has a range of extremely desirable features but is proportionate with Fijian poverty. The dichotomized view does not map at all directly the complex interpenetration of ceremonial activities and cash cropping, but it has motivated a very extensive discussion since the coup about the necessity, and difficulties, of bringing Fijians into commerce. This debate, which has actually been far more important than argument about constitutional and juridico-political restructuring, has featured an enormous amount of contradiction and ambivalence, and the extreme anti-custom option—which I have traced through certain adoptions of Seventh-day Adventism and which was most conspicuous in the Bula Tale case—does not necessarily have an especially wide following.[40]

The present thus amounts to an expression and an enlargement of the Fiji that was manifested in Sailosi's and Apolosi's political theater much earlier this century. In its stronger form this conception seeks a recovery of power on the part of indigenous people and their priests against both the foreigner-chiefs who abuse colonial or bureaucratic privilege and a range of actual foreigners, including Indians. Because there is at once a commitment to custom and an interest in material prosperity, which is perceived to be disabled by it, few can opt for the categorical rejection of hierarchy with which real economic advancement might be identified. But there is above all a sense that the tensions of the neotraditional order cannot be contained. Hence, while figures such as the high chief and administrator Ratu Sukuna are represented in official history as visionary architects of social compromise and the modern Fijian nation, Apolosi and Sailosi perhaps always had a sharper sense of the fractures in the edifice.

As a genre, biographies inevitably establish or restate the importance of their subjects. That is a convention that I do not resist here. But the story of Sailosi is intended to do more than disorient the conventional histories and anthropologies of Fiji. In *Crime and Custom*, Malinowski noted that the binding force of customary reciprocity was sometimes illustrated inversely in the ostracism of partly assimilated natives:

> Test cases are supplied nowadays, when a number of natives through laziness, eccentricity, or a non-conforming spirit of enterprise, have chosen to ignore the obligations of their status and have become automatically outcasts and hangers-on to some white man or other (1926, 42).

I have already noted that the neotraditional codification of culture in forms such as *kastom* or the Fijian way always permits certain forms of selective rejection, which often embody precisely a "non-conforming spirit of enterprise" of the kind mentioned. But this kind of cultural perversity has been engaged in by too many communities and is too closely connected with cult activities and prior social divisions for it to be regarded as an idiosyncratic non-thing, an exception proving the rule. From an anthropological perspective, the fact that a young Fijian man might say to me in a bar in town that "tradition is a lot of shit" means almost nothing; the complaint of the Assemblies of God woman about arranged marriage means almost nothing. Such people are educated, speak English, and are not Fijian to the same extent as the old men in the village who told those other stories I have used. But the associations between these statements could lead to a different investigation, one that deals precisely with this sort of abuse of the idea of culture. The forms of renaming discussed here at once permit the codification and subversion of hierarchies and customs and the parodying and appropriation of new religions. That is the process through which the cultural history of the present is being invented and contested.

PART II
COLONIAL IMAGES
AND
NARRATIVES

3

Liberty and License:
New Zealand Societies
in Cook Voyage
Anthropology

Over the last twenty years, studies of European "representations" and "images" of non-European peoples have proliferated. Much of this work has been of great interest, but certain widespread premises have arguably proved inhibiting. In the first place, it is frequently assumed that it was a relatively simple matter, in a perceptual and conceptual sense, for Europeans to apply their prior notions of savage or primitive life to whichever people they encountered. This is to preclude the possibility that particular circumstances might perplex travelers and prove difficult to reconcile with their more or less theorized expectations concerning other peoples—what we might call their anthropological ideas. Secondly, discussions have frequently focused on stereotypes or "images" of others, as though these were the basic units in the currency of colonial culture. Representations of Oceania are frequently seen to resort to either the notion of the noble savage or the opposed ignoble type. Certainly, among the constructions of indigenous people significant in the eighteenth and nineteenth centuries, these loom large, but I want to assert rather baldly that the concept of an image or type is far too static to account for the varying values and narratives that enter into assessments of particular indigenous societies. Contrary to both these assumptions, I want to suggest that such assessments were often hesitant and uncertain. In late-eighteenth-century perceptions, both virtue and vice or liberty and licence could be copresent among particular non-Europeans, who might therefore seem both noble and ignoble.

Finally, it is often supposed that colonial ideology works to distance non-European peoples such as Pacific islanders by emphasizing strangeness and denying shared humanity. While this distancing is conspicuous in some kinds of Orientalism, exoticism, and primitivism, contrary familiarizing tendencies are notable, and not only in the evangelical imaginings that of course sought to incorporate heathen people in the Christian community. In the philosophical writing of the eighteenth century, also, it can be suggested that Oceanic social relations and manners are represented and discussed through a European political vocabulary, and that metropolitan political arguments proceeded between the lines of ethnographic interpretation. We can be sure that the Oceanic societies were therefore misrepresented in various ways: but I aim to show in this essay that they were not "imaged" in any stable or stereotypic fashion.

In his *History of America,* published in 1777, William Robertson dismissed the notion that a "general state of promiscuous intercourse between the sexes ever existed" and asserted rather that "even among the rudest tribes" a regular form of marriage was universal. This was not to say that conjugality took a form that would have been familiar and pleasing to refined European persons: it was well known that women were invariably degraded among savages and marriage was accordingly less a union of equals than "the unnatural conjunction of a master with his slave" (Robertson 1777, 1:318–9). Parenthood among the native Americans, on the other hand, approximated a European sense of what was desirable and natural. Robertson noted that both parents in savage society were concerned to see themselves reproduced, and hoped to be cared for in their old age; they were therefore "not deficient in affection and attachment to their offspring." In no sense, however, did children reciprocate their parents' fondness, though the fault appeared to lie more in the latter's indulgence than in any constitutional peculiarity of the young in that region of the world.

> They suffer them to be absolute masters of their own actions . . . conscious of their own liberty, and impatient of restraint, the youth of America are accustomed to act as if they were totally independent, their parents are not objects of greater regard than other persons. They treat them always with neglect, and often with such harshness and indolence, as to fill those who have been witnesses of their conduct with horror (Robertson 1777, 1:323–4).

Participants in Cook's second voyage had been "witnesses," in another part of the world, to moments of violence in which children assaulted their parents. Two incidents are described in George Forster's *Voyage round the World,* which appeared in the same year as Robertson's *America.* Of these, one figured signally in *Observations Made during a Voyage round the World,* the remarkable synthetic work of natural history and ethic philosophy that was published a year later, in 1778, by the naturalist on the voyage, Johann Reinhold Forster (George's father). These incidents were, of course, not typical of the many acts of violence that were recorded over the course of the voyage, most of which were either perpetrated or directly provoked by Europeans; yet the way in which they were represented marks both the content and the limitations of an interpretative, ethnographic effort that can be traced through the writings of both Forsters, junior and senior, and those of Cook himself, among others. What allegedly occurred during the *Resolution*'s second visit to Queen Charlotte's Sound, in November 1773, does not simply exemplify the kind of fact that Robertson referred to; it was assimilated to a theoretical language, to a space of argument about the history of society, that the Forsters shared, broadly, with writers of the Scottish enlightenment such as Robertson, Kames, and Millar.

> A boy about six or seven years old demanded a piece of broiled pinguin, which his mother held in her hands. As she did not immediately comply with his demand, he took up a large stone and threw it at her. The woman incensed at this action ran to punish him, but she had scarcely given him a single blow, when her husband came forward, beat her unmercifully, and dashed her against the ground, for attempting to correct her unnatural child. Our people who were employed in filling water, told my father they had frequently seen similar instances of cruelty among them, and particularly, that the little boys had actually struck their unhappy mother, whilst the father looked on lest she should attempt to retaliate (Forster 1777, 1:511).

The other case occurred earlier, during the ship's period of refreshment in Dusky Bay in late March and April, 1773. Initially, it was supposed that the area was uninhabited, but on 7 April, an "Indian family" was encountered; it consisted of an older man, one older woman, two younger women, and several children. The older woman was distinguished by a wen or excrescence on the upper lip, which was said to render her ugly and thought to explain the man's apparent indifference to her. These people, depicted in William Hodges's *Cascade Cove* (figs. 7, 8) and certain associated works, were seen from time to time over the following days, and on the nineteenth, they were to come on board the ship.

> In the mean while they had a quarrel among themselves, the man beat the two women who were supposed to be his wives; the young girl in return struck him, and then began to weep. What the cause of this disagreement was, we cannot determine; but if the young woman was really the man's daughter, which we could never clearly understand, it should seem that the filial duties are strangely confounded among them; or which is more probable, that this secluded family acted in every respect, not according to the customs and regulations of a civil society, but from the impulses of nature, which speak aloud against every degree of oppression (Forster 1777, 1:160).

7. William Hodges, [*Cascade Cove*] *Dusky Bay*, ca. 1775–76, oil,
134.6 × 191.1 cm. National Maritime Museum, London.

In one case, then, the supposed daughter strikes the father; in the other the
son assaults the mother. The superficial symmetry between these incidents is
suggestive, precisely because the way in which they figure in the voyage literature is radically different. What transpired in Dusky Bay was perplexing; arguably, the whole experience of contact in that part of the South Island was pervaded by obscurity. In the passage I've quoted from George's *Voyage*, it is not
clear whether the "young girl" is one of the supposed "wives" he has just beaten;
that she strikes him "in return" suggests so, and she is in fact identified earlier
in the text, in the section describing the first encounter with these people, as one
of his wives: "He called to the two women . . . one of the women, which we
afterwards believed to be his daughter, was not wholly so disagreeable . . ." (Forster 1777, 1:138). In Forster senior's journal, upon which George's published
narrative was based, one of the wives or presumed wives is indeed younger than
the other, but it is quite clear from his description of the actual altercation that
the "young girl" was a third woman: "The old Man beat his two wives, & the
young Girl beat her Father & then fell a crying. He sent the wives & Children in
the Canoe out a fishing: but he & the Girl went round the Cove" and proceeded
to come on board the ship (Forster 1982, 2:258). The comparison between the
diary and the book suggests that there was more confusion in George's publica-

8. Detail of William Hodges, [*Cascade Cove*].

tion than there was during the encounter itself, and this is less surprising than might appear, given that George's only documentary source was presumably the diary, which was hardly unambiguous, and given that his memory at the time of writing, some four years after the event, must have been complicated by a considerable number of subsequent encounters with other Polynesians, both elsewhere in New Zealand and in the tropics.

James Cook's account of these people is generally less detailed, and he does not mention the quarrel in which the man both dispensed and received blows. He does, however, make it clear that there were three women and not two, which incidentally is the case in Hodges's painting, though Cook also, at one point, reproduces George's conflation of the "young girl" and the younger of the two wives; the confusion may have arisen because both appear to have been singularly forthcoming and talkative.[1] The point that Cook adds that is interesting is that the "girl" is supposed not only to be the daughter of the man, but of the woman whose countenance is disfigured by the wen. There is also, however, an emendation in Cook's manuscript journal that makes George's doubt concerning the relation between the girl and the older man categorical: "We learnt afterwards that this young Woman was not his Daughter" (Cook 1955–74, 2:122 n. 2). This prejudices the very perception of the group as a family, since the

9. *Family in Dusky Bay, New Zealand,* engraving by D. Lerpernière after William Hodges, from James Cook, *A Voyage towards the South Pole and round the World* (London: 1777), 2, plate 63.

woman with the wen is either not the girl's mother or not the man's wife, unless some polyandrous relationship or illegitimate parenthood is postulated. While the official published narrative does not reveal that the apparent daughter was not a daughter, other revisions of the journal, such as the addition of "as we supposed" in parentheses after mention of the man's two wives (Cook 1777, 1:75),[2] render identifications less, rather than more, certain, and this is still more the case in popular editions from 1780 onward, in which the relevant sentence is further altered to read: "We now saw all the man's family, as we supposed, which consisted of two wives, the young woman we mentioned before, a boy about fourteen years old, and three small children" (Moore 1780, 2:1125).[3]

The importance of these ambiguities is that it becomes unclear not only whether the man was struck by his daughter, a wife, or by an otherwise related or unrelated woman, but moreover whether he had one wife or two. Of course, the visitors were not even certain that either of the two women who were beaten were actually the man's wives, but the fact that an individual man, and especially an older individual, might not have a wife presented no particular problem to European understandings of conjugality or domesticity. In contrast, though George singled out the abnormality of the girl's behavior as the basis for his inference that these people were "secluded" in a domain beyond the regulation of civil society, it is hardly necessary to emphasize that a distinction between monogamous and polygamous unions was so significant to the interpretation of a people's form of civility that confusion on this point had to confound any larger assessment of their character and situation in the history of humanity.

Lerpernière's plate in the official publication (fig. 9) may well be a print after a lost sketch by William Hodges, but it appears rather more like an abstraction and repositioning of the figures in the painting *Cascade Cove* in the National Maritime Museum. While it is understandable that the engraver did not attempt to reproduce the disorderly complexities of the waterfall and vegetation, it is notable that the landscape is abandoned neither for the equivalent of a history painting (although the moment of contact between Cook and the old man would have been entirely amenable to such treatment, and such foundational encounters were in fact the subject matter of many of the plates in the third voyage) nor a set of portraits (though many of the second voyage plates were of course the *Man of Tanna,* the *Woman of New Caledonia* (fig. 10), and so on). Instead, this print claims to depict precisely what was elusive: *Family in Dusky Bay.* Not only the confusion concerning the number of the man's wives, but also some uncertainty around the character of conjugal relations, is suggested here by the fact that two contrasting dyadic relations are imaged—between the man and the standing woman on one side, and between the man and the seated woman with her baby on the other. The woman holding the spear figures as a companion and almost as a fellow warrior, given the evident strength and weight of her weapon; the other is by no means radically bestialized but is close and conspicuously

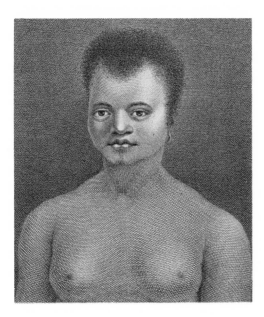

10. *Woman of New Caledonia,* engraving by Hall after William Hodges, from James Cook, *A Voyage towards the South Pole and round the World* (London: 1777), 2, plate 48.

subordinate to the man and seemingly carrying a good deal more on her back than her child. The burden is not only a recurrent emblem of women's denigration in unrefined societies but is resonant specifically of the debased situation of women in the western Pacific, New Caledonia, Tanna, and especially Malekula; in the texts from the second voyage, their condition is marked, or perhaps rather constituted by, the "fact" that they are treated like packhorses by their men (cf. Jolly 1992b). This is no more than a visual implication, but it is significant that the woman is in shadow if not definitely dark, and that her profile clearly displays frizzy hair that could very well have been taken by late-eighteenth-century viewers to be the "wool" supposedly characteristic of negroes, that moreover differs distinctly from both the merely wavy hair of the other two figures and that of this woman's original in the painting and in a sketch by Hodges (fig. 11).

11. William Hodges, [*A Maori Woman, Carrying a Child*], April 1773, red chalk, 17.0 × 8.7 cm. Department of Prints and Drawings, British Museum, London.

This woman seems therefore to be brought into conformity, in both her physical attributes and her conjugal subordination, with the typical "black" Melanesian woman, who is routinely contrasted with the lighter-skinned Polynesian and taken to be oppressed in the terms specified in the Enlightenment social theory alluded to earlier, that is, because she is dissociated from the martial pursuits that men value above all else. The other figure could be seen to personify quite a different construction of barbaric womanhood, one in which women are imagined to be affected by the martial environment to the degree that they carry arms themselves. Cook, not understanding that the spears were of a type used to hunt wood pigeons rather than engage in war,[4] presumed that this was the case, but did not draw the implication that women shared the liberty and independence of their men, as this woman's poise suggests.

Cascade Cove is neither explicitly nor implicitly titled *Family in Dusky Bay;* the relative isolation and foregrounding of the man surely renders peripheral the question of his relationship to any one or all three of the women. His rugged vigor and musculature might be taken first to echo the undomesticated strength of the rocks and the terrain, while the distinction between the seated girl and the standing adult women might imply, to any viewer concerned to speculate, that the man has two wives and a daughter, as the official narrative suggested. The engraving makes two figures of three by depriving one adult woman of her spear, reducing her to the seated position of the apparent daughter, and giving her custody not only of her child, but of a burden that she lacks in the painting; this merging of one wife and the daughter is, as it happens, the same conflation that is effected at points in both James Cook's and George Forster's texts.

But the young woman herself repaid this defect of recognition with interest— by mistaking a common sailor (and two or three others, officers as well as mere seamen) for a member of her own sex; it was a suggestive mistake, which the Tannese, among other Pacific islanders, were to repeat in the course of the same voyage. Though initially showing "a great partiality" to the young man, the woman "would never suffer him to come near her afterwards"; whether because "he had taken some improper liberties, or whether she had any other reason to be disgusted" was unclear, according to the *Voyage* (Forster 1777, 1:150). The diaries, on the other hand, make it clear that the woman discovered the sailor's true sex when she saw him urinating. The elision in George Forster's publication is motivated, of course, by delicacy, but it might be suggested that the step from a palpable circumstance to a point of ambiguity or uncertainty in the text resonates with the compounding of potential misidentifications in the matter of kinship; facts of a certain kind seem to produce here what Michael Taussig has called epistemic murk.[5] In Cook's published text, the matter is still more obscure: "Whether it was that she before took him for one of her own sex; or that the man, in order to discover himself, had taken some liberties with her which she thus resented, I know not" (1777, 1:77).

I am not arguing that the fabrication of obscurity is often attested to in the Cook voyage texts, though it is perhaps a generic feature of exploratory writing in the sense that moments of violence, and others that are peculiarly horrifying or astonishing, overwhelm the effort of apprehension and narration: "The mind is so entirely filled with its object, that it cannot entertain any other, nor by consequence reason on that object which employs it" (Burke 1987, 57).[6] The point is rather that the Dusky Bay encounter, unlike not only those at Tahiti and in other parts of Oceania but also those in other parts of New Zealand, was replete with aspects and ironies that were peculiarly difficult for these Europeans to comprehend; yet what was problematic tended to be paraded rather than disavowed in their texts. The want of comprehension was not, in any important way, the result simply of the fact that such knowledge of Tahitian as a few of those on board had acquired on Cook's first voyage scarcely enabled communication with these New Zealanders; attempts to converse proceeded mainly through gestures and mainly ineffectively. This deficiency of mutual understanding could, however, possess its own legibility for Forster senior, who wrote, "After half an hours unintelligible conversation at least as edifying as great many which are usual in the politer circles of civilized nations, & which here at least passed with a great deal more sincerity & cordiality on both sides, we took leave of our new friends" (1982, 2:249).

What, on the other hand, did lack legibility was the transparent fact that these few Polynesians abruptly broke off their intercourse with the visitors, much to the puzzlement of the latter, who saw the relationship as one characterized by friendliness and a degree of mutual generosity; as George Forster put it, "We never saw them again, which was the more extraordinary, as they never went away empty handed from us . . ." (1777, 1:172).[7] The sense that this was remarkable may be more directly connected than is initially apparent with a larger issue that I seek to address: the ways in which the interpretations of these events that are both implicit and explicit in what George and Johann Reinhold Forster wrote were at once enabled and deprived of coherence by an understanding of the antinomies of progress that they shared with the Scottish Enlightenment writers mentioned earlier, among others.

What is important about the incident in Queen Charlotte's Sound is not that the mother is abused by her son, but that the violence, and the accessory role of adult men, fathers of perpetrators and husbands of victims, is taken to be both endemic and diagnostic. George's description of the single occasion that his father witnessed is generalized on the basis of common sailors' observations (that are not mentioned in Forster senior's journal) and is followed by these remarks:

> Among all savage nations the weaker sex is ill-treated, and the law of the strongest is put in force. Their women are mere drudges, who prepare raiment and provide dwellings, who cook and frequently collect their food, and are requited by blows and all kinds of severity. At New Zeeland it seems they carry this tyranny to excess, and the males are taught from their earliest age, to hold their mothers in contempt, contrary to all our principles of morality (1777, 1:511–2).[8]

In Johann Reinhold Forster's *Observations*, the harsh treatment of New Zealand women by their husbands is similarly assimilated to a general condition in the first passage in his text in which these people are systematically discussed: women "are obliged to do all the drudgery, as is common in all barbarous nations" (Forster 1996, 159). Attached to this sentence is a long footnote that cites first Strabo and Tacitus, then a range of modern travel accounts from Africa, Asia, and America, to establish, at least to Forster's satisfaction, that both the ancient inhabitants of Europe and contemporary barbarians treat their women in the terms described. What I take to generate a distinctive ambivalence is not that Maori were thereby included in a capacious anthropological category, but that they were rendered similar to societies in earlier phases of European history, such as the ancient Germans, whose martial condition was understood less as an uncongenial belligerence than as the basis for an uncorrupted liberty that refined nations had lost.[9]

In the later section of Forster's book that is dedicated to an evaluation of the state of New Zealand society, the violence against the mother is positively determined, not merely by the general truth that women are badly treated among uncivilized people, but more powerfully and specifically by the effects of a certain mode of education. Forster considered and rejected the idea that the form of anthropophagy that prevailed in New Zealand, that is, the consumption of slain enemies, was motivated by hunger, as John Hawkesworth had asserted in the official narrative of the first voyage (1773, 3:43–4). Displaying almost exemplary anthropological relativism, Forster went to some pains to argue that the evident barbarity of the practice belied beneficial effects that it could well have in a longer view: warfare, conducted with such destructive effect, over a time could only in the end impress upon victors "that a living man is more useful than one dead or roasted"; hence, conquerors would eventually enslave the people they defeated and create more extensive and cohesive social unions. This seemed not merely a hypothetical development but already a fact in the North Island of New Zealand, according to reports from the *Endeavour*'s voyage (that have subsequently been considered inaccurate). Even if these were, in the first place, founded on the oppression of the conquered, any larger, more united society "prepares the way to a more humane and benevolent scene"; as Forster says, he "cannot help observing, that this barbarism is one of the steps, by which debased humanity, is gradually prepared for a better state of happiness" (1996, 214). This argument may appear eccentric, but Forster's contrived retreat from the immediacy of an atrocity to its historical causes and ramifications was a specifying operation—one that avoided attributing practices that happened to be repulsive to Europeans simply to a generalized want of civilization. He instead understood both cannibalism and the boy's violence as elements or effects of a warlike sociality.

In the section of *Observations* that I'm drawing upon, Forster is concerned especially to distinguish the relative advancement of the New Zealanders over a less improved population, that of Tierra del Fuego, whose inhabitants seemed striking for their apathy, misery, and indolence; in other passages of his book he was concerned similarly with accounting for the greater happiness of the Tahitians, relative to the inhabitants of New Zealand, the western parts of the Pacific, and Tonga. This exercise in ranking articulated with a narrative of progress that was animated by a grand analogy with stages in the human life cycle, from infancy to maturity, but differed from nineteenth-century evolutionist arguments in a number of crucial respects. Although Forster did make unpleasant and invidious comparisons between the physical appearances of various Pacific islanders, and especially islander women, he was not concerned with intrinsic racial differences, and rather saw stature, physiognomy, and color as effects of the mode of life, of forms of labor, of ratios of indolence and vigor, opulence and warriorhood; this comparative anthropology was thus political before it was physical.

Forster's particular arguments entered into a grand account of the effects of climate upon human happiness and progress; he imagined a general continuum between the most refined islanders in the tropics and the more debased peoples of temperate and frigid latitudes. While the Tahitians are certainly consistently celebrated and the Tierra del Fuegians harshly disparaged, the continuum was complicated by the differences between populations within broadly similar latitudes—notably between the Tahitians and other tropical Polynesians and the islanders of the western Pacific—but Forster did not in any case advance any rigid geographical determinism. Climate was arguably so important in the anthropological thought of this period, among thinkers who had all read Montesquieu, precisely because it was conceptually flexible. If it sometimes stood for mere latitude, the earth being divided into a series of horizontal zones within which temperaments were notionally similarly determined, at other times, it seemed to include the range of economic and political conditions that I mentioned—on the one hand entailed the broad nature of particular kinds of sociality, a martial or commercial character, but that on the other were recognized through, and constituted by, facts specifically related to the treatment of women and the form of the family (cf. Falconer 1781).

The animated character of the sociality of New Zealanders was certainly seen to arise from an intricate configuration of population, migration, education, and climate, and was understood especially as an advance upon the debased condition of the Tierra del Fuegians. The scattered and fragmentary nature of the society of the latter was taken to point out "the true cause of the debasement and degeneracy in savages; they can neither profit by the assistance, nor by the inventions and improvements of others, and the smallness of their numbers affords but a bad chance for a multiplicity of inventions or improvements" (Forster 1996, 207). Progress was associated with an increase in population, in part because a people's reserve of knowledge was thereby increased—in New Zealand, "their minds have acquired a larger and more liberal circle of ideas"— but more crucially because population pressure led to warfare, to efforts to extend a dominion and to acquire superiority. "All this of course rouses their minds from that indolence and inactivity with which they were oppressed, and they in every respect conquer somewhat of that degeneracy to which they were reduced" (208). Many cultural and technological accomplishments attested to the progress of the New Zealanders; Forster noted the elaborate decorations of tools, ornaments, dress, and arms, the "elegance and neatness" of the houses, the "easy and swift motion" of well-contrived and dextrously paddled canoes, and the elaboration of religious ideas that were not evidently merely superstitious. Most significantly, perhaps, he added that "the agriculture which is so well and so carefully carried on in many parts of the Northern island, incontestably proves the superiority of the New-Zeelanders over the inhabitants of Tierra del Fuego. So that it might be superfluous in me to take up more time in multiplying the proofs of this so evident truth" (210). It was unimportant for Forster that the South Island Maori he actually encountered did not appear to practice agriculture; by implication, even if the nomadic people around Dusky Bay did not institutionalize property and law to the degree that was understood to correspond, normally, with the cultivation of the ground, they were proximate enough to the "ideas and improvements" of their settled neighbors to be ranked, quite definitively, "higher in the class of rational beings" (1996, 208) than the Tierra del Fuegians.

Forster's arguments in favor of the "improved" state of New Zealanders, are, therefore, fairly elaborate, and refer both to what might be seen as indices of improvement, such as their refined arts, and to causes of a happier and more vigorous constitution, such as the relative mildness of the climate and the extent of the population. But against this, is, of course, the "one circumstance . . . which seems to degrade them," that is, their practice of cannibalism, which is the extreme expression of a martial spirit. The point is not that a remarkable vigor coexisted contingently and inconsistently with deplorable violence, but rather that, in this conceptualization, discrepant aspects of indigenous progress and custom were rendered indissociable in a martial condition: what roused a people from indolence and led to such a range of commendable aspects of their mode of life was precisely the cause also of their custom that Europeans could only find "horrid." Exactly what this understanding does not do is produce a coherent idea of Maori society; if the representation of Dusky Bay elevated merely perplexing facts to the level of epistemic obscurity, the understanding of sociality around Queen Charlotte's Sound produced a moral and political con-tradiction out of what was perhaps only a discrepancy between bad characteris-tics and good ones.

The contradiction, however, was in no sense obscure from the viewpoint of eighteenth-century political and historical thought. The martial condition was not so much a construction of a particular class of alien societies as a category evoked more commonly in diagnoses of the distemper of European societies. Progress tended to extinguish a military spirit and permitted men to lapse from military vigor and patriotism into indolence, vanity, and effeminacy; though property, opulence, and commerce might be conducive to refinement in the arts and to higher forms of civility and politeness, they also prejudiced public virtue, not least because commerce entailed a specialization of labor, knowledge, and interest that could only detract from a public and patriotic spirit. The decline of warriorhood as a general occupation and preoccupation of men also fostered licentiousness and corruption in the indirect sense that a standing army, as opposed to a civilian militia, facilitated a despotism that could not be sustained over a society of independent warriors; despotism was understood not merely to oppress but to impoverish those who were subject to it and to corrupt and debase both rulers and ruled in a variety of ways. All this, incidentally, is con-tained in the history of the word mercenary, which originally meant not a soldier who served a foreign power, but any soldier who was paid (as opposed to a civilian who took up arms to defend his land and his country); any paid pursuit, in fact, might be stigmatized by that word, which of course retains that original breadth of meaning in present adjectival usage. The tensions I'm exploring turn upon the fact that if the New Zealanders were cannibals, they were, at least, not mercenaries.

I am not concerned here with the significance of these ideas in European politics, but merely point out that an ambivalent or negative evaluation of commercial society and its attendant luxury and selfishness may evoke, as a foil, a positive, or at least correspondingly mixed, representation of a particular unrefined condition that was exemplified especially by the early Germans. Preeminent among sources was, of course, Tacitus. His *Germania* was read in a singularly eighteenth-century way that no doubt capitalized upon the critique of Roman debauchery suggested by German frugality and chastity but assimilated that moralizing geography to a distinctive political idiom. The absence of specialized occupations among the Germans is only implicit in Tacitus, but it assumes definite significance for Gilbert Stuart, whose history of "the progress from rudeness to refinement" in Europe was first published in the same year as Forster's *Observations:*

> The German . . . being unacquainted with particular professions, and with mercenary pursuits, was animated with high sentiments of pride and greatness. He was guided by affection and appetite; and, though fierce in the field, and terrible to an enemy, was gentle in his domestic capacity, and found a pleasure in acts of beneficence, magnanimity, and friendship (Stuart 1792, 2).

I noted earlier that Forster classed the New Zealanders among "barbarous nations," and it is therefore not surprising that the last remark here resonates with evocations of a manly simplicity that precedes refined disingenuousness and that might be extracted from many accounts of travels among people classed as barbaric (they are certainly scattered through Cook voyage accounts of New Zealand and some other Oceanic societies). Among the most significant, perhaps, is a passage in George Forster's narrative in which the violence of the Maori against Marion's party is explained and excused in terms consistent with Anne Salmond's recent reinterpretation: "The whole tenour of their behaviour to Europeans, seems to acquit them of treachery and cruel malevolence. It is therefore greatly to be suspected that they took umbrage at some affront, perhaps unwittingly committed by the strangers . . . " (Forster 1777, 2:465; cf. Salmond 1991, chap. 13). What is not commonplace in Stuart's representation of the German is the fact that the generic male is said to be "gentle in his domestic capacity." This assertion is especially striking given that this writer also observed that the government of "every rude community" had "a surprising affinity to that of the Germans, as described by Tacitus" (Stuart 1792, 158). This contradicts the claim, which I began by citing in Robertson and have found echoed in both George's *Voyage* and his father's *Observations,* that barbarians or savages or both were universally cruel to their women. Stuart disputed the readings of Tacitus—and the evidence from travel writers in America that Robertson, Millar, Kames, and others had drawn upon—and put forward a variety of empirical and deductive arguments for the relatively high estimation of women among Germans and barbarians generally.[10]

Stuart's relatively unqualified idealization of barbaric society is only salient to the other material that I've discussed because his celebratory account clearly depended upon dissent from the view that was generally subscribed to concerning the status of women among such people; this underlines the extent to which writers such as the Forsters, who both presumed that women were harshly treated by all barbarians and believed that this had been attested to by events that they had witnessed, were simply unable to produce an unequivocal estimate of society in New Zealand. This is also, incidentally, why the "noble savage," and for that matter, the "ignoble," are simply not adequate categories for the history of ideas in this period. When Forster wrote of the Maori, "Their principles of honesty, and public faith are noble," he was saying something that he never said, to my knowledge, of a European nation, yet he saw the liberal manliness of the New Zealand temperament as confounded by its excess:

> Their education is the chief cause of all these enormities. The men train up their boys in a kind of liberty, which at last degenerates into licentiousness: they suffer not the mothers to strike their petulant, unruly, and wicked sons, for fear of breaking that spirit of independency, which they seem to value above all things, and as the most necessary qualification for their societies (1996, 212).

In *The Machiavellian Moment*, J. G. A. Pocock has suggested that Scottish philosophy entailed "a theory of history which showed how virtue was built up and demolished by the growth of society itself," in which "contradiction was of the essence," and which "envisaged a future in which progress and corruption might coexist for a very long period" (1975, 503–4). Forster's interpretation of the societies of Queen Charlotte's Sound underlines the permanent character of this contradictoriness, which belonged as much to early phases of the history of civil society as to its maturity and future; the happiness of peoples other than refined Europeans was always enhanced by certain effects of their progress and marred or diminished by others. New Zealand and European societies, thus imagined, were not radically different, but were rather pervaded by analogous propensities and tensions; the extent to which this similarity could qualify or jostle with the historical evolution that certainly was present in Forster's text is suggested by the way in which liberty was seen by Millar and a number of other writers as a characteristic of both early and late phases of civil society rather than the periods in between (Millar 1990, 101).[11] The argument did not exactly postulate a circularity, but more the reappearance of a condition that was as unstable as it was generally desirable. Concluding a long section on the despotic character of paternal authority in unimproved societies and the gradual amelioration of this "excessive and arbitrary power," Millar notes that

> the tendency, however, of a commercial age is rather towards the opposite extreme, and may occasion some apprehension that the members of a family will be raised to greater independence than is consistent with good order, and with a proper domestic subordination (1990, 138).

Because Forster shared Robertson's sense that men might oppress and degrade their wives while their children were insufficiently restrained, it was possible to imagine something other than a long transition—instead, a simultaneity of a certain despotism and a certain independence. Liberty in barbaric societies, no less than in refined ones, was consistently vitiated in its excesses; the "licentiousness" thereby generated was as much there as here, as much here as there. All this is suggestive not only of the burden of the incident in Queen Charlotte's Sound in September 1773, but also, indirectly, of a further cause of the obscurity that Dusky Bay assumes in the voyage narratives and its relative insignificance in Forster's *Observations*. Both George Forster's and Cook's narratives mention but do not remark upon the fact that the supposed wives are carrying spears that were supposed incorrectly to be weapons of war; one of these is, as I noted, conspicuous in the engraving in the official publication. This must have been distinctly anomalous for anyone who shared the Forsters' understanding that women in barbaric societies were drudges specifically because they were strangers to the warlike pursuits that were valued by men alone. It is notable, if accidental, that a representation of Queen Charlotte's Sound Maori from Cook's third voyage presents a woman, a man, and a spear in a combination far more consistent with notions of martial patriarchy (fig. 12); and not surprising either, that later engravings based upon Lerpernière's print in popular editions of Cook and geographical compendia (figs. 13, 14, 15) radically alter the composition, further mutilating the "family of Dusky Bay" by changing the female warrior's sex or by rearranging the figures so as to diminish the independent status and martial character of the woman.

Forster's identification, which I quoted earlier, of savages as those who were unable to profit from others' inventions or improvements resonates with many observations he and others made in the course of Cook's voyages and subsequent journeys. Time and again one finds a people's civility or superiority correlated with their openness to strangers and their goods, or their standoffishness and lack of interest in cloth or iron interpreted as belligerence, as a sign of a more

12. *View in Queen Charlotte Sound, New Zealand,* colored aquatint, from James Webber, *Views in the South Seas, from Drawings by the Late James Webber, Draftsman on Board the Resolution,* published by Boydell & Co. (Cheapside: 1808), plate 1. National Library of Australia, Canberra.

debased and primitive state. The positive side of this, which connects improvement with an interest in wider intercourse and foreign objects, echoed an argument of David Hume's concerning the positive effects of foreign commerce:

> In most nations, foreign trade has preceded any refinement in home manufactures, and given birth to domestic luxury. The temptation is stronger to make use of foreign commodities, which are ready for use, and which are entirely new to us, than to make improvements on any domestic commodity, which always advance by slow degrees, and never affect us by their novelty . . . Thus men become acquainted with the *pleasures* of luxury, and the *profits* of commerce; and their *delicacy* and *industry,* being once awakened, carry them on to farther improvements in every branch of domestic as well as foreign trade. And this perhaps is the chief advantage which arises from a commerce with strangers. It rouses men from their indolence . . . (1882, I: 195–96).

While Hume was more balanced in his assessment of the effects of commerce than many of his contemporaries, and while he believed that the opulence of private men might make the public more powerful, the language he employed is plainly ambivalent in a sense that resonates with the debate referred to earlier. Commerce may lead to refinement and may invigorate men, but it is evidently also feminizing and infantilizing: the restless and superficial passion for novelty, which is clearly the animating force behind commerce, is particularly an attitude of children and women (see especially Burke 1987, 31). Exchange between indigenous peoples and Europeans, which attested to at least a limited civility on the part of the former, thus possessed an uncertain signification. On the one hand, an anxiety to acquire new things indicated a capacity for learning and improvement; on the other, it suggested that mercenary practices were not wholly alien to barbarism, even though the latter was understood as the antithesis of commercial society.

Much was said about the corrupting effect of commerce in Tahiti, where aristocrats as well as common women prostituted themselves for curiosities and luxuries, but corruption was also pretty evident in New Zealand, or rather in Queen Charlotte's Sound. There, "the New Zeelanders went through the whole vessel, offering their daughters and sisters promiscuously to every person's embraces, in exchange for our iron tools, which they knew could not be purchased at an easier rate" (Forster 1777, 1:212). Here, the degeneracy of the British crew not only caused this sexual corruption but augmented the oppression of indigenous women by their menfolk. If the latter had always treated the former brutally, they only now used them as commodities; as George noted: "It may therefore be alledged, that as the New Zeelanders place no value on the continence of their unmarried women, the arrival of Europeans among them, did not injure their moral characters in this respect; but we doubt whether they ever debased themselves so much as to make a trade of their women, before we created new wants by shewing them iron-tools; for the possession of which they do not hesitate to commit an action that, in our eyes, deprives them of the very shadow of sensibility" (1777, 1:212).

In Dusky Bay, there had been no such articulation of modes of licentiousness. Exchange, certainly, took place, and the Maori were not stupidly indifferent to foreigners in the way that the Tierra del Fuegians had been; as George noted, they, on the contrary, possessed a singular courage: "In spight of their inferiority of force, they cannot brook the thought of hiding themselves, at least not till they have made an attempt to establish an intercourse, or prove the principles of strangers who approach them" (1777, 1:171). On the other hand, the interest in novel foreign goods appeared restrained and provoked no unbounded passion for ornaments and no subordination of virtue to trade. What George took to be extraordinary in the unexpected departure of the group from the area was not really inconsistent with the degree of improvement of the Dusky Bay people: they were evidently less polished, less unified, less commercial, and less cor-

13. *A Family in Dusk Bay* [sic], engraving from George William Anderson, *A New, Authentic, and Complete History of Voyages round the World* (London: 1784–86). Anderson's collection, published in eighty sixpenny parts, was the first popular subscription edition of Cook's voyages.

14. *Habitants de Mallicolo—Nouvelles Hébrides,* engraving from Domeny de Rienzi, *Océanie ou la cinquième parti du monde* (Paris: 1836–37). Though clearly derived from the Lerpernière image, these people are transposed to Malekula in the New Hebrides (now Vanuatu). De Rienzi's compilation was the most important synthesis of geographical knowledge of Oceania in the first half of the nineteenth century; this engraving also appeared in Italian, Spanish, and German editions.

15. *Famiglia della Baja Dusky, nella nouva Zelanda,* engraving from Theodoro Viero, *Raccolta di stampi . . . di varie nazioni* (Venice, ca. 1791). Although there are faint connections with the 1777 plate, the figures are dramatically altered and the man in particular brought into conformity with a generic barbarian, combining traces of a Maori-style curvilinear facial tattoo and a feather headdress with native American rather than Oceanic associations.

rupted than the related populations in Queen Charlotte's Sound and further north. The problem, I suggest, emerges also from a discrepancy between the characteristics of these particular people, in terms of the salient anthropological language, and the essentially positive response that the Europeans had toward them. In fact, in terms of the criteria generally adduced in stadial categorizations, the Dusky Bay people were savages rather than barbarians: their numbers were tiny, their material culture appeared rudimentary, and their conjugal forms were uncertain and possibly even promiscuous; most importantly, they shifted from place to place and engaged in no agriculture. At two points, George goes so far as to remove them from civil society and from the regulation of custom altogether, yet these people were patently not debased into something like the indolent stupor of the Tierra del Fuegians, who were supposedly removed but in the first degree from absolute animality. The Dusky Bay people were only at one further remove, in terms of the continuum from pole to tropic, but were clearly courageous, open, and honest.

It was the practical character of the encounter and the responses of particular Europeans to particular Maori that seems to have overdetermined one set of discriminations and left much indistinctness. The ambiguities were distilled, with the most delicate irony, by George, who wrote of an early stage of the encounter:

> The next morning we returned to the natives, and presented them with several articles which we had brought with us for that purpose. But so much was the judgment of the man superior to that of his countrymen, and most of the South Sea nations, that he received almost every thing with indifference, except what he immediately conceived the use of, such as hatchets and large spike-nails (1777, 1:139–40).[12]

From the perspective of the discourse that I've discussed, the superiority of this man is not merely anomalous. The superiority so starkly and plainly expressed in the man's indifference to trifles and baubles was in a way consistent with the uncommercial character of savagery, yet it mocked the elaborate efforts of both Forsters to specify and account for the advancement of the Tahitians and the other tropical Polynesian populations over peoples who were secluded, who were isolated from larger reserves of knowledge and education, who eked out a straggling existence in a cold climate, and who left nature in a chaotic, absolutely unimproved state. At the beginning of this essay, I emphasized that I was concerned to draw attention to the contexts and ambiguities of exploratory writing, not to recuperate it. But if there's anything that we might salvage from this discourse, it is this: that a natural historian could turn this little specimen of resistance into a joke at the expense of his anthropology.

4

Objects of Knowledge:

Oceanic Artifacts

in European Engravings

"The real voyeur is engraving."—Picasso

In *Modern Painters,* Ruskin suggested that it was especially characteristic of modern engraving that everything was "sacrificed to illegitimate and contemptible sources of pleasure," which were "vice throughout," possessing "no redeeming quality nor excusing aim" (1898, 1:43 n). However idiosyncratic this peculiarly forceful condemnation may be, Ruskin's more specific references to the inadequacy of the media—for instance, for conveying Turner's atmospheres—resonate with art history's enduring attachment to what is original rather than derivative, to higher genres and proper forms of art. If prints were ever only cheap or not-so-cheap reproductions of paintings that were themselves available for inspection, this consignment of poor copies to a wilderness beyond critical vision might be justifiable; but from a historical perspective concerned with the circulation and effect of representations, it would seem desirable to put together some sort of critical and interpretative technology that takes the various forms of prints seriously as singular cultural products.

As with video, there are obvious sociological propositions—for instance, that the technology permits the "copies" to be circulated far more extensively than the original or prior media such as paint or film—in differing class contexts and in a fashion less accessible to policing. Observations of this kind may do something to account for persisting aesthetic hierarchies, but they don't take us far toward a positive account of what exactly prints are. Just as video is something other than film on tape (especially when a movie has been shot on video, rather than transferred, as Wim Wenders demonstrates in his *Notebook on Cities and Clothes*), engravings have effects that are specific to their techniques and materiality.

Benedict Anderson (1992) has drawn attention to the crucial significance of what he has called "print capitalism," and especially newspaper publication, for creole nationalism. Linda Colley (1992, 41, 220–1) has similarly suggested that newspapers "made it easier to imagine Great Britain as a whole" even in the early eighteenth century; they later created a more intense and general awareness of events in the life of the monarchy, in parliamentary business, and in other political processes. While these arguments concerned printed *texts*, it is obvious that the reproduction of visual material, and especially of political cartoons and satires through mass-circulation engravings, was equally crucial to the articulation and shaping of public political sentiments. The power of such images derives from their condensed character, from the use of icons such as John Bull, and often from simple and direct appeals to moral responses—for example, toward the barbarous treatment of women (Colley 1992, 264), or toward behavior that may not be savage but is manifestly ridiculous or effeminate. Of course, the truth in such images does not arise from any literally accurate representation of circumstances but from their capacity to anticipate and immediately resonate with truths perceived by a viewing public, an audience that has prior interests and preoccupations yet may be refashioned as it consumes visual representations and self-representations.

The particular power of engravings may also be derived from the long-prevalent notion that visual images have a special capacity to convey truth that words do not. It is, of course, a fact that certain kinds of information—concerning botany and architecture, for instance—may be far more readily conveyed graphically than verbally, but I am less concerned to extend fairly tired arguments on this point than to note that one of the specific correlates—the idea that a text is less sufficient than an engraving—is attested to for the period I focus on in this essay, implicitly by the singular importance of prints in travel books, and more explicitly by the common reference to an illustration that gives "the best idea" of an object, building, or scene. In the radical novel *Hermsprong*, Robert Bage heightens his readers' anticipation and makes his account of a near fatal riding accident more compelling through appeal to the graphic texture of an absent print, while ironically parading the modest status of his own book: "Without an engraving, I despair of making my readers understand the ensuing description; and the patrons of this humble sort of book-making are not sufficiently liberal to enable a poor author to gratify his readers and himself in this particular. However, when the public ask a fourth edition, I will certainly give it, with a map, at my own expense" (1985, 17).

I am suggesting that what made prints important was not merely the technological and social facts of their mass distribution, which enabled the anticipation of certain public audiences, but also the notion that some kinds of prints were taken as vehicles for peculiarly objective representational truths, such as those evoked through charts, diagrams, and anatomical profiles (while others, if possessing truth of any kind, might be allegorical or exemplary). This could not have been asserted in any vehement way for the prints associated with travel books in the sixteenth and seventeenth centuries, which were usually produced without reference to primary sketches and often on the basis of images borrowed from other travel books or from Biblical iconography, of peoples or places remote from the region notionally depicted (van Wyk Smith 1992; Smith 1992, 173–4). For these imaginings, which were in significant senses preracist, the differences between African and native American bodies, even European and native American ones, were not of such importance that they needed to be accurately conveyed through visual representations. In the eighteenth century however, and particularly after 1750, it became more common for engravings to be based directly on the traveler-author's sketches or those of an accompanying artist; a degree of ethnographic specificity emerged, and glaring contradictions between texts and images (the one denigrating, the other idealizing native peoples) became less common. By the early nineteenth century, when techniques were considerably diversified and improved, it was claimed that engravings were not merely accurate but possessed an indexical relation to what was depicted: "The pencil is narrative to the eye . . . its representations are not liable to the omissions of memory, or the misconceptions of fancy; whatever it communicates is a transcript from nature" (Daniell and Daniell 1810, ii). This rhetoric, which was subsequently appropriated by the advocates of photography, had its technical correlate in the use of devices such as the camera obscura, which artists such as the Daniells, Fraser, Salt, and others employed in India and elsewhere. The tone and light of their aquatints was remarkable; the use of color conveyed the distinct exoticism of plants, landforms, buildings, costumes, and bodies as never before.

At the same time as prints were being authorized or championed with the aid of this prephotographic rhetoric, the adequacy of their representations was constantly questioned. Lord Valentia, traveling through north India, found fault with a number of the plates in William Hodges's *Select Views in India* (1785–88): one of a gateway "had no resemblance to it," while it was sardonically presumed at Juanpore Bridge that "Mr. Hodges's view seems to have been drawn from memory" (Valentia 1809, 1:82, 89, cf. 125). These statements were no doubt motivated by the fact that Valentia was accompanied by his own secretary and artist, Henry Salt, whose rival works illustrated the publication quoted. It may similarly be noted that a good deal of the acrimonious debate surrounding the publication of the findings from Cook's second voyage—between the naturalists Johann Reinhold Forster and George Forster, the astronomer William Wales, and in the background, the Admiralty and Cook himself—turned upon the accuracy or otherwise of engravings published in the official account of the voyage. The costume of the Malekulan man, the dress and physique of the Tongans, the form of indigenous artifacts and ornaments—the published representations of all of these were challenged and debated (Joppien and Smith 1985–87, 2:72–3, 87–92).

In the context of the travel publishing business, the idea that a print is above all a derivative image is inappropriate. Portraits and even landscape views were often based not upon oil paintings that would have been exhibited as works of art in their own right but upon watercolors or sketches prepared specifically for reproduction. In the case of natural history illustrations and a closely affiliated genre that I consider here, which consists of representations of exotic ethnographic implements, ornaments, and weapons, it was still less the case that the "original" drawings or paintings had any status as art works in themselves; like a typescript, they amounted merely to a stage in the preparation of a printed work.

In the case of eighteenth- and nineteenth-century political prints, the most obvious matters to be analyzed are their content, stance, and ambiguities; however, one of the questions that may be of greater interest to the historian concerns the kind of public or audience the images sought to address and what wider assumptions about political opinion and active citizenship they therefore registered. Similarly, an analysis of travel prints can address the issue of how distant peoples and colonized or prospectively colonized places were represented (were they feminized? bountiful? neglected? archaic?). Though such studies certainly contribute to the rapidly accumulating corpus in colonial cultural studies that is concerned with European representations of non-European "others," we may discover more that we do not already know if we ask about producers and audiences rather than about what is depicted. In the case of travel, as distinct from that of the political caricatures, there might be less of interest to say about the public projected by the images and more value in attempting to establish what the visual representations implied about travelers and the work of travel itself. It is something of a cliché to say that the traveler uses the experience of the foreign to fashion himself or herself; familiar as the proposition may be, it is relevant for the grand tour, because that was understood specifically as a methodical and pedagogical exercise (cf. Stagl 1995), and in a different way for scientific travel, which was not unambiguously celebrated or approved of. Though many critics have argued that science legitimized imperialism, natural history and antiquarianism were not themselves definitely legitimate: scientific travel, like collecting, was often considered trivial or promiscuous, a mask for espionage, commerce, or licentiousness. How, I ask in this chapter, does a rather odd class of visual representations relate to the effort of self-definition, which I take not as an interior psychological process but as a public project of intellectual and moral authorization, not strictly of the self but also of the endeavor of natural history and scientific travel?

Artifacts

The kinds of prints that I deal with here have been ignored not only by art historians but also by the wide range of scholars dealing with European representations of non-Western peoples. While anthropologists, for instance, have been increasingly concerned with the ways in which European uses of artifacts have encoded interests in the exotic and the primitive, discussion thus far has mainly been oriented to institutions such as museums and international expositions (Stocking 1984; Clifford 1988; Price 1989). There has been less work on the agendas of particular collectors and on the representation, as opposed to the arrangement and display, of objects (but see Cardinal and Elsner 1994; Bann 1995). Of course, plates such as those from the publications of Cook's famous voyages of the 1770s (figs. 16–19) might seem merely an esoteric or very minor class of images undeserving of critical attention, but it is important to note that these books and similar voyage works were extremely popular and were frequently reprinted; the pictures, which included landscape views and portraits of islanders but often also numerous arrays of artifacts of this kind, were considered particularly attractive. Fashionable interest in the ethnographic specimens known as curiosities was moreover unprecedented, such that common sailors could augment their incomes considerably by selling collections on returning from voyages; some of the material ended up in major private collections such as the Leverian Museum. Although museums existed earlier in Germany, Italy, and France (Impey and MacGregor 1985; Pomian 1990), the period was one in which the interest in both European and colonial antiquities was expanding and becoming a matter for larger public institutions and societies as well as notoriously fetishistic private collectors: the British Museum, seemingly the paradigmatic repository of imperial loot, was established in 1753; the Royal Asiatic Society, which collected material and published information concerning antiquities and anthropology exhaustively in India, was founded in 1784; early in the nineteenth century, organized excavations were proceeding under British sponsorship in Egypt and material flowed steadily to London. In retrospect, these institutions and projects epitomize colonial collecting, which seems rapacious, extraordinarily self-confident, and absolutely indissociable from military, political, and economic dominance. Leaving aside the question of whether this is adequate even for interests in specimens, artifacts, and collections during the Victorian period, this perception would radically overstate the degree of author-

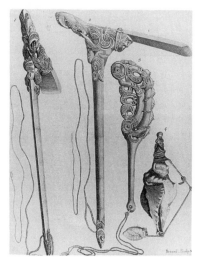

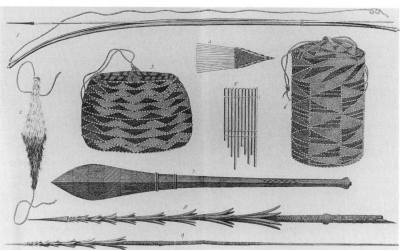

16. (top left) *A Chest of New Zealand, As a Specimen of the Carving of the Country*, engraving after R. Ralph, from John Hawkesworth, *An Account of the Voyages undertaken by the order of His Present Majesty for Making Discoveries in the Southern Hemisphere* (London: 1773), 3, plate 15. The Maori feather box depicted is in the British Museum.

17. (bottom) *Ornaments, Utensils, and Weapons in the Friendly Islands*, engraving by Record after Chapman, from James Cook, *A Voyage towards the South Pole and round the World* (London: 1777), 1, plate 21.

18. (top right) *Specimens of New Zealand Workmanship, &c.*, engraving by Record, from James Cook, *A Voyage towards the South Pole and round the World* (London: 1777), 1, plate 19.

19. *Various Articles of Nootka Sound, Various Articles of the Sandwich Islands,* engraving from George William Anderson, *A New, Authentic, and Complete History of Voyages round the World,* (London: 1784–86). National Library of Australia, Canberra.

ity and coherence that collecting—and the scientific travel that facilitated it—possessed earlier. The ways in which artifacts were depicted in the late eighteenth century are thus of some salience for the longer history of Western interests in exotic material things and peoples. They are not self-evidently part of an imperial, totalized knowledge "of the other"; rather, they are somewhat opaque images that attest more to insecurity than to mastery, and to a disputed knowledge of the exotic.

I have argued elsewhere that there was a good deal of enthusiasm about Pacific curiosities in the late eighteenth century, but the attitude is marked by a puzzling lack of content and specificity; exotic objects commanded attention but were not subject to articulated aesthetic assessment, classification, or enframing in any comparative discourse concerning peoples or technologies (Thomas 1991; 1994). This is manifest in the kind of text that accompanied figures of "weapons and implements":

> 20. Is a kind of Battle-axe, used either as a lance or as a patta-pattoo. The length of these is from five to six feet. The middle part of them is very ingeniously carved . . . 24. A Whistle, made of wood, having the out-side curiously carved. Besides the mouth-hole they have several for the fingers to play upon. These, which are worn about the neck, are three inches and a half in length, and yield a shrill sound (Parkinson 1784, 130–1).

Both textually and visually, things are represented in a rigorously objective fashion, yet also in the most radically uninformative way; their uses may be obvious or may be referred to in captions of the kind quoted, but relevant comment is almost always rigidly neutral. While remarks are occasionally made upon the dexterity or ingenuity of carving, especially in New Zealand material, inflected moral or aesthetic adjudications, or narrative associations, are hesitant or absent from descriptions of the baldest sort.

The absence of any twentieth-century interpretative discourse concerning plates depicting ethnographic specimens is thus matched by an absence in eighteenth-century commentary; the very lack may itself be an index of the objects' identities as appropriated European exotica and of the cultural and political interests inscribed in the images' production. If scholars who have otherwise found Enlightenment workings of the exotic a remarkably complex and rich field have apparently had nothing to say about these illustrations, this lack may manifest not just a simple absence of interest but also perhaps a fact—that in a sense there is nothing that can be said about them. A marked degree of illegibility might, of course, merely reflect our own lack of awareness of the ways in which these engravings were responded to at the time of publication, but in this case there is arguably a singular kind of discursive vacuity that can be seen to positively express the conflicted interests in the things represented and in the broader work of representing the exotic in the late eighteenth century.

This vacuity of meaning emerges, I suggest, from the extreme decontextualization of the pieces depicted, from the kind of space that they occupy, and from the absence of clear adjudications or narrative positioning in the texts within which these plates were physically bound. The extent of discursive deprivation can be signaled crudely by the contrast with another set of engravings in the same publications (figs. 20, 21), which depicted Cook's landings on various islands and meetings with indigenous peoples after the paintings of William Hodges and John Webber. Some of these showed peaceful encounters; others violent ones. All embodied the sense of historical significance that the voyage of exploration possessed, which was manifested not only in the expansion of strictly geographical knowledge, but also in the commerce and intercourse that ensued between European civilization and islanders; commerce, which was considered fateful and morally ambiguous, would induce progress through trade and the introduction of manufactured articles as it would also corrupt the characters and bodies of natives, emblematically through prostitution and the introduction of venereal disease in the fashion discussed in the previous chapter. The topographic sites of these encounters on the edges of land and sea, civility and barbarity; the inclusion of the ship, expressive of the voyage and British naval power; and the juxtaposition between the dignity of the classicized islanders and the grandeur of Cook's arrival are immediately reminiscent of established traditions of history painting—which found subject matter still more appropriate in Cook's death on the beach in Hawaii during the third voyage (Joppien and Smith 1985–87, 2:71–3). The landing and meeting pictures are, in other words, saturated with human purpose, with human difference, with an encounter that was (and was at the time understood to be) historically constitutive.

It is precisely this contextualization in human action—action that is accorded some moral or historical significance—that is at the greatest remove in the images of curiosities. Though the objects are of course the products of human work and craft, they are abstracted from human uses and purposes; the very possibility of displaying "weapons and ornaments" in a single assemblage indicates the extent to which the things imaged are decontextualized and their uses become irrelevant. While the meanings of objects normally subsist in their functions and in their perceived and encoded significance, and they are hence clubs and headdresses rather than merely pieces of wood or shell, such differentiations seem subordinated or forgotten here in the perception of forms; it would no doubt be going too far to suggest that the associations with particular practices are entirely erased, but we are, I think, at a severe remove both from any sort of narrative and from the ordinary flow of experience, when fighting, fishing, and self-decoration can be equated in this fashion.

While these images are essentially variants of natural history illustrations, there is also a kind of painting that they remind us of. The genre of still life, Norman Bryson suggests, offers several insults to the kind of "human-centered dignity" we are used to in other genres of painting and of course in narrative and representation more generally: "In history painting we see the human form more or less idealized, and in portraiture we see the human form more or less as it is, but in still life we never see the human form at all." The viewer is, moreover, "made to feel no bond of continuous life with the objects which fill the scene"; the objects depicted "lack syntax: no coherent purpose brings them together in the place where we find them" (1989, 228–34; see also Bryson 1990). Bryson argues that some still life, and particularly that of Chardin, humanizes and refamiliarizes its objects through a casualness of vision that implies households and domesticities rather than showcases, and hence, that there is scope for a counterbalancing contextualization that mutes the genre's objectifying fetishism. I will suggest that in just a few of the images of artifacts, there is a comparable amelioration. These, however, are exceptional, and Bryson's proposition that the genre displaces or excludes humanity is true in a more extreme way of the engravings; this is perhaps not surprising, since a variety of parallels and continuities might be noted between Dutch still life, the business of collecting, and eighteenth-century scientific illustrations, with respect not

20. *The Landing at Middleburgh, One of the Friendly Isles*, engraving by J. K. Sherwin after William Hodges, from James Cook, *A Voyage towards the South Pole and round the World* (London: 1777), 1, plate 54.

21. John Webber, [*Captain Cook in Ship Cove, Queen Charlotte Sound*], 1777.
Pen, wash, and watercolor, 60.7 × 98.5 cm. National Maritime Museum, London.

only to the decontextualizing mode but what was decontextualized (fig. 22). The
still life paintings frequently included rare or Oriental commodities and natural
curiosities such as shells (which like flowers, are identifiable as species or varieties); the realism of their precise vision was also combined with bizarre and
unreal juxtapositions and combinations that emphasized the material character
of objects and neutralized their diverse uses. The minute descriptive vision of
the Dutch painters—"the little style, where petty effects are the sole end"—was
censured by Joshua Reynolds; in much the same language, he criticized the
unaesthetic visual empiricism that some landscape painters were beginning to
adopt and which was present to some degree in paintings from the Cook voyages, caught as they were between neoclassical aesthetics and scientific interests
in novel atmospheres, plants, and bodies (Reynolds 1878, 1:359; Smith 1985, 111;
cf. Alpers 1983, 19–22). This attitude has no particular bearing on the representations of artifacts, which were simply subaesthetic rather than inadequate or
imperfect forms of something else; but if "minute particularities" led the artist
not simply to produce inadequate work but to "pollute his canvas with deformity," as Reynolds suggested, it is possible that the engravings express more
substantial transgressions of value, which arise from the wider moral status of
particularity and novelty.

The disconnection between human viewer and an array of things has more
particular determinations than those in still life painting (a defamiliarizing

22. Frontispiece to *The Catalogue of the Portland Museum*, engraving by Grignon after Burney. (London: Skinner & Co., 1786). National Library of Australia, Canberra.

treatment of otherwise familiar bread, fruit, and vessels); dissociation is magnified not only by the peculiar conjuncture of objects belonging to quite different domestic and nondomestic domains of human activity—tattooing and warfare—which has already been mentioned, but also by a simple fact that can only be considerably less arresting for the museum-going, late-twentieth-century viewer, namely, that in the 1770s, Maori carving was indeed radically novel and strange and, to a greater or lesser degree, so were many of the other artifacts and designs brought back from the Pacific on Cook's voyages. Of course, some things were readily recognizable as spears, bows, or bowls; but others, such as a Marquesan headdress of feathers, shells, and tortoiseshell fretwork and the garment of the chief mourner in Tahitian funeral processions, were considered extremely curious and perplexing.

Let me return briefly to the space that the imaged things occupy, which I suggest is what makes their exclusion of humanity still more radical than that typical of still life painting. In the second half of the nineteenth century, artifacts were sometimes arranged on walls in a fashion reminiscent of the printed images of that period, which gave much greater emphasis to symmetrical appropriations of form, but there is no sense for the earlier period that what confronts us is a representation of a wall or of any other natural space upon which or within which we see things that are set out. Rather, the absence of shadow, the de-emphasis of tone associated with any particular light source, the frequent lack of any framing or border on the page, and the inclusion of a variety of implements of quite distinct sizes presupposes an abstract, nonspatial field in which weightless things might equally be standing vertically or laid out on a surface. The strange counterpoint to the uninflected realism of the objects' treatment is the wholly imaginary field that they occupy, which could be seen as no less abstract and unnatural than the painted surfaces of Pollock or Rothko. If the latter immediately strike us as paintings rather than paintings *of* anything, the former is just an area of blank paper upon which things have been printed, rather than an area that imitates a real space of any other kind. The suppression of scale and the fact that one piece can appear twice within an image—from different angles or in its entirety and in a detail—not only suggests a comprehensive abstraction from any normal physical domain but raises a question about the position and the character of the viewers: is there some correspondence between the unworldliness of the specimens' nonspace and their own vision and interest in the objects? That is, can that interest be positively constructed as an engagement that is correspondingly dehumanized and objective, free of inflected motivation, or is it intelligible only as a kind of alienation, a failure that is ensured by the severity of the images' decontextualization?

Curiosities

This is the point at which it becomes important to ask what it meant to call artifacts "curiosities." Of course, this term had been employed earlier, as it was subsequently and is sometimes still (though after the mid–nineteenth century "curio" was more widely used); given this diversity of context it cannot be suggested in some transhistorical way that this labeling is especially revealing. For the second half of the eighteenth century, however, it is notable that travel writing (concerning Europe as well as more distant regions) is pervaded by the idea of curiosity, that the nature of curiosity is not fixed but morally slippery, that its associations with legitimate authority and inquiry are disputed and ambivalent, and that this area of semantic conflict is directly associated with responses to ethnographic specimens, since "curiosities" were frequently characterized as being "curious" and as arousing the "curiosity" of people for whom they were exotic. In Cook's own journals, and in the voyage accounts of the naturalists and officers, there are a plethora of references to "curious" garments, ornaments, adzes, caps, and the like, as well as to "curious" carving, staining, tattooing, and so forth (Smith 1985, 123–5; Thomas 1991, 129–32).

Given that the artifacts were found to excite a passionate acquisitiveness among sailors (who, it was said, preferred to barter for them rather than for fresh fish and fruit) and that the Cook voyages in general were said to excite an eager curiosity for geographical knowledge among the British public, what seems specific to the moment is a field of meaning within which subjective response, adjectival characterization, and naming would seem intimately if not harmoniously connected. In the late nineteenth century, in contrast, a "curio" was more immediately legible as a sign of idolatry or cannibalism, which would provoke quite specific moral responses rather than the form of desire that I will suggest was marked by its ambivalence and vacuity. To put this another way, and in quite anachronistic theoretical terms, the eighteenth-century associations implied a relationship between exotic object and knowing subject that was profoundly hermeneutic—a thing could not be considered a curiosity without reference to the knower's intellectual and experiential desire; discourses, inquiries, and relations, not just their objects, were curious—while subsequent attitudes tended to objectify the tribal specimens as expressions of a savage condition, a barbaric stage founded in the order of social development rather than in the responses and pleasure or displeasure of a particular civilized person. There is an implication of risk for the eighteenth-century engagement with an exotic object that appears not to arise in other contexts.

This implication may be read as positively hazardous if the wider associations of curiosity are taken into account. Though the idea of legitimate inquisitiveness is often encountered, there are many forceful expressions, in a variety of genres, of the notion that curiosity is infantile, feminine, somehow tarnished, and licenced in the sense of licentiousness rather than authorization. In fiction, curiosity is often explicitly promiscuous. It might be suggested that its dependence on external things, and its arousal and risk, in the context of a masquerade in Fanny Burney's *Cecilia*, is paradigmatic: "In her curiosity to watch others, she ceased to observe how much she was watched herself" (Burney 1988, 106). The peculiar blending of illegitimate and laudable aspects is captured by the paradoxical gloss in Johnson's dictionary: to be curious is to be "addicted to enquiry." While enquiry would usually seem a proper and essentially masculine activity, addiction, entailing abandonment or at least a partial surrender of self-government before an external agent or object, is certainly illegitimate and excessive.

What is infantile, insecure, and morally problematic in society at home nevertheless figures as an appropriate disposition abroad: Gibbon expressed the commonplace with respect to his own grand tour that "in a foreign country, curiosity is our business and our pleasure" (1984, 134),[1] and it seems entirely natural for Johnson to note censoriously that a writer who failed to ascertain the correct breadth of Loch Ness was "very incurious" (1968, 307). The apparently logical character of this shift, which arises from the different status that a preoccupation with the novel has in familiar circumstances and in foreign parts, does not, however, render curiosity unproblematic in the context of travel; it is not as if the external situation of the objects of inquisitiveness insulates knowledge from the implication of impropriety. For John Barrow, in 1801, discursive authorization was evoked through the curiosity's exclusion: "To those whom mere curiosity, or the more laudable desire of acquiring information, may tempt to make a visit to Table Mountain [above Cape Town], the best and readiest access will be found directly up the face next to the town . . . " But what was the difference between being curious and desiring information? Barrow wrote that the mountain's summit was "a dreary waste and an insipid tameness" that prompted the adventurer to ask whether "such be all the gratification" to be gotten after the fatigue of the ascent:

> The mind, however, will soon be relieved at the recollection of the great command given by the elevation; and the eye, leaving the immediate scenery, will wander with delight round the whole circumference of the horizon . . . All the objects on the plain below are, in fact, dwindled away to the eye of the spectator into littleness and insignificance . . . The shrubbery on the sandy isthmus looks like dots, and the farms and their enclosures as so many lines, and the more-finished parts of a plan drawn on paper (1801, 37–8).

In Barrow's account, the exhausted body doubts the worth of a short excursion because of the dullness of the immediate surroundings; on the other hand, for the mind, the value of the ascent is established by the panorama that it affords, which is marked by the fact that the traveller can experience the surrounding world as a picture. The association of the mind, the larger view, and information prompts an opposed series of implications—of curiosity and a kind of vision that responds to proximate surroundings and is overwhelmed by the condition of the body rather than delighted by the larger scene. This overdetermination of intellect by corporeality is of course expressed in the vocabulary of curiosity, which, like hunger and lust, is not governed by the mind but is "aroused," "gratified," and so on. This is hardly specific to the period, but it is notable that the aim of a desire "more laudable" than curiosity is the subsumption of other lands to the form of representation over which one possesses a "great command." It is as if picturing, understood immediately and explicitly as an operation of power, somehow establishes the legitimacy of a kind of knowledge or interest that is otherwise problematic, otherwise anxious and giddy. This is highly suggestive insofar as the imaging of the objectifications of curiosity, of ethnographic specimens, is concerned, and this is a point I'll return to.

Enduring proverbs (e.g., curiosity killed the cat) and more recent texts such as the Curious George children's stories (e.g., Rey 1954) and *I Am Curious (Yellow)* (Sjoman 1968) tell us that curiosity's connotations of risk and licence were not specific to the eighteenth century. The question therefore arises as to precisely why they should have been discursively conspicuous in that period, rather than merely semantically present. I suggest that curiosity was a problem because it shadowed another term that had the same attributes—one that was also a matter of passion and particularity, of the attraction of what was novel. Unlike curiosity, commerce was central to eighteenth-century British political debate, and attitudes toward it were similarly profoundly ambiguous. Even in a relatively neutral account such as David Hume's, it was as directly associated with novelty and passion as we have already seen curiosity to be:

> In most nations, foreign trade has preceded any refinement in home manufactures, and given birth to domestic luxury. The temptation is stronger to make use of foreign commodities, which are ready for use, and which are entirely new to us, than to make improvements on any domestic commodity, which always advance by slow degrees, and never affect us by their novelty. The profit is also very great, in exporting what is superfluous at home, and what bears no price, to foreign nations, whose soil or climate is not favourable to that commodity. Thus men become acquainted with the *pleasures* of luxury and the *profits* of commerce; and their *delicacy* and *indus-*

try, being once awakened, carry them on to farther improvements, in every branch of domestic as well as foreign trade (Hume 1882, 1:295–6).

As I noted earlier, Hume sees an appetite for the novel as improving, but his own observations on the "uncertain signification" of luxury adumbrate the negative dimension of the process, which receives a good deal of attention also in the works of Lord Kames, John Millar, and Adam Smith (Pocock 1975, 430–1; Copley 1984; Raven 1992). One argument was that luxury was feminizing and corrupting; Britain could be identified with earlier empires or societies that had declined as opulence sapped their martial vigor and public spirit. Another was that the particularization of labor removed one of the bases of active citizenship; not only were men therefore cheapened, the state of the body politic as a whole was prejudiced by the scope for despotism. These debates, which of course have a complex relationship with class instability and social rivalries between trade and landed property, need not be discussed further here. My point is simply that curiosity, in its canonically impassioned and infantile form, was both metonymically situated within the process of trade—as the form that desire for novel foreign commodities took—and metaphorically associated with the whole. A vocabulary of corporeal desire governed both; the fetishism of the bauble, the particularism of the flycatcher, had as problematic a relation to public virtue as the "petty effects" of the empirical painter had for Reynolds's aesthetic universalism. One's interest in a specimen or object might indeed be definitely scientific; but the fact that this interest could not be apprehended as the appreciation of some general truth, but took the form of a desire for particular things, meant that one's project could only be polluted and deformed, if the implications of the neoclassical dicta were taken to their limits. This characterization is not as extravagant as it may seem. We will see below that some forms of collecting and antiquarianism really were licentious, and sometimes preoccupied by literal deformity, or imagined deformity, that certainly deformed the business of inquiry. This is all too well attested to by the shocking case of the "Hottentot Venus" (Gould 1985, 291–305); let that stand for the plethora of expressions of colonial prurience that are too sad and objectionable to be rehearsed.

Risks

A suggestion that curiosity, a kind of interest that fetishized novel objects, actually entailed some "risk" to the knowing subject may seem itself to fetishize some textual ambiguities and unduly amplify their significance for any concrete, historical, knower. In the case of the Cook voyages, however, the identity and authority of scientists and others arguably *was* open to being mocked and disfigured, both in the experiential context of contact with islanders, and in the theater of British public debate, within which the self-presentations and motivations of scientists were not always represented in the terms they themselves projected.

The form of ambiguity and risk that is of more direct relevance here relates to the status of the natural scientists—Banks, on the first voyage, and Forster on the second. The editor of Cook's account, John Hawkesworth, was less circumspect than he might have been in alluding to the sexual contact between the sailors generally and the Tahitian women, and the prominence of Banks in his account suggested to many that his botany was fraudulent, "that he was more interested in exotic women than exotic plants" (Smith 1985, 46). This was the theme of a number of satirical poems, such as the 1788 *Transmigration:*

> ATTEND, ye swarms of MODERN TOURISTS,
> Yclept, or Botanists or Florists:
> Ye who ascend the cloud-capt Hills,
> Or creep along their tinkling Rills;
> Who scientifically tell
> The Wonders of each COCKLE-SHELL;
> And load the Press with Publications,
> With *useless, learned* DISSERTATIONS.
> Ye who o'er Southern Oceans wander
> With simpling B——ks or sly S——r;
> Who so familiarly describe
> The Frolicks of the wanton Tribe,
> And think that simple Fornication
> Requires no sort of Palliation.
> Let wanton Dames and Demireps,
> To *Otaheite* guide their Steps;
> Their Love's delicious Feasts are found;
> There Joys *so innocent* abound!
> Behold, a Queen her Gul o'er reaches;
> First steals, and then she wears his Breeches.
> Such luscious Feats, when told with Ease,
> Must Widows, Matrons, Maidens please;
> Nor can they blush at having read
> What ye so modestly have said:
> Yet though ye strive to dress your Story,
> And make (what is your Shame) your Glory,
> With us this makes no Variation;
> Still is it simple FORNICATION,

Whether in DRURY'S ROUNDS ye sport,
Or frisk in OBEREA'S COURT.[2]

Here, the ambiguity of licensed or licentious authority is most conspicuously at issue; science is not only a cover for fornication, but even in its public character, is shown to privilege trivial objects such as cockle shells, and to express itself in works that are equally effusive and useless. While Banks could hardly respond to such a categorical rejection of natural history, he could dispute the extent to which his interests were professed rather than genuine, and he effected this by presenting himself, in a portrait that was published as a mezzotint (fig. 23), not only with curiosities but with a folio of botanical drawings that together mark the accomplishments of the voyage. If this picture is ambiguous, if it suggests vanity and personal acquisitiveness with respect to the curiosities that surround the subject, this implication is counterbalanced by the presence of the strictly scientific image of the plant, which is obviously not an ornament but a specimen. I suggest that the plates depicting plants and ethnographic artifacts do more or less the same work for the project of natural history in the voyage publications as the drawing does for this portrait: the evocation of "specimen-icity" affirms the vacuity, the dispassionate character, of a natural history that was striving to differentiate itself from avaricious commercial collecting, and from inconsequential "fly catching" at the same time.

While my concern here is not with the origins of the representation of artifacts in a dehumanized, abstract, fashion—which might be traced through a variety of earlier modes of depicting medallions, agricultural implements, and classical antiquities—it is clear that the immediate model for the Cook voyage productions derived from the conventions of natural history illustration; most of the images published with the account of the first voyage were drawn by Banks' own draftsmen, who treated the objects in the same way that they depicted birds, fish, flowers, and so on. Artificial and natural could even be placed together, as in a plate (fig. 24) in another work from the 1770s, Forster's translation of Osbeck's *Voyage to China*. If there is nothing striking or remarkable about this, that fact itself attests to the extent to which we are now accustomed to the idea that artifacts are specimens; it requires a certain defamiliarization to see this identification as contingent and historical, as something that has a genealogy that had to be struggled for at a particular time. The effort to make this identification in the field of vision must be seen as a difficult one, not only because it entailed a struggle with private and unscientific interests in curiosities, but also because it was internally duplicitous and dishonest. In fact, artifacts were not specimens in any meaningful sense; they were not the objects of any theoretical discourse or systematic inquiry. There was, in this period,

23. J. R. Smith's mezzotint after Benjamin West, *Joseph Banks*, ca. 1772. Dixon Library, State Library of New South Wales, Sydney.

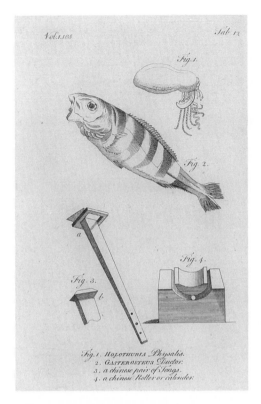

24. Marine life and Chinese implements illustrated in Pehr Osbeck, *Voyage to China and the East Indies* (London: 1771). Cambridge University Library, Cambridge.

nothing like Linnean classification that could be applied to artificial curiosities: they were not drawn into any comparative study of technology or craft; they played no significant part in the ethnological project of discriminating and assessing the advancement of the various peoples encountered (which instead turned upon distinctions in the condition of women and political forms). They were specimens because they were treated as such, and their display in the space of the specimen, which abstracted them from any immediate human interest (in ornament, for instance), was part of an expressive work that evoked the science of men like Banks and licenced their curiosity. Once less youthful, Banks did in fact find his status legitimized and endorsed, even if with gentle irony:

> Sir Joseph was so exceedingly shy that we made no sort of acquaintance at all. If instead of going around the world he had only fallen from the moon, he could not appear less-versed in the usual modes of a tea-drinking party. But what, you will say, has a tea-drinking party to do with a botanist, a man of science, a president of the Royal Society? (Burney 1904–05, 3:481).

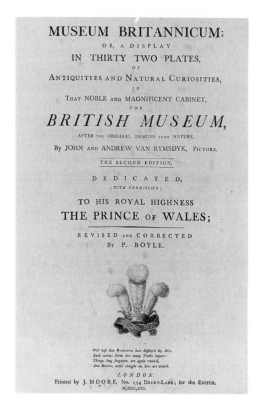

25. John and Andrew Van Rymsdyk, *Museum Britannicum*, 2d ed. (London: 1791) title page.

And he has since of course become part of the British imperial pantheon and the prehistory of white settlement in Australia, where substantial primary school time is still devoted to the "explorers." From this vantage point, the effort to discredit natural history as trite and promiscuous seems merely an evangelical irrelevancy, a misconstruction of real scientists whose work participated in a wider, highly consequential, expansive project; but the suggestion that I've advanced, that licentiousness was an ambivalence internal to curiosity rather than merely an external deprecation of it, is directly expressed by some others who claimed a scientific interest in the rarities of the British Museum.

In 1788 John and Andrew van Rymsdyk, pictors, published *Museum Brittannicum,* a set of plates of curiosities in the British Museum (fig. 25); this unusual work made much of its precise mimesis, true imitation being the "solemn Law" guiding the artist, who declared "himself an enemy to Nature-Menders, Mannerists, &c." The plates are indeed fetishistic in their attention to the appearances and details of particular antiquities and natural curiosities. To say that the volume was a work of entertainment rather than science is to understate its flagrant disinterest in any classificatory systematization and the corresponding extremity of its enthusiasm for the singular and bizarre.

> Now, in a Work of this kind, some Objects will always be found more *pleasing* than others, according to the different *Tastes*, Studies, and Geniuses of particular Men:—this I was soon made sensible of, for when I began to shew my Designs to the Ladies and Gentlemen, some wished my Work had consisted of BOTANY; others of BIRDS, BUTTERFLIES, or QUADRUPEDS; some again of FISH, SHELLS, and FOSSILS; a few wanted them all ARTIFICIAL &c. . . . Therefore I came to a Resolution to chuse an Intermixture, which will be found to consist of some things fine, others but middling, and a few perhaps quite indifferent (van Rymsdyk and van Rymsdyk 1791, iv).[3]

The giddy and random vision that this eclecticism prompted is distinctly Borgesian: the plates include tailorbirds' and wasps' nests; the *oculus mundi*, or eye of the world, a Chinese pebble that becomes transparent in water; a penknife with a gold tip, employed in an alchemist's sleight of hand; a brick from the Tower of Babel; "A very curious *Coral*, modeled by Nature, in the form of a Hand or Glove" (fig. 26); Governor Pitt's brilliant diamond; and some weapons including the *flagello*, an unlawful instrument said to have been extensively used "in the *Irish* massacre of King *Charles*'s time; though far be it from me to advance any thing that is not true." Lest these oddities testify insufficiently to the perversity of interest, we also find stones from the urinary tract, one "with a Silver Bodkin" within: "It is generally supposed that the lady had an obstruction in the urinary passage; she made use of the Bodkin, (to remove it) which by some accident slipt and remained in the bladder; the stony substance forming itself gradually *Stratum Superstratum* round it.—The same case happened to a woman, who made use of a large nail; the stone and nail may be seen at a friend's of mine" (van Rymsdyk and van Rymsdyk 1791, 49, caption to pl. 19). Another illustration showed "One of the *Horns* of Mrs. *French*," who was exhibited at shows; this caption detailed a number of other cases of women who grew horns like rams, cast them, and grew further pairs; despite the sex of the ram, this proclivity was evidently unknown among male humans. Though he of course had entirely different things in mind, this does suggest another relevance for Ruskin's references to "vice" and "illegitimate and contemptible sources of pleasure"; the van Rymsdyks hardly excluded improper constructions of licence when they wrote that "Drawing and Studying these Curiosities" was "like a luxurious Banquet, to me indeed the most voluptuous Entertainment" (iii). An association with corruption and debauchery is still more explicit in one of Hogarth's *Marriage à la mode* engravings (fig. 27), in which curiosities

26. John and Andrew Van
Rymsdyk, *Museum Britannicum*,
2d ed. (London: 1791), plate 20.

are part of a scene full of allusions to adulterous liaisons, effeminacy, sexual rapture, corrupt wealth based in slaveownership, false connoisseurship, and so on (Dabydeen 1987, 74–89).

For the natural historians, the abstraction of artifacts into a scientific enclave was a double operation that recursively authorized the natural philosopher's travel and collecting by making the particular claim that a curiosity was a specimen, something in a scientific enclave, rather than an object of fashion or mere commodity that those lacking scientific authorization might traffic in and profit from. The difficulty of the first aspect of this project, displayed in the *Museum Brittanicum* and in the absurdities of societies of antiquaries (cf. Johnson 1751), was that it was readily imitated and appropriated in a fashion that might not so much have deployed an authoritative cover for licentious, trivial, or fetishistic pursuits as it parodically exposed the licence and ambivalence internal to proper

27. *The Countess's Levee*, from William Hogarth's *Marriage à la mode*, series of six plates, June 1745, plate 4. Second state, engraved by S. Ravenet.

forms of inquiry, a voluptuousness subsequently exploited by Max Ernst in his own "natural history" engravings (fig. 28). In this sense, the conflicted character of the interest in curiosities is not simply a peculiar response to a particular, though not particularly important, set of novel things, but it is also emblematic of the whole project of expansive curiosity, which sought to abstract, generalize, and dehumanize particular and contingent forms of knowledge that in fact often did spring quite directly from passion and private interest.

   The difficulty of the second aspect of the effort, which still arises between indigenous peoples, or others whose artifacts or "heritage" have been appropriated, and private collectors and institutions, arises from the conflicts between scientists' assertions of their rights to control specimens and the interests of others who seek to deal in them or use them. There is not much direct information concerning the purchasing and display of curiosities in the late eighteenth century, but there are suggestive allusions, such as Keate's observation that the hatchets of the Pelew Islanders "were not unlike those of the South Sea islands, of which so many have been seen in England" (1789, 312). It is clear, however, from the voyages themselves, that many common sailors acquired substantial

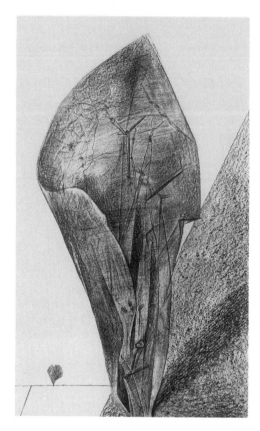

28. Max Ernst, *Elle garde son secret*
(*She Guards Her Secret*), sheet 10
from *Histoire naturelle,* Editions
Jeanne Bucher (Paris 1926).
Collotype 42.8 × 28.0 cm.
Reproduced by permission of the
National Gallery of Australia,
Canberra. © ADAGP, Paris, and
DACS, London, 1997.

collections, often with a view to sale at home. J. R. Forster found that the thirst of
the ship's crew to acquire curiosities conflicted directly with his own interest,
especially when common sailors sought to resell items (here natural rather than
artificial specimens) to him at exorbitant prices. Forster associated his own
interest with that of the government and the public, while he represented the
sailors as acting from base passions and commercial motivation that directly
conflicted with "the common cause." Forster sought to illustrate his own publication from the voyage—a work of geographical and ethnological exposition
rather than the standard narrative—with plates "of Natural History, Utensils,
Implements of War, etc.," while the official history would have included the
views, landing scenes, and portraits of islanders; Forster would have supervised
the drawing and engraving of the weapons and utensils, but in the course of
protracted negotiations, he quarreled with Cook and the Admiralty, and finally
published separately with none of the plates (Hoare 1982, Dettelbach 1996).
Given the extent to which Forster's status had been at issue—on the voyage

itself, and in the course of postvoyage disputes, which need not be entered into here—it becomes increasingly clear, I suggest, that what the images of curiosities depicted was rather less important than what they evoked. The sense in which this required a positive effort to decontextualize objects that were not quite specimens, insofar as they remained connected with human interest or a scene of human life, is manifested in the difference between John Webber's drawing of a Kamchatka sledge (fig. 29), and the plate published in the account of the third voyage (fig. 30). This became an object of reason, dissociated from passion, commerce, and luxury, and from the base avarice of the common sailors who were so readily mistaken for women.

Variations

I stress that the arguments that I've advanced do not relate to the whole genre of artifact depiction, which had earlier manifestations, for instance in Lafitau's crucial work of comparative ethnology (1724), and which developed, with an increasing emphasis on the symmetrical arrangement of forms, throughout the nineteenth century (see, for example, Thomas 1991, 159–60). The former was distinguished by its classicizing rather than natural-historicizing orientation toward non-Europeans, and the latter by greater emphasis on the distinctive characteristics of particular races; their coherence as human types was expressed materially through a distinct assemblage of implements that also displayed their degree of technical advancement. This shift is notable primarily from the 1840s on: in the 1820s it was still the case that the suggestive vacuity of the specimen was unqualified either by the local human context or by a theoretical operation on material culture. Though some voyages, such as Freycinet's, included substantial numbers of artifact plates (fig. 31) in their *atlases historiques*, actual commentary on the pieces that went beyond the baldest description remained limited.

While the discursive configuration that encompassed a particular, unstable, and contested association between curiosity and curiosities was arguably specific to the period I've discussed, the construction of the images was also historically mutable. As comparison between the plates from the official publications and, say, Parkinson's work (1784), makes clear, these were not in any case homogeneous even within the Cook voyage works; over the first decades of the nineteenth century, the use of lithography as opposed to line engraving sometimes gave artifacts a more tangible and less "clinical" appearance, but this concretizing trend was suppressed by the inclusion of larger numbers of pieces, which were recognizable less in their individual usefulness or specificity than as an array or assemblage. The conflation of different scales, the incorporation of

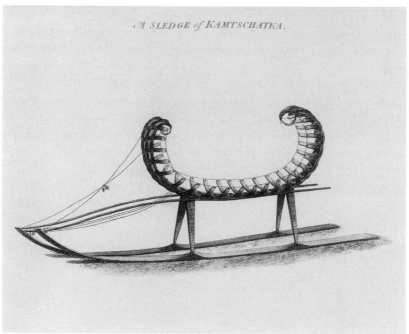

29. John Webber, *A Sledge of Kamchatka*, ca. 1781–83. Pen, wash, and watercolor. 18 × 22.3 cm. Mitchell Library, State Library of New South Wales, Sydney.

30. *A Sledge of Kamtschatka*, engraving by Woodyer after John Webber, in James Cook and James King, *A Voyage to the Pacific Ocean* (London: 1784), plate 71. National Library of Australia, Canberra.

elements of detail and different views, and the apparent randomness of the kinds of things selected were all features that produced images that were, no less than those from the Cook voyage texts, almost willfully meaningless.

However, there were ways in which the scientific vacuity I've described was obviated by different textual and graphic treatments of curiosities in certain works. While the plates (fig. 32) in the initial published edition of Labillardière's *Voyage à la Recherche de La Pérouse* (1800a) were of the same general kind as those in the Cook publications, just as the natural-historical and scientific aspirations were similar, a cheaper edition in English had less interest in the authorization of curiosity and more in compelling narrative.[4] The "fact" that the people of New Caledonia were warlike cannibals had been proved to the mariners by the islanders themselves, who acted out their method of cutting up a victim in a playful fashion that probably responded more to the visitors' preoccupation with the topic than it reflected their own practices; this savage character was also expressed in an engraved portrait of a particularly aggressive islander (see chapter 5, figure 43). The specter of cannibalism was, however, incorporated more directly in a redrawn engraving of weapons in the English edition (fig. 33), in which the array was broken up into individually captioned pieces, most of which were weapons or were otherwise associated with fighting and anthropophagy; for instance, the *nbouet* was "used by these Cannibals in dissecting their enemies."

The engraving of curiosities was open to being modified in a different way, compatible with the idealization of the noble savage rather than the denigration of the ignoble. Keate's *Account of the Pelew Islands* was not in any sense an official account; written by a man of letters on the basis of interviews with the sailors, rather than personal participation in the voyage, it was effusive in its sentimental appreciation of the inhabitants of the island now properly known as Belau, whom he regarded as "an *ornament* to human nature" (1789, xiii). The book was extremely popular partly because the son of the paramount chief, Prince Leboo, like Omai a decade earlier, had been brought to London and was lionized by society; a *History of Prince Lee Boo* (1844) was in its nineteenth edition by 1844. Keate's work took up the fashion in curiosities by devoting seven of its seventeen plates to artifacts, after watercolors by John Plott (figs. 34–35). What is striking about these, in contrast with the Cook voyage images, is that the largeness of the pieces within their engraved frames, which fill the page, produces a tangible proximity, a sense of texture and function, that derives partly from the use of stipple engraving, which is not typical of the genre. While the conventional line engraving of the Cook voyage usually privileges form, sometimes reducing things to two-dimensional shapes, and draws attention to elements of design rather than substance, stipple gives a far more definite sense of tone and material—of knives and baskets as cutters and containers, as jagged and envel-

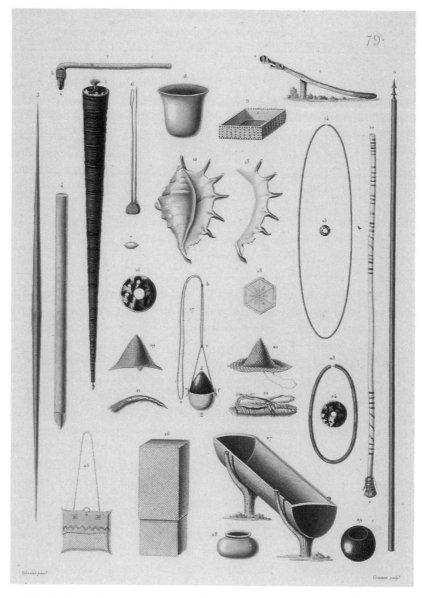

31. *Isles Mariannes: divers objets à l'usage des anciens habitans,* hand-colored lithograph by Coutant after Bévelet, from L. C. Desaules de Freycinet, *Voyage autour du monde . . . pendant les années 1817–20* (Paris: 1827–39), atlas, plate 79.

32. *Effets des Sauvages de la Nouvelle Calédonie,* engraving after Piron, from J. J. de Labillardière, *Voyage à la recherche de La Pérouse* (Paris: 1800). Mitchell Library, State Library of New South Wales, Sydney.

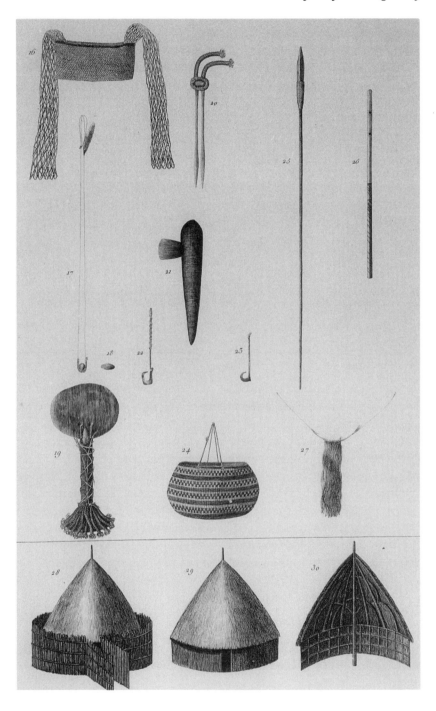

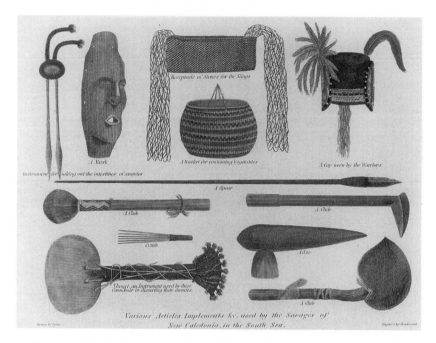

33. *Various articles, Implements, &c.,* engraved by Hawkesworth, from J. J. de Labillardière, *Voyage in Search of La Pérouse* (London: 1800).

oping things. The external appearance of tortoiseshell may not be effectively communicated, but the sheer body of the vessel, and its associated spoon, are immediately available for recognition and use, just as the "basket for common purposes" indeed seems common and accessible (the portraits in Keate's book, prepared by the same engraver from the work of a different artist, were similarly humanized and were markedly individual and sentimental [cf. Smith 1985, 134–5]). The distance of these images from the abstraction of the Cook voyage specimens is moreover marked by the emphasis on light and shadow; the things are resting on a surface and are in a worldly space inhabited by the artist, or equally by the viewer, rather than in a nonspatial and comprehensively dehumanized domain.

What perhaps seems the most striking departure within the genre that I have reviewed is manifest in some publications from the 1840s. George French Angas produced a lavish series of lithographs under the titles *South Australia Illustrated* (1847c), *The New Zealanders Illustrated* (1847a), and *The Kaffirs Illustrated* (1849); the folio volumes included portraits of individual natives, landscape scenes, and, especially for New Zealand, many examples of Maori archi-

34. John Plott, [*Belauan Imple-ments*], watercolor. National Library of Australia, Canberra.

35. *Ornaments. 1. A small Dagger. 2. the sheath made of Bamboo. 3. a Wooden Basket inlaid with Shells. 4. an Apron of Cocoa Nut Husk.* Stipple engraving by H. Kingsbury after John Plott, from George Keate, *An Account of the Pelew Islands*, 3d ed. (London: 1789), plate 5.

tecture and artifacts (figs. 36, 37). These plates of objects were not on the whole dissimilar to the lithographs of ethnographic specimens published in the atlases of major French voyages to the Pacific a few years earlier, except that Angas frequently included a vignette of some kind of human activity in the center of his plates. In one dominated by fishing equipment—lures and the like—a canoe at a radically smaller scale is seen out on a lake; in another, a woman is preparing food, and so on.

If the key to the earlier images is their dehumanization, might these scenes of ordinary domestic life and subsistence rehumanize the arrays of material culture that are displayed? There is a clue in the images themselves, in the extent to which the scenes of activity seem radically shrunk in relation to carvings and artifacts, some of which might be held in the palm of one's hand; so far from abstracting these things from the condition of the specimen, indigenous life has itself arguably been reduced to the status of a collected item or exhibit. This would make sense if the differences between the Cook voyage encounters, and

36. *Women of the Nga-Ti-Tor Tribe,* from G. F. Angas, *New Zealanders Illustrated* (1847), plate 42. Mitchell Library, State Library of New South Wales, Sydney.

other eighteenth-century visits, and the colonial encounter in the south Australia of Angas's time are taken into account. The early voyages dealt with dynamic populations that were in no significant sense oppressed or subordinated by the European presence; though venereal disease had an immediate effect, there was no sense that their numbers would be severely reduced as a result of introduced diseases. Nor did the circumstances of contact compel Europeans to denigrate indigenous peoples in any extreme fashion. By the late 1840s, on the other hand, there was a real commitment to permanent and large-scale white settlement in Australia and New Zealand; the contradiction between indigenous occupation and white demands for land would lead almost inevita-

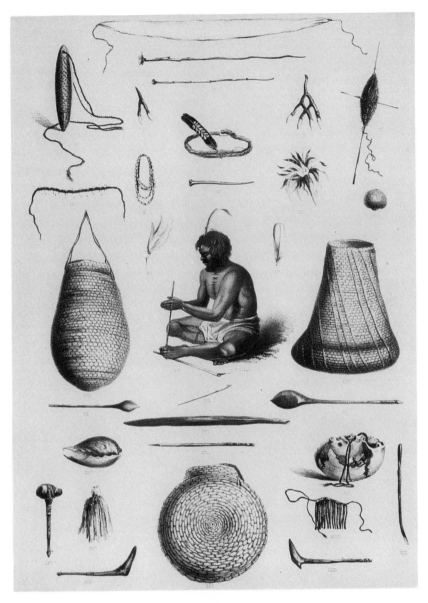

37. *Aboriginal Inhabitants—Ornaments and Utensils,* from G. F. Angas, *South Australia Illustrated* (1847), plate 27. Mitchell Library, State Library of New South Wales, Sydney.

bly to open conflict, and to attitudes that legitimized European appropriation, such as the idea that natives were passing away before the stronger race. The struggle did not flare up in New Zealand until the wars of the 1860s, and in Australia there was of course no concerted war but rather a prolonged invasive process that took place in remote regions much later than those around sites of early settlement. The inevitable and necessary transformation was, however, already clear at the time that Angas wrote:

> As British civilization is daily spreading over the Australian continent, so the degraded natives of the soil are fast disappearing; and, in New South Wales especially, they will, ere long, have totally disappeared. During my stay there, I made constant search and inquiry into the past history and customs of the aborigines; and, combining my own observations with those of others who have been eyewitnesses to their ceremonies, I have been enabled to preserve such records of these people as may prove interesting to ethnologists at a future day (1847b, 2:210).

Although Angas did not express such a categorically pessimistic view of the fate of the Maori, he clearly detected degeneracy in their superstition and in the indolence of chiefs; his positive remarks were generally reserved for converted, assimilated natives, who made themselves useful by growing food to trade with Europeans (2:20). What I want to draw attention to, however, is not his commonplace racism, but his confident engagement in an ethnological project and the peculiar temporality it imposed. The project documented a vanishing people and could equate a graphic record of some aspect of their manners or behavior with an artifact; anticipating the extinction of a degenerate people in Australia and at least the eradication of what was barbaric or degenerate about the people in New Zealand, Angas could treat the present almost nostalgically. Taking the anachronistic character of the native for granted, he did not need to struggle for, or overemphasize, the sense in which native artifacts and native life itself amounted to specimens; they were not so much things amounting to or belonging to anyone's experience, but facts of natural history and facts from the past.

The reincorporation of humanity in the ethnographic engraving thus consummated, or rendered redundant, the twin effort initiated in the Cook voyage prints: it was now evident that exotic cultures were objects of scientific knowledge, and, while colonial science was at least as prurient or compromised as ever, its intellectual and cultural status was more secure. While, in the late eighteenth century, Joseph Banks's botanizing seemed to lapse into womanizing and was the subject of evangelical censure, less than a century later one of the most famous evangelists almost subordinated his missionary work to scientific collecting. David Livingstone's hybrid commercial, evangelical, exploratory practice could not have possessed the same legitimacy seventy, or probably even fifty, years earlier.

Exhibitions

The forms of curiosity that I've discussed here have been various, but none of them licensed the representation of objects by their indigenous former owners and users; the conflict-ridden discourse was united by its appropriative character, which commoditized artifacts and made the variety of utensils, implements, weapons, and ornaments the instruments of intellectual powerplay, a conflict that largely or absolutely excluded the meanings attached to things by their producers. This silencing or displacing effect of Orientalism and associated forms of colonial discourse hardly requires further documentation on the basis of the material considered here.

The objects depicted in Keate's book are in the ethnographic collections of the British Museum; they have been displayed at various times in the Museum of Mankind and will no doubt be exhibited again, perhaps in new permanent displays to be established in the museum's future galleries in the old British Library. Some contemporary curators would reject the distinctions between Western and non-Western art and present the bird-shaped "tureen" and similar objects as magnificent works, their labeling confined to minimal facts of provenance, type, and age. In some institutions, "ethnographic" items, understood as masterworks, are even displayed with the masterpieces of European art: Indonesian textiles, Melanesian ancestral figures, northwest American masks—all old and anonymous—can share a gallery with Tiepolo, Rubens, Monet, and Fred Williams. A less-encompassing exhibition may be restricted to the work of a particular people, or to some of their work, as the famous Te Maori exhibition was dedicated overwhelmingly to early ancestral sculpture. Te Maori nevertheless presented particular works, isolated in dark spaces, as remarkable individual artworks; even the smallest jade ornament was transformed into a peculiarly heavy monument, its spirituality and authenticity bearing down upon the viewer. Museums, it would seem, are forever humorless. This kind of display, and especially also the kind of catalogue photography that goes with it, reproduces the old operation of decontextualization, but to different ends. If, earlier, the thing was appropriated into a vacuum so that it could be declared a specimen, it is now appreciated into a vacuum as a work of art and an expression of the complexity of tribal culture. What is crucial for the politics of the process is not, of course, the question of how current strategies differ or don't differ

38. Dagmar Dyck, *Manu kalapu,*
1995, screenprint, 50 × 56 cm.
By courtesy of the artist and the
Lane Gallery, Auckland. Photo:
Mark Adams.

from colonial curiosity, but the context and effects of the approach in the making and reception of particular shows. Adjudications about the merits and limitations of exhibitions cannot be read off exhibitions in a formalistic manner; they may prove very difficult to read at all.

While this treatment of "ethnographic art" is common enough, the directions in curatorial strategy at the British Museum are such that any new exhibit of the Belauan material is likely to favor more or less the opposite approach and contextualize the objects in the culture and history of Belau. If the exhibit is consistent with strong shows that the museum has put together over the last decade on the Amazon, Madagascar, the Inuit, and Papua New Guinea over recent years, it will present living traditions, evoke the feel of the place, display contemporary artifacts and imported goods, and present, in a consciously anti-exoticist fashion, a dynamic rather than a static culture. Rather than frame the exhibits with the texts of white anthropologists, it will incorporate some Belauan voices, people's explication of their own culture or of the artifacts. This kind of exhibition, in other words, could make a space for listening beyond the silence that Orientalism seems to have imposed for so long. Even if it were inevitably open to charges of ventriloquism—asking "the Other" to enunciate what "we" want said—this would be an appropriate and honorable redemptive strategy, one that ameliorates some of the many disquieting or reprehensible aspects of imperial museums. It could, however, also be seen as one that is untrue to the significance and history of these objects as exotica within Britain. The identities of material things are not fixed and founded but mutable and prone to both subtle and radical historical reformulation; ethnographic artifacts, like other things, have biographies marked by different contextual meanings and uses and punctuated by appropriations and recontextualizations (Appadurai 1986; Thomas 1991). These are hybrid objects that lack purely "Pelew," or Belauan, identities; they have also had lives as foreign things within Britain, as things seen and manipulated themselves and imagined via Keate's plates and text. One kind of exhibit, which displayed not only the things but their engraved images and which conveyed something of their British as well as their Belauan meanings through captions and commentaries, could make these exotic things not only the pawns for further operations of scientific or curatorial authority, but also signs of their own migrant histories, which display the history of collecting and the anxiety of curiosity.

Finally, it is worth noting that just as curiosities were decontextualized by explorers, ethnographers, and engravers, Polynesians are now able to decontextualize the genre of prints that I have discussed and reappropriate the imagery to their own purposes. Happily ignoring all the issues of scientific voyeurism that

39. Poster promoting a Pacific cultural event, produced in Auckland, 1994, incorporating a watercolor of Pacific artifacts in the Berne Historical Museum by Emmanuel Otto Bay, ca. 1890. (See Kaeppler 1978, 22, fig. 46).

once surrounded the images, contemporary islanders have both borrowed the mode of illustration in their contemporary art (fig. 38), and also directly re-produced images of the type I have discussed in this chapter (fig. 39). The images serve simply as illustrations of their artifacts and art traditions that are appropriately used to promote cultural events and the affirmation of identity. The future values and uses of representations, like artifacts, are never defini-tively inscribed in the things by their producers.

5

Melanesians
and Polynesians:
Ethnic Typifications
inside and outside
Anthropology

The chief aim or function of colonial ideology, it is often asserted, was or is the affirmation of the superiority of white colonizers over non-Europeans or natives. It can hardly be disputed that reinforcement of such a basic racial hierarchy is conspicuous, but one premise of a more adequate account of the representations produced by colonial travelers and ethnological writers might be that they were (and are) concerned, not simply with white superiority, which of course was often too obvious a "fact" to require substantiation, but with the superiority of some indigenous peoples over others. In any journey, a traveler encountered a variety of groups; administrators were likely to deal with distinct populations; and the ethnological theorist was of course often specifically concerned with defining and ranking different "races." Despite their inevitable diversity and inconsistency, these comparisons did not proceed in a totally haphazard way, but tended to be reiterated to the point that they acquired, as Edward Said says of the basic geographic difference between East and West, the status of an external and axiomatic truth. On the other hand, what was at issue in such discriminations, what kinds of criteria mattered, might be disputed and might vary over time.

The example I explore here is the enduring geographic-cum-ethnological division of Oceania into "Melanesia" (in the west) and "Polynesia" (in the east). Although nineteenth-century representations privileged color (the Melanesians being black and the Polynesians lighter skinned), the crucial point in modern anthropological comparison was until recently that Melanesian societies were egalitarian and Polynesian societies hierarchical; the division thus articulated with social evolutionary oppositions between tribes and chiefdoms, the more centralized and hierarchical Polynesian polities providing grist for the "origins of the state" mill.[1] There would, perhaps, be nothing to discuss if the categories mapped real differences, on the basis of biological variation, language, social forms, ancestral groups, or whatever, but they do not: it has been argued by archaeologists, linguists, historians, social anthropologists, and others that the dichotomy is basically misleading (see Thomas 1989 for full references). "Melanesia" lumps together populations with quite different backgrounds (Papuans and Austronesians), while "Polynesia" is better understood as an offshoot or subgroup within Austronesian "Melanesia" rather than a comparable entity. I do not wish to belabor the point that the ethnological categories are invented, which is in any case made irrelevant by the fact that they have acquired substance through their use by scholars and by many Pacific islanders: while people from the western Pacific might identify themselves first as members of immediate groups, second as Tolai or whatever, and third as Papua New Guineans, there are also contexts where they see themselves as "Melanesians," and there is certainly a transnational indigenous elite that would often identify itself in this way. The term "Polynesian" is widely used of and by migrants in New Zealand from Niue, the Cook Islands, Tonga, Samoa, and elsewhere. The point, then, is not that the categories are false, but that their persistence is sustained through reiteration and redefinition, rather than on the basis of self-evident human differences.

In this chapter I do not attempt anything like a comprehensive review of the way in which the juxtaposition has evolved (which, to be complete, would need also to consider the specific values attached to a third region, Micronesia, in the northwest Pacific). Rather, I aim to illustrate the proportion of continuity and discontinuity in the values that each term possessed. As Bernard Smith (1992, 189–90) has pointed out, the problem with an account of colonial discourse such as Edward Said's, from the viewpoint of the ways in which Oceania has been represented, is that the enduring and internally consistent character of whatever we would see as the counterpart to Orientalism is overstressed. What is important, of course, is not the pursuit of empirical particularity for its own sake, but what the nuances suggest about wider shifts in aesthetic and ethnological projects, and in the stakes that those projects had in hierarchizing operations.

Encountering Difference: Eighteenth-Century Perceptions

The number of descriptions and observations of Pacific peoples that can, in some sense, be called ethnographic, is of course very considerable, even for early periods of contact; systematic ideas about cultural or "racial" difference across Oceania were, however, shaped by a relatively small number of key texts emerging from the late eighteenth century. The voyages of Captain Cook were of great importance in the formation of representations of Oceanic peoples for two reasons: First, contact was made with a wide range of native peoples particularly in the South Seas, but also in Tierra del Fuego, eastern Australia, northwestern America, northeast Asia, and insular Southeast Asia. Of the many explorers who had earlier passed through the Pacific, most made only fleeting contacts, but the participants in the Cook voyages had protracted encounters with the peoples of places such as Tahiti, Tonga, Hawaii, Tanna, and parts of New Zealand; these were complemented by briefer visits to many other islands—Niue, Easter Island, New Caledonia, and so on. Secondly, participants in the voyages included scientists or natural historians who were disposed to describe and speculate about the "varieties of the human species" among other matters; their publications, and the well-illustrated official accounts from the voyages, became influential, and frequently conditioned the perceptions of subsequent mariners who read the books during their own travels and encounters. (Golovnin, for example, who visited southern Vanuatu in 1809, included several quotations from George Forster's narrative of the second voyage in his journal, adding phrases such as "We experienced the very same thing" [Barratt 1990, 55]).

Notice was of course made of language, and it was quickly recognized that Easter Islanders, New Zealand Maori, Tahitians, Marquesans, and Tongans spoke what were evidently dialects or related languages. The similarity of the words for numbers alone made this clear—to Joseph Banks, among others (Banks 1962, 2:35–7). Contact with unrelated groups on the Pacific Rim, such as the people of the American northwest coast and Kamchatka, reinforced the sense of the underlying homogeneity of what was later to be called the Polynesian population. Though ancestral links with Malays were immediately identified, the recognition that this was a cohesive grouping to be distinguished from the peoples of the western Pacific emerged especially from Cook's second voyage, when Kanaky (New Caledonia) and parts of Vanuatu (the New Hebrides), as well as many Polynesian islands, were visited. A number of the voyage writers speculated about the relationships between these peoples and about the migrations across vast Oceanic distances that seemed so extraordinary, given the relatively low level of seagoing technology; in so doing, they were broaching issues that have continued to fuel inquiry ever since, which has drawn upon archaeology, linguistics, computer simulations, even experimental reenactment of canoe voyages. Here I do not explore the complexities internal to the Cook voyage accounts (but see Jolly 1992b), but focus on the most systematic exposition, part of Johann Reinhold Forster's "Remarks on the Human Species in the

South-Sea Isles," which occupies almost four hundred pages of his 1778 *Obser-vations Made during a Voyage round the World* (1996). It had already been noted, on the first voyage, that the inhabitants of parts of New Britain and New Ireland were "Negroes" (Hawkesworth 1773, 599); the people of eastern Oceania were obviously not:

> We chiefly observed two great varieties of people in the South Seas; the one more fair, well-limbed, athletic, of a fine size, and a kind benevolent tem-per; the other blacker, the hair just beginning to become crisp, the body more slender and low, and their temper, if possible more brisk, though somewhat mistrustful. The first race inhabits O-Taheitee, and the Society Isles, the Marquesas, the Friendly Isles [Tonga], Easter-Island, and New-Zealand. The second race peoples New-Caledonia, Tanna and the New Hebrides, especially Mallicollo [Malekula] (Forster 1996, 153).

Here, the word "variety" is supplanted by "race," and these are elsewhere interchangeable in Forster's usage, which follows that of Buffon closely and is similarly ambiguous with respect to the stability of a class of this kind. While environmentalism prompted an interest in the mutability of animal species and kinds of people (as they were domesticated or moved into different climates, for example), there was a tendency to represent these types as if each were pos-sessed of a singular nature or character. Subspecies, races, or varieties might be written about as if they possessed the stability and distinctness of species—even though they of course lacked formal singularity in the sense that they could interbreed and produce fertile offspring. A claim that there were "two great varieties of people in the South Seas" is thus far from a casual observation. It is a statement that effects a basic partitioning of humanity, that makes comprehen-sible a series of further distinctions and differentiations in both the physical characters and forms of civility discerned amongst the peoples observed. (See Thomas 1996 for further discussion of Forster's ethnology).

As is already clear, comparisons were made at the level of physique and temperament; they were also noted in technology, in forms of government, in responses to foreigners, and in the treatment or standing of women. Though the notion that there were two distinct peoples or races was enunciated by a number of writers as well as Forster, discriminations were also made within each group. Assessments of particular peoples could be ranged along a con-tinuum, with Tahiti at one end and Malekula at the other; among those later called Polynesians, the Maori and the people of Niue were considered more debased, while in the western Pacific, the New Caledonians were more favorably regarded than those of the New Hebrides. Adjudications concerning particular peoples took elaborate and considered forms in the texts of the Forsters and

Cook, but were also expressed more summarily in the journals of others on the voyage, such as Lieutenant John Elliot:

[Tahiti] appeared to us to be the Paradice of those Seas, the Men being all fine, tall, well-made, with humane open countenances; the Women beautiful, compaired with all those that we had seen, of the Middle Size, zingy, suple figures, fine teeth and Eyes, and the finest formed Hands, fingers, and Arms that I ever saw, with lively dispositions . . . when we were on shore here we felt ourselves in perfect ease and safety (Elliot and Pickersgill 1984, 19).

The Men of this [Tanna], and other Isles in this neighbourhood are as active as Monkies, running about the Rigging in the same manner, and something like them in face. Their Wast[e] nipped in with a Cord, like a Wasp—those are the Shortest Race of Men we saw (34).

Here [New Caledonia] we stayed a few days . . . The People, both Men and Women, are tall, robust, and generally well made, but large Limbed and heavy looking; the Men generally approaching 6 foot . . . the Women in proportion—but mild, humain, and civil (35).

Tannese and Malekulans were bestialized in this racist fashion in a number of accounts; though George Forster dissented from such "ill-natured comparisons," Cook and most others regarded them as an "Apish nation" (Jolly 1992b). While considered less debased, the New Caledonians were grouped with the people of the New Hebrides even at the time of initial visits. In Johann Forster's 1774 voyage diary, he found the people "very swarthy, & pretty much alike to the people at *Tanna*" (1982, 643); later reflection emphasized a more definite, and more definitely inferior, grouping. In notes on a set of artifacts sold to a Florence Museum in 1778, the Forsters wrote:

In the westernmost part of the Pacific we have discovered several new islands, hitherto unknown and inhabited by black peoples very different from all the others in the Pacific. These peoples, less civilized than the others, go about quite naked, without any clothing except some leaves . . . They always carry arms, that is to say bows and arrows, javelins, and bludgeons (Kaeppler 1978, 72).

While readers accustomed to nineteenth-century evolutionary thought and its refinement by such twentieth-century writers as V. Gordon Childe might have expected technology to operate significantly as a measure of evolutionary advancement, this text in itself suggests that a lack of civilization was not directly expressed in the crudity of artifacts. In fact, evaluations of the material culture of those later known as Melanesians were mixed, and in some cases the fine carving and polishing of the weapons was noted (cf. Thomas 1991). The twentieth-century reader might similarly assume that the degree of inequality, stratification, or political "advancement" would provide an important measure of the progress toward civilization, and there are certainly statements that appear to bear such expectations out. For Johann Forster, Tahitian government

> is a kind of feudal system; but it has much of that original patriarchal form, blended with it, which rectifies the many defects of the feudal government, and for that very reason is infinitely superior to it, being founded on principles of kindness and benevolence, and on that primitive simplicity which bears always the stamp of perfect undegenerated nature (1996, 227).

A linear trajectory may be postulated here, but it is subordinated to Forster's negative views of feudalism and does not correspond directly with progress toward civilization in a moral sense; from the point of view of his liberalism, the Tahitians are more civilized than the Tongans because the former have abandoned "part of that stiffness, formality, and humiliating respect paid to their chiefs," thus arriving "at that happy mean which assigns the just bounds of prerogative to each rank of people" (1996, 361). That these views had at least as much to do with eighteenth-century political debate as comparative ethnology hardly requires emphasis.

Therefore, while there are predictable observations on the elementary patriarchy prevailing on islands such as Tanna, it would be wrong to see social "complexity" or the development of rank and hierarchy as central elements of Forster's comparative apparatus, or as significant indices in the more casual observations of other Cook voyage participants. What was more fundamental was the status of women. As Margaret Jolly has pointed out with specific reference to Cook voyage perceptions of the people of Vanuatu, "All observers are united in a chorus of complaints about women's hard manual work and men's forceful control over them" (1992a, 342). The women were regarded as ugly, but their unattractiveness was traced as much to their debasement by their men as it was grounded in any prior physical nature. Cook noted that the Tannese men made

> the Women do the most laborious work, of them they make pack-horses. I have seen a woman carrying a large bundle on her back, or a child on her back and a bundle under her arm and a fellow struting before her with nothing but a club, or a spear or some such like thing in his hand; . . . I cannot say the women are beauties but I think them handsome enough for the men and too handsome for the use that is made of them (1955–74, 2:504–5).

Forster presented a congruence between the treatment of women and the elevation of a particular society as both an empirical fact and a general axiom:

The more debased the situation of a nation is, and of course the more remote from civilization, the more harshly we found the women treated (1996, 258).

The males in barbarous nations look upon the women as their property, and this went so far, that in New-Zeeland the fathers and nearest relations were used [i.e., were accustomed] to sell the favours of their females to those of our ship's company, who were irresistibly attracted by their charms (259–60).

In O-Taheitee, the Society, the Friendly Isles, and the Marquesas, the fair sex is already raised to a greater equality with the men; and if, *from no other reason, from this alone,* we might be allowed to pronounce, that these island-ers have emerged from the state of savages, and ought to be ranked one re-move above barbarians. For the more the women are esteemed in a nation, and enjoy an equality of rights with the men, the more it appears that the original harshness of manners is softened, the more the people are capable of tender feelings, mutual attachment, and social virtues, which naturally lead them towards the blessings of civilization (421–2; emphasis added).

An ambiguity might arise here, since civility and peacefulness are associated with a progressive feminization of society; where would this place Europeans, who are clearly more civil than even the most feminized of South Sea islanders? Though just this problem—of associations between opulence, luxury, and ef-feminacy—pervaded eighteenth-century fiction, political thought, and the social theory of writers such as Kames and Ferguson, Forster was not obliged to address the issue directly. This gendering of the Melanesia/Polynesia division was, however, to endure.

It is apparent particularly from George Forster's views that the construction of the peoples of the western Pacific was not unambiguously negative; even the harsher assessments of Malekulans were to some extent particular to that island and were qualified by more positive assessments of New Caledonians. This mixed perception was gradually to resolve itself into something harsher: if in the 1790s there was no generalized opposition in European discourse between Melanesians and Polynesians, those later classed among the former were being represented in an essentially different way from the latter. This was effected in Labillardière's *Voyage in Search of La Pérouse* (1800b) not so much at the level of ethnological theory as through illustration and emphasis on the cannibalism of the New Caledonians. As Jolly (1992b) pointed out, the west/east differentiation

40. William Hodges, *Woman and Child of Tanna*, ca. August 1774, chalk drawing, 54.2 × 37.3 cm. National Library of Australia, Canberra.

41. *Man of the Island of Mallicolo*, engraving by J. Caldwall after William Hodges, from Cook, *A Voyage towards the South Pole and round the World* (London: 1777), 2, plate 47. It has been frequently noted that the figure has been classicized through the addition of the cape, which is absent from Hodges's chalk sketch.

in the Cook voyage publications had been somewhat subverted by the engravings that were published with the official account: these approached ni-Vanuatu and New Caledonians in basically the same manner as the Tongans and Tahitians, and though the pictures of Polynesians were mostly of named chiefly men and women, the individuals from Tanna, Malekula, and New Caledonia were ennobled or at least presented sympathetically. As is even more apparent in the Hodges drawings upon which the engravings were based, particular people, not exemplars of racial types, were depicted (figs. 40–42). The fact that this treatment may arise more from the conventions of sketching and portraiture than the attitudes of Hodges or those of the engravers (neither of which are accessible to analysis) is beside the point: the plates failed to print the distinction that was so textually prominent—that between the "two great varieties" of South Sea islanders.

The images in Labillardière's book are wholly different. The Tongans (and the eastern Indonesians) are shown in much the same way as they were in the Cook publication, in head-and-torso portraits of individuals, mostly identified as aristocrats. The New Caledonians, on the other hand, are full figures, though that fact is less important than their particular disposition (figs. 43, 44). The man,

42. *A Woman of Easter Island* and *A Man of Easter Island*, engravings from George William Anderson, *A New, Authentic, and Complete History of Voyages round the World* (London: 1784–86). These very free adaptations of the plates in Cook's *Voyage towards the South Pole* further diminish the illustrations' ethnographic specificity. Pacific peoples are rendered as essentially European, in a fashion at odds with the descriptions of exotic manners and customs in the accompanying texts.

whose head seems disproportionately small, has a malevolent expression, is obviously physically strong and aggressive, and is in the act of throwing a spear. While the Tahitian men of some of Hodges's paintings were feminized, depicted as indolent, and luxuriant almost in proportion to the luxuriance of the foliage, the masculinity of this figure is emphasized, not only by his musculature, but more by what is rendered quite central: his conspicuous testicles and penis-wrapper. The image of the woman would be perplexing out of context; the awkward pose might almost be a dance movement, but that interpretation is excluded by her wariness and apprehension. Given that this plate directly follows the previous one, an implication of the cowering attitude is that she is being attacked or threatened by the warrior. Though she faces the wrong way, and though his aggressiveness, considered in isolation, is likely to be interpreted in terms of something like intertribal (male) warfare or belligerence toward visiting (male) Europeans, the suggestion of an excessive form of domestic violence is consistent with the eighteenth-century notion that has already been referred to, the correlation between the lack of civility and the brutalization of women. Savagery, as an evolutionary stage, was thus imaged through savagery toward women.

The distinctions put forward by Forster and by other participants in the eighteenth-century voyages acquired wide currency. For example, the ethnological "preliminary discourse" to a major evangelical publication, the narrative of the voyage that established the first stations of the London Missionary Society (LMS) in the South Pacific, presented a similar view of Oceanic human variation in 1799. The lighter-skinned peoples were contrasted with a "darker race," which occupied Australia, New Guinea, New Caledonia, the Solomons, Vanuatu, and Fiji. These people were presumed to be the "original inhabitants" of at least the larger Asiatic islands, who had been conquered by the Tahitians and others; "the astonishing migrations of this race seem to have originated, like those of the northern Europeans, from designs of conquest" ([Haweis] 1799, lxxxv–lxxxvi). The evolutionary implication here was rather different to Forster's. He had differentiated western and eastern Pacific islanders within a grand narrative of natural history, associating the former with the childlike state

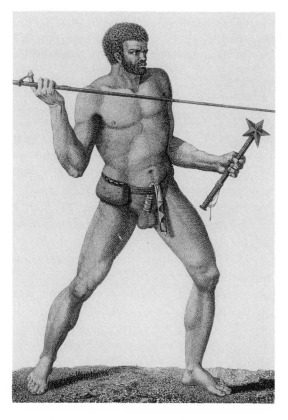

43. *Sauvage de la Nouvelle Calédonie lançant une zagaie*, engraving by Copia after Piron, from J. J. de Labillardière, *Voyage à la recherche de La Pérouse* (Paris: 1800), plate 35. Mitchell Library, State Library of New South Wales, Sydney.

44. *Femme de la Nouvelle Calédonie*, engraving by Copia after Piron, from J. J. de Labillardière, *Voyage à la recherche de La Pérouse* (Paris: 1800), plate 35. Mitchell Library, State Library of New South Wales, Sydney.

of savagery and the latter with the more advanced if unstable adolescence of barbarism; the evangelical ethnologist took it for granted that the lighter race was higher than the darker, but suggested a parallel internal to European history with warriors such as the Saxons and Danes. While equations between distant others and antecedent forms of Western sociality have generally been funda-mental to evolutionist thought, the nuances of these identifications have been variable: in this case, what was important was perhaps the fact that the European barbarians had been persuaded to reject their pagan priests and idols by mis-sionaries in a manner that the LMS hoped to, and in fact later did, emulate. "All the islands of this ocean presented fresh ground for missionary labour." From this point of view, a population's station on an evolutionary ladder was not the most important question. In the penal colony of New South Wales, the writer noted, "we find the gospel preached with purity and zeal to a herd of our own countrymen, whose vices reduce them below the most abject class of the hea-then world around" (lxxxvii).

Mapping Oceanic Races: Nineteenth-Century Perceptions

While the broad contrast between eastern and western Oceania was expressed in many texts, the ethnological distinctions as understood in the twentieth century were not clearly defined until the 1830s. Even subsequently, there was a good deal of ambiguity; the general term "the South Seas" was extensively used in the nineteenth century and even now retains some currency, mainly in travel writing rather than scholarship, and in the late nineteenth century indentured laborers from the Solomon Islands and Vanuatu were referred to as "Polynesians." However, the boundaries of Melanesia, Polynesia, and Micronesia as they have been understood in modern anthropology, geography, and related disciplines were set out by the navigator Jules-Sébastien-César Dumont d'Urville in an article in the *Bulletin de la Société de Géographie* in 1832; his scheme was similar to that of Rienzi (1836–37), whose *Océanie* had been translated into German, Spanish, and Italian and provided the key synthesis of ethnographic and geographic knowledge concerning Oceania for the mid–nineteenth century. Their maps (fig. 45), though differing in certain respects, represented the divisions very much as they have been perceived since—the Polynesian "triangle" included Hawaii, Easter Island, New Zealand, and the islands of the central Pacific; Micronesia included Kiribati (the Gilbert Islands), the Marshalls, the Marianas, and so on, but did not extend as far west as the Philippines; the boundary between Polynesia and Melanesia was drawn between Tonga and Fiji. The most significant difference from subsequent conceptions was the inclusion in the latter region not only of New Caledonia, New Guinea, and the Solomon Islands, but also of Australia. This approach to dividing up the Pacific was reproduced in a French atlas that appears to have been regularly reprinted during the nineteenth century (fig. 46).

Like the earlier writers, Dumont d'Urville stressed that the Polynesian region was inhabited by a distinct race, "a single great family whose members are spread across tremendous distances" (1832, 4). The similarities were not only physical: "The language is everywhere exactly the same" (something of an exaggeration). The Polynesians were slaves of the *tapu* "superstition," were kava drinkers, and were notable for their developed arts, civilization, regular government, royal dynasties, castes, laws, etiquette, and organized religion (4–5). Variation was acknowledged, but within the framework of the underlying family relationships:

> The political condition of the Samoans, of athletic physique, is virtually unknown; but the account of La Pérouse permits one to suppose that it closely resembles that of Tonga. The Marquesan form of government is

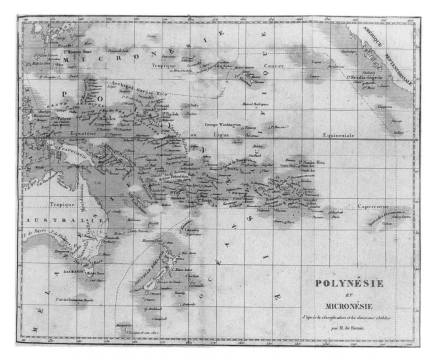

45. "Polynésie et Micronésie," map from Domeny de Rienzi's *Océanie* (Paris: 1836–37).

closely connected with that of the Society Islands [i.e., Tahiti] but it is simpler and more patriarchal . . . the inhabitants of the Low Islands, or [Tuamotus], to the east of Tahiti, stripped of institutions and dispersed in small tribes, live in a state little removed from that of the Melanesian tribes and perhaps show the transition between the two races (8).

The Melanesians were characterized by their blackness, by their "hideous" women, by the great diversity of their languages, and by the attenuated character of their polities:

These blacks are almost always grouped in very fragile tribes, the chiefs of which exercise arbitrary power, often in a manner as tyrannical as that of many petty African despots. More degraded towards the state of barbarism than the Polynesians or Micronesians, one encounters neither a form of government nor laws nor established religious ceremonies amongst them. All their institutions appear still to be in their infancy; their dispositions and intelligence are also generally inferior to those of the tan race (Dumont d'Urville 1832, 11).

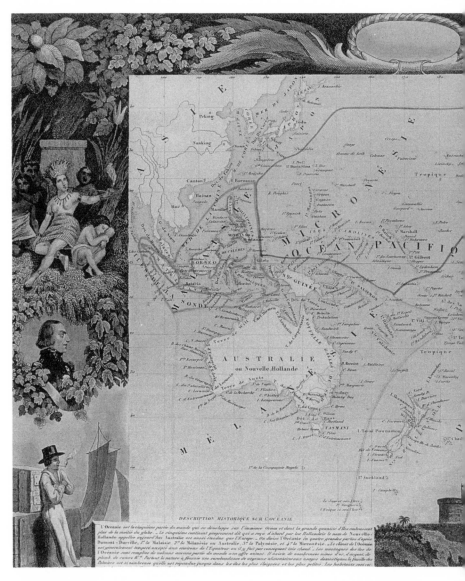

46. 'Océanie,' map attributed to Emile Levasseur, from *Atlas universel de géographie physique* (Paris: 1854). The hand coloring accentuating the divisions between Melanesia, Polynesia, Micronesia, and Malaysia is similar in all copies sighted and was therefore presumably done in the workshops of the publisher or printer, rather than being the idiosyncratic addition of a particular purchaser. Several earlier and later editions are documented; the first incorporating d'Urville's ethnic divisions apparently appeared in 1838.

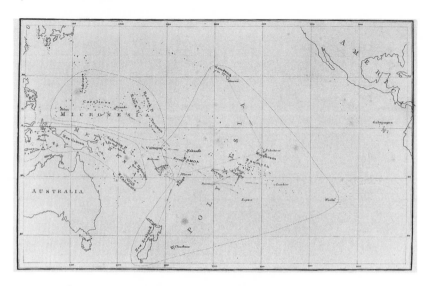

47. "Map of Pacific Regions," from Horatio Hale, "Migrations in the Pacific Ocean," *American Journal of Science* 2d ser. vol. I, no. 3 (May 1846). National Library of Australia, Canberra. This is similar to the map in Hale's *United States Exploring Expedition: Ethnography and Philology* (Philadelphia: 1846).

Another point present in earlier writers was restated by Dumont d'Urville: unlike the hospitable Polynesians, the savage Melanesians always met Europeans with defiance and hostility (1832, 11–2). There was thus a convenient congruence between the advancement of the different peoples and their sense of appropriate behavior toward foreigners, and specifically Europeans; this willingness to enter into relations was often equated with a desire to engage in commerce, itself generally interpreted as a civilizing influence despite the patently corrupting element of prostitution and the harmful ramifications of the introduction of alcohol and firearms. What had in effect been an assumption of the Cook voyage commentators was restated as an axiom: "The difference of character in the three Oceanic races is most clearly displayed in the reception which they have given to their earliest civilized visitors" (Hale 1846, 73).

This writer, Horatio Hale, was one of those responsible for drawing Dumont d'Urville's scheme into English-language geography and anthropology. An important participant in the United States Exploring Expedition to the Pacific of 1838–1842, Hale acknowledged the work of "French voyagers and geographers" in mapping out Pacific migrations and voyages along lines very close to those of Dumont d'Urville (1846, 3–8; fig. 47). Like the earlier writers, he approved of various characteristics of the Polynesians, such as their innovative "readiness to adopt new customs and new modes of thinking" (13)—by this time the Tahitians, Hawaiians, and various others had converted to Christianity, which made little progress in Melanesia until considerably later. The paramount feature of Polynesian society, though, was not this flexibility and responsiveness, but the degree of political organization, "a grade of civilization nearly as high as their circumstances would permit," which took the general form of divisions between chiefs, landholders, and common people (14, 29).

Hale's work exemplifies a refocusing of the contrast that had been defined initially in the Cook voyage texts. While the regions that had been discriminated were essentially the same, the key marker amongst the plethora of those juxtaposed had, in the eighteenth-century accounts, been the treatment of women. Their lack of equality with men was measured by their engagement in a corrupting and debasing form of labor, namely, agriculture, and this was held to impede a generalized softening and refinement of the other sex and of society. While both Dumont d'Urville and Hale persisted in referring to diverse physical and mental attributes in contrasting the two "races," gender lost its privileged position, and (particularly for Dumont d'Urville) the form of social organization instead acquired more significance: an equation along the lines of "Melanesia is to Polynesia as equality is to hierarchy" began to emerge, though the Melanesian condition was initially expressed more in terms of a lack of coherence and regularity of organization, rather than as a positive condition of equality.

A second significant shift was that the assessment of bodies moved from a frankly subjective aesthetic register toward an objectifying phrenology or physical anthropology. For Johann Forster and his contemporaries, their own responses to the physical appearances of Tahitians, Tierra del Fuegians, and others were not out of place in a discourse of natural history; in fact it was quite appropriate to order the description of the differing varieties of eastern Pacific islanders on the basis of their relative attractiveness, the Marquesans being discussed second since they were "the variety of men, next in beauty to those of the Society-Isles" (Forster 1996, 155). The elaborate atlases published with the narrative of Dumont d'Urville's expedition included cranial studies of almost photographic accuracy of virtually all the peoples encountered, and in subsequent decades a vast statistical literature emerged that would establish, for example, that the cranial capacity of Polynesians was greater than that of Papuans.

Dumont d'Urville's ideas acquired wider circulation and authority through James Cowles Prichard's *Researches into the Physical History of Mankind,* one of the most widely read anthropological syntheses of the mid–nineteenth century (cf. Stocking 1973). Though calling for some terminological revision (finding "Kelaenonesia" more etymologically satisfactory than "Melanesia"), Prichard was faithful to Dumont d'Urville's ethnological distinctions, and he elaborated on their imaginative and evolutionary dimensions by associating the "Black nations" with a more rugged and less appealing topography shrouded in primeval forests:

> To the beautiful groupes of islands inhabited by the Polynesian tribes, covered with rich vegetation and spread out like clusters of gems under the sunny sky of the Great Ocean, a striking contrast is presented when we turn towards the adjoining region on the west. The more concentrated and extensive lands of this western region contain long ranges of primeval forests. The tribes of human beings who inhabit them are equally unlike the people of the eastern groupes. Ferocious and sullen, of savage and menacing aspect, naturally averse to intercourse with strangers, they have ever shunned the approach of civilised people as uniformly as the Polynesians have courted it . . . Their physical characters are likewise very different from those of the agile, graceful, and comparatively fair Polynesians. Among these tribes are to be seen some who recede farthest from the almost European or Asiatic beauty of the Tahitian and Marquesan islanders, and exceed in ugliness the most ill-favoured brood of the African forests, whom they rival in the sooty blackness of their complexion (1836–47, 4:212).

A further dimension of the contrast arose from the interest in the different attitudes of the two varieties to Europeans: Prichard follows others in finding the Melanesians resistant to contact, and though he exaggerates the uniformity of responses within each of the juxtaposed "races," it had certainly been the case that, in general, the western Pacific peoples had been more hesitant and cautious than most Polynesians. This distinction, between openness and closure, had implications for the prospects for advancement of the different peoples. While racial ideas often embodied some essentialism, which attributed to particular races stable characters that were resistant to modification or amelioration, it is interesting that Hale could identify a capacity for change in the Polynesians that the Melanesians lacked. His view was advanced in the course of a brave attempt to plausibly discriminate between western Polynesians and the "Melanesian" Fijians with whom they clearly shared so much in political forms, language, and custom. The problem was not one that had arisen for the earlier commentators because contact with Fiji that had resulted in any widely available published information had been negligible before the visit of the United States Exploring Expedition. The Fijians represented something of a paradox for the major ethnological division because they seemed physically Melanesian yet had a "regular and artificial system of government" and were skilled in various crafts:

[The Fijians] are spoken of by all voyagers as savages, and uniformly treated as such, while the Polynesians are regarded rather as a semi-civilized race. Nor can there be any doubt that this distinction, so universally and involuntarily made, is a just one. Yet it is difficult to perceive, on first view, the grounds on which it rests . . . The truth perhaps is, that the difference in character . . . lies not so much in any particular trait, as in a general debasement of the whole,—a lower grade of moral feeling, and a greater activity of the evil passions . . . The Feejeean may be said to differ from the Polynesian as the wolf from the dog; both, when wild, are perhaps equally fierce, but the ferocity of one may be easily subdued, while that of the other is deep-seated and untameable (Hale 1846, 50).

Shifting Evaluations: The Twentieth Century

It is apparent from George Brown's *Melanesians and Polynesians* (1910) that the harsh racism of writers such as Hale could be abandoned, while basic elements of the ethnological juxtaposition were preserved. Brown was a Methodist missionary cum missionary-ethnographer with extensive experience in Samoa and various parts of the western Pacific. He was writing in a period when many Melanesians had been converted to Christianity and many were also pacified, though a secure colonial order was yet to be established in much of Papua New Guinea, and in enclaves in many other areas the generalized hostility and resistance that informed the extremely negative mid- to late-nineteenth-century views of Melanesians was being qualified in the light of more differentiated perceptions of particular populations. Like many missionaries, Brown had a sympathetic though patronizing attitude toward the people with whom he had worked; in *Melanesians and Polynesians*, however, he refrained from making his attitudes toward particular peoples explicit, instead expressing his concern to present a clear account of the facts in accordance with the questions raised in the Royal Anthropological Institutes guidebook, *Notes and Queries in Anthropology*. Brown's lack of interest in physical anthropology made him pass over the features of Melanesian bodies, which so many other writers had stigmatized, and on many points he was surprisingly relativistic. "Many cannibals, indeed, are very nice people," he wrote, "and, except on very special occasions, there is no apparent difference between them and non-cannibal tribes." For most writers since the Cook voyages, cannibalism had been emblematic of savagery, but Brown emphasized that it was "a semi-sacred rite," mostly "practised to discharge an obligation to the spirits of the dead" (1910, 140–1). He thus contextualized the practice anthropologically (and, at the same time, marked himself as a scientific, anthropological writer rather than a missionary propagandist).

Brown's aspirations to objectivity led him toward a methodological relativism that was apparently disengaged from the Manichean coding of pleasure and displeasure that had pervaded earlier formulations of the Melanesia/Polynesia division. Each people or race constituted a field for a neutral and specifically ethnographic description: the nature of the colonial history did not measure anything of significance for this account, while the responses of a European man to their bodies were still less relevant. If, in fact, many ethnological descriptions of this period did continue to incorporate some of the earlier and frankly subjective responses of travel writing, Brown's work excised them more rigorously. This is not to say, however, that an evolutionary perspective was disavowed. Reflecting the widely held view that matriliny was an archaic and antecedent stage, Brown wrote that

> the system of government in Samoa shows a very great advance upon that which existed in most of the Melanesian groups. The exogamous system existing in Melanesia has practically passed away . . . With the decay of that system and the advance of culture, descent through the father replaced the old custom of descent through the mother. The immediate effect of this was the establishment of hereditary chieftainship (1910, 282).

He also followed many earlier writers in seeing Fiji as an evolutionary step higher than the rest of Melanesia: a custom at chiefly installations marking inheritance of the title through the mother and father differently showed "that in the advance in Fiji from the old Melanesian descent through the mother to that of descent through the father, the change was made gradually" (1910, 40). This perception of Fiji as a kind of transitional region between Melanesia and Polynesia was reiterated in many twentieth-century anthropological studies and accorded with the general image of "an upward west-to-east slope in political development," to use Sahlins's later expression (1963, 286). It also enabled readings of the prehistory in which the migrations and invasions of two distinct races were downplayed as an evolutionary narrative became more prominent. The ranking of one society or population in relation to another was thus disconnected more radically from avowed pleasure or displeasure on the part of the analyst; it was not a matter of whether "negroid" people were more primitive than those with lighter skins, still less of whether their bodies were less appealing or not, but simply of the archaic and antecedent character of their societies.

The Recuperation of Representations

Rather than trace the usage of Melanesia/Polynesia through the twentieth century, I turn briefly in conclusion to the issue of how the baggage of the terms figures in contemporary indigenous self-representations. The term "derivative discourse," used in this context particularly by Partha Chatterjee (1986), is a provocative one in the sense that it emphasizes the dependence of certain nationalist and anticolonial ideologies upon the regimes they opposed; some anthropologists take arguments of this kind to diminish the agency of the colonized, or reduce it to a reaction against colonial hegemony in an unacceptable way that recapitulates the worn "fatal impact" account of the experience of colonization (see chapter 1). Again, hybrid forms appear to be unusually indeterminate and contentious in their political meanings and values. I do not wish to argue in principle either that "derivation" is in fact a matter of "appropriation" and therefore attests to the effectiveness of indigenous agency or the reverse, that even if appropriated institutions and objects are accorded novel and distinctly local content, an imposed homogeneity is manifest at the level of the forms that indigenous nationhood, citizenship, and history can take. Both of these things might be true for different phases of a particular colonial or postcolonial history, or for different kinds of derivation (or appropriation) at one moment. I can only make superficial observations on contemporary ethnic categories in this context, but these are sufficient to establish what are essentially negative points.

These questions of derivation are important, but turn out to be substantially irrelevant in the case of recent and contemporary indigenous discourses. So far from being dupes who are unwittingly reproducing colonialist ideology, the politicians and others interested in defining identities on a larger regional scale—whether Melanesian or Polynesian—seem virtually uninfluenced by prior outsiders' images. This is certainly true of the single most elaborate and significant effort to define Melanesian cultural identity. In his series of newspaper articles, which were extensively debated within Papua New Guinea and subsequently published as a book entitled *The Melanesian Way,* the politician Bernard Narokobi defined the Melanesian way as "a total cosmic vision of life in which every event within human consciousness has its personal, communal, spiritual, economic, political and social dimensions. It is, by its very nature, inherently open to change" (Narokobi 1980, 20; for extensive analysis see Otto 1996). Narokobi's discussion incorporated brief essays on many topics, such as the centrality of the village in traditional and modern Melanesian life, the emblematic use of betelnut, and the compatibility of tradition and Christianity, which I need not go into here: the point is that these issues either did not feature in colonialist typifications of Melanesia or were not central to them. Insofar as this is "derivative" at all, the influences are from African negritude thought, which Narokobi knew of through a Nigerian philosophy lecturer at the University of Papua New Guinea.

When Narokobi affirmed the importance and strength of indigenous spirituality and the dignity of the wisdom that had been passed down by ancestors, he could be seen to put forward a "nativism" that celebrated the features of indigenous culture that were typically denigrated in Western discourse, but he was also writing from experience of the continuing strength of what were real features of local culture in village situations. In chapter 8 I take up the question of how far this kind of objectification of indigenous culture is a reactive formation arising from the cultural dynamics of colonization. Here my point is simply that even if Narokobi's notion of the Melanesian way could be seen primarily as a contradiction of Western denigrations of a generic "primitive" or "traditional" mode of life, it drew little on Western representations of Melanesia.

Narokobi's exposition of the Melanesian way can profitably be compared with contemporary expressions of Polynesian identity in New Zealand. While he was writing deliberately as an ideologue in the years immediately after independence, the expressions of Polynesian identity I will briefly mention do not take this theorized form. Their context is moreover quite different, in the sense that they emerge not in a national context but among migrants from Samoa, the Cook Islands, Tonga, Niue, and elsewhere, who collectively form a substantial Polynesian or Pacific islander population, especially in Auckland. Although a shared Pacific culture flourishes, and although a number of Polynesians have senior positions in universities and the bureaucracy, there has been little overt political mobilization and no explicit formulation of the nature of the Polynesian way comparable to Narokobi's text. What is conspicuous, in contrast, is rather the highly visible expression of Polynesian identity through food, material culture, dress, and sociality. Polynesians buy island vegetables such as *kumara* (sweet potato) and taro. They wear brightly colored *lavalavas* (sarongs), some of which bear patterns derived from barkcloth and carry bags woven from either pandanus or plastic. Their houses are decorated with framed photographs of relatives, around which are often hung shell necklaces. Appliqué quilts and other forms of islands needlework are conspicuous in their homes. They get together for church occasions and huge extended-family ceremonies and picnics. In addition to these practices of identity, there are certainly contexts in which the character of islands sociality is discussed; these include court cases in which the traditional cultural background of offenders may be considered. In these instances, the importance of respect to elders and the incidence of violent punishment are far more likely to be cited than questions of hierarchy and chieftainship. The same might be said of the substantial body of contemporary Pacific literature that naturally contains much observation and reflection upon the burden of tradition and the defining characteristics of indigenous sociality (see, for representative selections, Wendt 1980, 1995). Ideas of Pacific culture have clearly been shaped by Christianity and are thus not isolated from a wider dynamic of indigenous and introduced categories; what is conspicuous, however, is that the ethnic typifications that have been generated over the past two centuries in ethnological discourse and travel writing have had a negligible impact on either the practical expression of Polynesian identity or Polynesians' statements about the nature of Polynesian culture. In this respect at least, European and indigenous ideas about Oceania have been linked, but not shared.

6

Fear and Loathing

in the South Pacific:

Colonial and Postcolonial

History in Popular

Fiction

Histories are told in films and novels as well as in academic texts. In this chapter I am concerned with a zone of intersection between scholarly and popular understandings of both colonial conflict and contemporary change in the Pacific. The three texts I discuss index differences between the meanings we are able to extract from colonial and postcolonial histories, and, most strikingly, the temptation to lapse into denigration that marks responses to the latter. The problem seems to arise in part from globalization and cultural hybridity: if neither of these conditions are as novel as often seems supposed, if hybrid actors and cultural products were in fact conspicuous and important at quite early stages in colonial histories, they suddenly become more visible and central in postcolonial circumstances because the primary opposition between whites and natives that structures our understanding of colonial history gives way to a succession of other differences. If this is to some degree a positive shift— because we are forced to recognize and deal with a range of complexities that were previously marginalized—it has a more negative dimension. For some writers, "acculturated" actors are not so much morally ambiguous figures such as Joe Leahy; they are merely inauthentic.

Oceania, understood in so many different ways by Europeans over the last few centuries, is no longer dark and mysterious, inhabited by headhunters or cargo cultists. The islands are still idealized as tropical paradises and largely safe holiday destinations; but in addition to these images, this periphery is now considered dangerous, the bearer of ill-adapted forms of metropolitan politics, business, and consumer culture: in his ironically titled *Happy Isles of Oceania*, Paul Theroux writes, "The Solomon Islanders in Honiara were among the scariest-looking people I have seen in my life—wild hair, huge feet, ripped and ragged clothes, tattoos on their foreheads, ornamental scars all over their faces, wearing broken sunglasses. They loped along in large groups, or else idled near the stores that played American rap music and looked for all the world like rappers themselves" (1992, 201). The sense of things transplanted and gone wrong is attested to by *Black Harvest,* but that film offered no simple reduction of the failure of modernization in Papua New Guinea. But in some popular narratives, there is another response to contemporary developments, one that leaves us with little more than a sense that Pacific societies and politics bear only shadows of meaning and value, only thin allusions to projects that happened genuinely elsewhere and before.

The novels of Peter Corris are appropriate to any discussion of an interplay between scholarship and popular fiction because Corris was trained in Pacific history and published a major study of the labor trade to Queensland (1973), among other works, before leaving academic life to take up more commercial writing. In 1980 he published a popular history of boxing in Australia and the first of some dozens of thrillers, many of which have been private investigator stories that could be said to transplant a Ross Macdonald approach to Sydney. Although these tend to be as formulaic as much else in the genre, there can be no question of Corris's essential competence, and he is now certainly among the most prolific and widely read Australian thriller writers. A number of these books have drawn upon Corris's earlier interests in Aboriginal and Pacific history and in boxing, and he must be credited with having done much to give complex, nonstereotypic, and basically sympathetic Aboriginal characters greater presence in pulp fiction, but I cannot say anything so positive about one of his recent books set in the Pacific.

The Cargo Club (Corris 1990a)[1] opens with a brief prologue, a clip brought forward from the action of the story's climax: Ray Crawley is on a tropical beach, backing away from a black man with a machine gun, whose immediate identification as a priest suggests liberation theology, Latin America, and Catholic guerrillas. A variety of attitudes could, of course, be taken toward this kind of revolutionary; but Crawley's mind, wandering from exhaustion, fear, and thirst, recalls that in the Philippines, there are resorts "where left-wing holidaymakers could play at being insurgents. What would happen here if a couple of 'Che Guevaras' appeared on the beach? Probably nothing, all part of the fun" (20). Our first take on this South Pacific country thus places it under the shadow of a kind of hyperreality: though the priest is evidently a real guerrilla rather than a player in some theatrical performance for political tourists, there is something false about him or the scene that prompts a sense of derivative inauthenticity.

For all that, he is no less threatening: "The priest, sucking at his abscessed tooth, and his eyes mad and bulging but with his machine gun held steady, kept coming. *Crawley, you bloody idiot,* he thought, *how did you get yourself into this?*" (23).

The next few chapters tell us how, and elaborate on the implication of this opening passage, that however real and violent any political confrontation is in these islands, it is caught up in dissimulation, in a tangle of excess, insanity, and falsity. The appropriate response seems to be one of wonder: how did we outsiders ever get involved? This sense of surfaces, of meanings without substance, is not specific to the nation Corris calls Vitatavu but pervades the whole novel, just as the question of notionally postimperial involvement in decolonized nations is hardly specific to the imagination of Australian security in the Pacific.

Crawley is a jaded intelligence agent; his is said to be "a family in name only" because he rarely sees his wife, who is preoccupied with her feminist history doctoral research, while his son is "allegedly" doing the higher school certificate by correspondence, while surfing up and down the coast. Bored in Canberra, Crawley agrees to take on an undercover job to discredit a Soviet-leaning minister for resources in the recently independent South Pacific state of "Vitatavu," which is being destabilized by the "Pacific Liberation Army" (PLA) and the "Movement for Melanesian Unity" (MMU). A security force battle with militant rebels recalls the Kanak hostage taking and cave massacre on Ouvea (in New Caledonia) in April 1988, but "Vitatavu" is otherwise a thinly disguised Vanuatu. Soon after he arrives, Crawley encounters a PLA operative, trained as a soldier by the French, who had joined guerrilla units after decolonization and "responded to the arguments of leaders demanding more changes, different boundaries, greater rights for indigenes, the expulsion of Europeans not born in the islands, and all Asians. There was plenty of fighting to be earned, and money to be earned doing it" (Corris 1990a, 42). Rattled off in that fashion, these claims or demands sound like mere rhetoric: there is no sense that there might be a real set of problems arising from the incompleteness of decolonization, from various systems of regional or provincial administration, or from the persisting privileges and machinations of expatriates; any political substance or justification behind such a program is subverted, in any case, by the suggestion that this guerrilla is motivated less by the issues than by the opportunity to fight and the financial benefits.

Crawley is taken into custody by the security forces and witnesses the torture of an MMU militant; when the latter is rescued, as part of a wider rebellion, he is taken along and forced to march up to a jungle hideout, which is later shot up by the same murderous paramilitary troops. The sexual interest is not so much conveyed through James Bond-like conquests on Crawley's part (he is too cynical and battered to be particularly appealing) but in an affair between a lesbian journalist from the Australian Broadcasting Corporation (ABC) and Françoise Beni, an adviser to the Soviet-leaning politician: the old colonial-pornographic interest in black women's bodies and cross-racial sex is thus augmented and taken into another domain of taboo, much to the titillation and frustration of various male spies and cops, both black and white, who in the end have the satisfaction of shooting Françoise to pieces. Back in Canberra, Crawley recalls his father's summation of experience in the island fighting of the Second World War: "My old dad told me that Pacific was a good spot except for all the bastards shooting at you. I guess I found it pretty much the same" (Corris 1990a, 186).

What takes place in these allusions and events is a displacement of Pacific nationalist and subnationalist politics into an internationalized and denatured terrorist mode, marked particularly by the insurgent groups' sinister acronyms. The local peculiarity and history of the islands' political problems is submerged as the characters of insurgents and bureaucrats alike are assimilated to types equally familiar from the Middle East, Africa, or anywhere else. Vitatavu's capital is called Kwaxat, an impossible name in a Pacific language but vaguely reminiscent of the Gulf and unearned oil wealth, or a generalized third world. Jo Willis, the ABC journalist, has a sense of the scene because she has "encountered nationalism in every hemisphere, burning in the eyes of very different people—hawk-nosed Afghans, bland-faced Tibetans, suicidal Palestinians" (Corris 1990a, 119). Nationalism, then, is associated with the third world, with other people's violence, and apparently doesn't exist in Australia, Europe, or North America. All of this can be objected to on a simple level, because it magnifies out of any proportion the actual levels of political dissent and violence in the Pacific. Most of the consequential political differences are expressed by different regions and church denominations, not in rival militias; sermons, court proceedings, and ordinary factional and bureaucratic conflicts, rather than street battles, are the main theaters of political competition and debate. Even in the protracted tensions and many demonstrations that occurred in the lead-up to the Fiji coup and in the period since, no one was killed as a direct result of violence (though the impact of reduced funding for health facilities, and of shortages of supplies and trained staff, has had tragic ramifications that are difficult to assess precisely). Where, on the other hand, there actually have been major confrontations—as in Bougainville, for instance, where many have died— it would be very misleading, not to say offensive, to characterize these in the terms implied, as if a bunch of hotheaded militants had finally found an outlet for their aggression (which is not to say that both the Bougainville Revolutionary Army and the PNG Army have not been unnecessarily destructive and irresponsible), and it would be still more absurd to suggest that those involved were being financially rewarded.

Of course, the book's exaggerations could be excused on generic grounds: given that the real Pacific is too boring for the purposes of a thriller (and apparently one originally plotted for a television series), we should only expect the scene to be spiced up and overdrawn. This would be to ignore the particular properties of certain characters and the way in which one perspective on the whole affray is privileged. Paul Beni, the MMU leader, is almost the only ambiguous character: of the others, some are thugs and opportunists (neither the violent militants nor the degraded expats are rendered appealing), others are more principled but shown to be out of touch with the harsh realities of corruption and power. Paul Beni's ambivalence is not simply an incoherence but a duality that expresses a particular racial politics; he plays a role similar to the millenarian leader Reverend John Laputa in John Buchan's *Prester John* (1910), a role marked by the combination of authenticity and savagery (cf. Thomas 1994, 144–9). Both figures are genuine in the sense that they are real leaders—intelligent, principled, visionary, unambiguously dedicated to the cause of their people rather than some personal gain. However, what is positive in these portraits only underlines their negativity because in both cases readers are presented with necessary failures: Laputa is ultimately a prisoner of superstition and Beni is ultimately a crazed militant. The former's fall into futile violence and irrationality indicates that indigenous resistance cannot transcend savagery; the latter's loss of self-control and descent into terrorism is similarly not a narrative of individual failure but a larger projection that imagines the limits of anticolonial and postcolonial politics. Colonialism is replaced only by corrupt independence; further democratization is an unreality fantasized by hotheads who mimic the violence of more important international terrorists.

Beni's subjectivity is not the voice of the narrative, and the book might have been more interesting if it had tried to construct his imagined contradictions from the inside rather than from a distance. What is in a grammatical sense a third-person narration is, however, very close to one character's perspective: Crawley is very definitely the protagonist. Though he, like some of Le Carré's spies, is not an especially sympathetic figure, his body is produced as a primary point of reference and identification—through physical struggles, drinking bouts, threats of torture, injuries, and exhausting marches through the jungle. What happens to *him* hurts; the sufferings of other characters are seen from a distance. Crawley's proximity to the reader's sense of events authorizes his way of seeing things and allows it to frame and inform not just evaluations of particular characters, but also the whole moral topography of the work. From the start, this vision is pervasively cynical; with respect to his dropout son, for instance, he reflects:

He was glad that his son spent most of his time unencumbered in the outdoors—driving the highways in jeans and a T-shirt; in nylon bathing trunks, trying for a one minute perfection, instead of wrestling with questions like duty, sex, respectability, and freedom. He'd never resolved them; he doubted that they could be resolved. So why not ride horses and surfboards into the twenty-first century? (Corris 1990a, 4).

Crawley's disenchantment applies to all politicians, not just those seeking "true independence for Vitatavu . . . social and economic justice and environmental protection" (Corris 1990a, 14). The fact that they are all the same, whether they "represent" Australians or Pacific islanders, neutralizes these concerns and evacuates their significance: as if one government in a Pacific state would be the same as any other, as if nothing consequential might be changed by their particular projects or policies. The appropriate attitude is thus one of disengagement from the mess; the Pacific would be a nice place "except for all the bastards shooting at you" (186).

Naismith's Dominion (Corris 1990b) contains this variant on the usual disclaimer: "The Jeremiah Islands do not exist and the people whose lives and actions are portrayed here have never existed." This isn't even in small print on the page with the copyright notice and cataloging data, but conspicuously faces an admittedly imaginary map of the "British Jeremiah Islands Protectorate." A reader familiar with Pacific islands history is likely to find this statement alarming, at least in retrospect as he or she gets into the book and finds the Solomon Islands, the Kwaio of Malaita, the strongman Basiana, and the 1927 killing of district officer Bell all too recognizable (especially since this reader will also know the best account of these events, the 1980 book *Lightning Meets the West Wind*, which was written by Roger Keesing with Corris and draws on the former's fieldwork and oral history as well as the latter's archival studies in his earlier career as Pacific historian). So, given that numerous specific incidents in this effective historical novel, and not merely the bare outlines of the story, derive from documents and oral histories, are we to see the nonexistent Jeremiah (Solomon) Islands and their inhabitants merely as discursive surfaces that exist only as we reinscribe them in the present? Hardly; it is no doubt the very truth of the narrative that requires its facticity to be denied.

Murdo (Malaita) is the most problematic island in the protectorate, from the viewpoint of the colonial administration; it is peopled by recalcitrant warriors who refuse to adopt Christianity but whose toughness makes them valuable to recruiters for the canefields in Queensland and Fiji. Hence, there are a number of killings of white traders to avenge men who died while away, and confrontations over trade goods and apparent kidnappings. This history of skirmishes provides the background for the novel: specifically, it is the unpopular head tax levied on the islanders and government efforts to collect firearms that fuel resistance on Murdo. The key indigenous actor is Eglito, who as a child, witnesses his father's hanging by the colonial administration and who subsequently becomes a *lemo*, or bounty-hunting warrior, a figure of ancestral power and violence, a type whose strengths have been consolidated by contact and new weapons but who stands to lose all under pacification and Christianity. The book's dynamic is fatal, but islanders such as Eglito are not victims of a colonial impact they cannot control; the confrontation and mayhem are prompted and fashioned by their honor, by their will to defend their autonomy, and by the efficacy of their spells, curses, and ancestors.

Naismith, the district officer on Murdo, is not such a fool as most of the colonial officials, who inhabit an inebriated fantasy world around the Tulagi golf course. He is an isolated man and a teetotaller, closer to the "natives," ethnologically astute, ambiguously alienated from the civilizing mission yet concerned to give it a decent and effective face. He is also distrusted by his superiors and subordinates, intrigued against by an evangelical missionary, and distracted by a visiting American woman who reminds him of a lost fiancée; his vision and authority become unstuck as the book proceeds, and he drifts into a confrontationist policy in which he fatally overestimates his own capacity to dominate the Murdoans. The upshot is a bloodbath at a tax collection point: Naismith himself is clubbed with a venerated, ancestrally empowered rifle by the warrior Eglito, and a number of native police are shot or knifed. Baekani, a renegade assistant of Naismith's, kills Eglito and two or three others before being shot himself, not by an agent of the state but by an anthropologist about to begin fieldwork in the area. As the epilogue informs us, the anthropologist is later awarded an Oxford doctorate for his thesis on "Conflict and Resolution among the To'beli of Murdo."

It's obvious that *Naismith's Dominion* is a far more satisfying book than the thriller, but if this is so just because one book is faithful to an ethnographic and historical understanding from which the other is remote, it may seem a peculiarly academic complaint that makes unreasonable demands of the thriller genre. Certainly, my problems arise partly from a view that works such as *The Cargo Club* convey a false and misleading idea of contemporary Pacific societies. But this is not the main problem: what is important for an assessment of the cultural politics and effects of the book is not some proportion of fantasy and truth, but a diagnosis of the metanarrative that is made available to shape further perceptions and responses to the peoples concerned. Just as films such as *Dances with Wolves* and *Black Robe* inform and refashion perceptions of native

Americans in ways that have wider implications and are inevitably contentious, the Corris stories make statements about Pacific islanders that are enunciated within a highly differentiated field of representations that includes ethnographic television documentaries, journalistic reports, folkloric reenactments for tourists, anthropological texts, and paperbacks. The audiences for these kinds of works are certainly diverse, but they would be inadequately summarized by labels such as "scholarly" and "popular," which might exempt both from particular kinds of scrutiny. The questions that we can and should ask concern the metanarrative: the way in which the particular history suggests a moral landscape inhabited by actors of a type, certain peoples, certain nations, and the ways in which a past and an imagined future have particular values, which might foreshadow resistance and triumph, growth and fulfilment, uneasy resolution, decline and sterility, or hypocrisy, indulgence, and junk.

I argued in chapter 1 that the context in which Pacific history is written has undergone a shift from a colonial context, in which decolonization is envisaged, to a postcolonial one, in which the "two worlds" starkly juxtaposed in colonial relations give way to a plethora of morally ambiguous differences. I have described this as a shift over time, but current writing concerned with the colonial period, such as Anne Salmond's book *Two Worlds* (1991), may preserve the European-native or colonizer-colonized opposition, as does Corris's Naismith novel. That book is "historical" in the loaded sense of a history painting: it dramatizes a conflict beyond particularities and ennobles the actors in an honorable, fatal dignity. Eglito is a violent man but one acting to defend his culture and autonomy. Naismith's decency is underlined; for all his detachment and misjudgment toward the end, his death manifests a cruel irony—since he is the colonizer who makes the most effort to understand those receiving the blessings of empire and is largely shorn of illusions concerning that mission. In this respect, the novel's judgments echo the earlier coauthored work of "nonfiction." As Keesing and Corris claimed, quite appropriately, in their foreword, the story possessed "the sense of Greek tragedy in a collision between two ways of life, between indigenous order and colonial power, and between protagonists whose strength of will could not be turned" (1980, vi). While these dramatizations of a tragic confrontation were patently saturated with meaning and value, the postcolonial muddle in *The Cargo Club* is marked, as we have seen, by a deprivation of significance. The struggles that are described proceed in the name of "true independence for Vitatavu," "social and economic justice," and so on, but these causes can only figure as the hollow appeals of politicians whose actions evince self-interest rather than an exemplary historical project. What was in fact at stake in the colonial period, and could be shown to be at stake in a historian's narration, becomes matter for dissimulation in the inauthentic voice of the postcolonial leader. While the colonial confrontation can be imagined from two points of view, which possess conflicting but equivalent authenticities, the meta-narrative of postcoloniality in *The Cargo Club* differentiates among both indigenous and expatriate actors but refuses to accord legitimacy and authenticity to any perspective except that of Crawley. He regrets his involvement and regards the whole scene as a bloody shambles, something we appropriately can only wash our hands of.

The transition from a colonial to a postcolonial politics of knowledge is marked in the writing and controversial reception of the Keesing/Corris study *Lightning Meets the West Wind*. The book was substantially researched and written in the years before independence in 1978, but it was not published until 1980. In a key passage, the authors explored rival accounts of Basiana's motivations and emphasized not their particularity in oaths or head taxes, but their position in the colonial struggle: "What Basiana and his comrades were doing was making a final and desperate stand against the subjugation of their way of life by an alien power. They were striking a last blow for their independence—an independence now being nominally granted to their children and grandchildren fifty years later" (1980, 195). Keesing and Corris, who hoped that a "corrective view of this much-distorted event can be important to an emergent new Solomons nation" (3), were thus writing within the earlier of the two paradigms that I identified: the fundamental political opposition that structured the history of the islands was the colonial confrontation, and the task was to recover the other side, that is, the story from the point of view of the colonized. The way the book was received by at least a few Solomon Islanders, however, manifested the new circumstances of the postcolonial epoch: it was attacked, in particular, by the premier of Malaita, a Christian man related to members of the native police who had participated in a bloody punitive expedition that followed the massacre. So far from being a narrative that in some sense addressed the concerns of all Solomon Islanders, the book was represented as an offence that unnecessarily stirred up old conflicts among islanders (rather than between them and colonizers). In an essay reflecting on the controversy surrounding the book, Keesing acknowledged that *Lightning*, like so much revisionist colonial history, possessed the flaw of turning the heroes into villains and vice versa, but he suggested that the source of criticism lay in the book's privileging of the voices of a marginal minority (the Kwaio), who tend to be regarded as backward pagans or thugs and criminals by other Solomon Islanders:

In situations such as that of the colonial and postcolonial Solomons, the politics of representation and the identification of subalternity are by no means simple matters. Solomons politicians have more power than expatriate scholars, and they use it to further their personal, class, and sectarian interests. Cleavages of class . . . now overshadow cleavages of language and culture in the Pacific . . . the Kwaio pagans . . . constitute both an underclass and a persecuted and marginalized cultural minority. The cultural nationalist discourse of a postcolonial elite, counterposing the indigenous and authentic to the foreign, alien, and exploitative, lays down ideological smokescreens that cover and hide the realities of class interest, neocolonialism, and the exploitation and pauperization of hinterlands villagers. To find the subalterns, we must penetrate the smokescreens laid down by the "insiders" who have the power to represent the present and claim the past: and these subalterns too, if we find and hear them, speak with discordant voices (1990, 298–9; see also Keesing 1992a).

In effect, Keesing rejects the moral and historical paradigm of pre-Independence Pacific history, which enabled expatriate scholars to identify with, and sometimes speak on behalf of, generalized indigenous "insiders." The mantle of the insider is now seen as a cover for the particular interests of a new elite, a postcolonial class that deploys many of the forms of colonial hierarchy but is not thereby engaged in some empty simulation: the perpetuation of various forms of real political and economic dominance is all too apparent. Keesing takes sides by drawing attention to enduring inequities within the Solomons, but he does not now claim to present or represent any unitary Kwaio perspective on the Bell massacre: he is unable to do so, in part because of differences with some of his informants on points of considerable significance. His assessment of the numbers of Kwaio killed in the punitive raids that followed the massacre are much smaller than those of some local leaders, who have put forward claims for large sums in compensation from the British and/or central Solomons governments. Scholars are clearly no longer in a position to claim to represent or write for either the dominant or the dominated within postcolonial Pacific states. They may present the stories of particular people, or of particular groups, but can only narrate these as they see them, in a fashion that must be perspectival and politically inflected. This is so, whether the scholar in question acknowledges the fact or not.

If there is a persisting difficulty in Keesing's 1990 formulation, it is the implication that the subalterns are more worthy of attention than other actors and classes. This is, in effect, an answer to the question that I posed in chapter 1 with respect to Nicholas Dirks's discussion of decolonized history: who now plays the part of the privileged actor in the narration of postcolonial stories and histories? One justification for embracing the perspective of people such as the Kwaio would be that the perceptions of the dominated have frequently been obscured and ignored, and that a major task for historians and anthropologists is the recovery of "histories from below," of forms of resistance that have been recognized only as criminality, childishness, messianic sedition, laziness, and so on. This—and the Subaltern Studies project that Keesing draws upon—is indeed an appropriate response to one set of historical absences. There may, however, be a risk of introducing a new kind of authenticity in which the rebels and intransigent underclasses attract our empathy while diverse other Pacific islanders do not.

This is particularly a problem in the Pacific because—outside Bougainville and New Caledonia—overt militant resistance has been relatively exceptional, and most Pacific islanders have accommodated various colonial impositions, absorbed some (such as Christianity) in locally appropriate forms, and maintained their autonomy as much through sheer disengagement from state institutions as through active resistance to them. The effectiveness of these strategies has often been marked by their ambiguity in the eyes of colonial authorities: Was an agricultural cooperative a healthy sign of economic development or a cover for sedition? Was one population's shift in adherence from one mission to another a sign of "genuine" religious choice or a way of subverting their chiefs' authority? Such indigenous tactics (exemplified by the new religions of some of the Fijians in chapter 2) within a zone of apparent order tend, however, to be indistinct, not only for colonial officials, but also for historians and sympathetic political activists. It is therefore easy to itemize, and privilege, a series of recognizable rebellions in the Pacific—as David Robie has done in *Blood on Their Banner* (1989)—while devaluing the politics of islanders who appear merely to be quiet collaborators or apathetic villagers. If this sort of narrative is attuned to local counterparts of global liberation movements and marginalizes peculiarly Melanesian responses and strategies, Keesing's subaltern perspective authenticates the anticolonial tribe become postcolonial underclass while dismissing national politicians and bureaucrats. Even if this new elite is in fact corrupt, isn't there a risk that we evoke a caricature of natives unfit to govern themselves when we should be contextualizing corruption and inefficiency in the problematic relations between new and weak states with considerable natural resources, and multinational capital and aid bodies? Isn't there also a risk that we might overstate this corruption and subsume those engaged in attempting to administer necessary health and education services to the figure of a self-serving bureaucrat? Is there any story or history in which these hybridized "natives" can be protagonists?

If a subaltern perspective risks lapsing into a romance of resistance, *The Cargo Club*'s privileged actor is the jaded outsider who discovers that the contemporary Pacific—now manifestly a region that cannot be tightly controlled by neocolonial regional powers—is not worth owning or governing. A writer who could endorse an anticolonial warrior acting to defend custom and the old ways must, it seems, reject the postcolonial militant in town, who by contrast is merely a deluded by-product of liberation theology or a thug after cash, dosed up on all-purpose third world ideology.

Corris's thriller is intelligible partly because so much has been said about the globalization of culture, the multiplication of simulacra, the creeping specters of hyperreality. These international processes have received a good deal of attention in recent cultural studies and anthropology, but those outside academia are hardly oblivious of them; innumerable tourists nostalgically regret the proliferation of poor copies of Western commodities and styles and travel further and deeper into the third world in search of receding authenticities, only to encounter more garish and disharmonic exhibits and performances. Contemporary travel writing—like Theroux's 1992 book and much of what appears in *Granta*, for example (see Sugnet 1991)—now transcends the overplayed interests in discovery or adventure and instead finds all this curiously satisfying: the failures of nationalism, the flaking paint, the natives with personal stereos, the fake tribal dances, are dull and sleazy and tell us little about a wider world except that we are the only ones able to detect the ironies.

Both the popular discourses and the cultural critiques that are labeled postmodern of course take many forms. It is possible to be interested in transnational cultures and scenes of hybridization without regarding everything that is imported or transposed as a mere surface that lacks its own presence and distinctiveness. It is indeed important, in the Pacific, to deal with the variety of global forms, the folkloric reifications of culture, the appropriations that may appear, at first, to be merely derivative and inauthentic (Jolly 1992c). Corris's thriller is, of course, not an application of postmodern theory to the postcolonial scene, but the book's inability to make a positive statement about contemporary Pacific societies does carry a warning about the ironic distancing that often characterizes postmodern writing. The idea that the cultural world is pervaded by simulations and quotations is often illuminating and can be subversive when, for instance, it is deployed to undo the privileged originality and authority of high art. Subsuming island nations to resorts in which political fantasies can be acted out does not, however, provide anyone with a novel or consequential understanding of either the political situations that are notionally described, or our own involvements (as tourists, as ethnographers, as historians) with them. It is rather a strategy of writing that precludes recognition and even apprehension of the political meanings and values that do persist, to our evident discomfort, in the postcolonial Pacific.

PART III

BEYOND

THE INVENTION OF

TRADITION

7

Tin and Thatch

Korolevu is not Electricityland; it is not a motorcar place. But this Fijian village is at the end of a road, eighty dusty kilometers up valley from the coastal market town of Sigatoka on the dry western side of the big island of Viti Levu. So it is not that far to the shops, not even that much farther to Nadi, and the journey—usually four uncomfortable hours in the back of a Japanese truck crowded with village people—seems somehow insufficient to transport you into the radically different domain of the city. There are moments of noise and anger here, as there are anywhere else, but Korolevu is typically a tranquil place: its sounds are those of talk, birds, and the breeze through coconut palms; its time is unhurried; the food is from gardens and the river; and the language is a local dialect that feels entangled with the bare hills and the daily gifts by which kinship in the place is made— one cannot imagine it in print or in radio commercials like standard Fijian.

In June 1988 I drove up the valley road to live in Korolevu to do anthropology and oral history. In some ways this felt like the end of a journey rather than a beginning, since for some years I had been pursuing old letters and notes bearing on the area's history under British colonial rule, and I wanted to know how struggles of which I had a partial knowledge from these faded pages were regarded by those old enough to have waged them and their children. But I was distracted by what mattered to the people who welcomed me, who made much in the present of a past other than the one I had thought of pursuing. This is not an attempt to speak on behalf of these Fijians of the interior, but only a reaction to some of their self-accounts.

In contemporary Oceania, the relationships between tradition, identity, and change are crucial. These keywords at once figure in national political discourse and underlie what rural people say of their own situation. The former kind of talk exploits rather than expresses the latter, and the continuities between the two are mainly ironic. Despite much rhetorical abuse, the loaded triad is crucial, yet neither in the way we expect nor in quite the way village people themselves maintain. So this is about how we foreigners are utterly misled by appearances, while indigenous people sustain useful and probably essential mystifications.

A specific perception of tribal tradition and social change is so widespread in Western representations of many parts of the world that it clearly derives less from actual transformations anywhere than from features of our own ideology. This is the "transistors among the Tasaday" view. We noticed that tee shirts, manufactured tools, canned food, cigarettes, and other such things have found their way into areas that should be remote and tribal. These material objects are in themselves signs, not simply of change, but of a loss of distinctively primitive identity: to the extent that they are conspicuous, introduced goods reflect the degree to which some group has abandoned or lost its authentic cultural heritage. Thus, a tribe amongst whom grass skirts are still worn will be seen as comparatively untarnished by foreign intrusion, while it is obvious that Samoans or Tongans who wear digital watches and possess radios or videos have leapt across the gulf between the traditional and modernity and can no longer be expected to have any distinctively native culture. In this understanding, it is a dead material thing like a Coca Cola bottle that impels change, rather than living people. These ideas echo widely in scholarship and popular accounts, especially television documentaries of the "vanishing peoples" genre, but they also have a real hold on the way we spontaneously react to images: after I once showed a film on Papua New Guinea highlands ritual to students, the first questioner pointed out a few shots that included such things as umbrellas and asked, Did the people *therefore* have some problems about their identity?

This assumption expresses a kind of tragic romanticism over the fall of the noble savage from a gracious state, free of commodities, and tells the wrong story about tribal histories and the present for several reasons. People who look extremely authentic have often had their social lives transformed by such things as population movements and disease as an indirect result of colonialism. Here I do not dwell on the absence of societies outside wider and ultimately global histories but stress the converse point that the introduction of foreign goods does not in itself bring the values of the countries in which such articles are produced. Things are often not sought out of a newfound consumerist desire but instead are actively appropriated by the local culture and used in ways consistent with some modification of prior sets of ideas.

As you move up the Sigatoka Valley toward Korolevu, you pass Fijian villages in which only one or two houses are traditional Fijian *bure*, built up on mounds

48. The *were levu*, or "big house," Korolevu Village, Noikoro District, central Fiji, 1988.

faced with river stones and with steep, thatched roofs. All the others are made from some combination of corrugated iron, concrete, timber, and some bush materials. Farther up the valley, the proportion tends to change. Korolevu is dominated by its *bure,* especially by what is simply known as "the Big House" (fig. 48). Raised above all the others on a huge foundation mound, this is notionally the house of the paramount chief of the district but in fact is used exclusively and rarely for ceremonies such as the welcoming of important groups of visitors. Other interior villages, frequently inaccessible by car, have very few nontraditional houses, and Navala, in the province of Ba, has none at all. This symbol of the perpetuation of Fijian custom appears on the front of the 1988 Fiji phone book (somewhat ironically, since the village contains no telephones).

These interior villages thus look different and are sought after by those travelers who would differentiate themselves from resort-going tourists by getting into the back blocks and seeing a bit of "real" Fijian life. The villages to which they are directed by guidebooks are certainly attractive visually, but they are also supposed to represent something that corrugated iron and proximity to town and money depletes: the reserve of Fijian authenticity.

But there is a big discrepancy between this kind of view and the way important features of tradition and identity are seen by Fijians. The key concepts are to do with sharing and hospitality, and respect. Nearly every casual visitor to a Fijian village will be told that the crucial feature of the Fijian way of life is embodied in one's willingness to share. You don't let somebody walk past your house without calling out, "Come and have a cup of tea," "Come and eat," or "Here is your lunch." This sort of thing is not exactly said in the expectation that the invitation will be taken up, but nor is it an empty assertion: people do actually eat and drink tea in others' houses almost daily. One should not think of accumulating for oneself, but rather of getting kin and visitors into the house to partake of what one has, and they are always urged to eat abundantly, to have another bowl of tea. This is closely connected with the suffusion of village life by kin bonds that extend not merely beyond villages but across traditional tribal polities as confederations. Many of those close by are one's "siblings," fathers, mothers, or children, while those from farther away, with whom one is not already related, tend to be classified as cousins. The classifications crosscut those of English terminology so as to make translation free of anthropological terminology difficult. As in many other parts of the world, the crucial opposition is between those to whom one is related by same-sex ties in previous generations (e.g., father's brothers' children) and cross-cousins (e.g., father's sisters' or mother's brothers' children). The former group is hierarchically differentiated into elder and younger, while cross-cousins are supposed to be more equivalent in status, less constrained by forms of respect, and potential sex/marriage partners. But the central point with regard to the perception of Fijian life is that in another village one meets not strangers but people one calls younger sister or mother—terms that restate and reinforce the relationship whenever they are used. This extension of family and mandatory hospitality toward visitors are linked in the notion of *loloma*—"love," in the sense of affection and Christian caring.

Relatedness is not an unstructured net of mutual obligations but is organized rather by status differences and asymmetries manifested in expressions of respect. Any mature person is respected: this is reflected in the fact that a parent of either sex should not be addressed by name but rather as "Naomi's father" or just "Naomi." This means that both parents and a child may all routinely be called by the latter's name, but in practice this does not lead to the confusion one might expect. Respect, however, is really based on a more complicated combination of principles that are more or less metaphorically associated: chiefly/commoner, male/female, visitor/native (i.e., *taukei*), elder/younger—the last, both in the sense of absolute age and of seniority of family line deriving from birth order (the two, of course, do not necessarily correspond, even among those closely related).

The context in which this social order is manifested and re-created more centrally and conspicuously is in the kava ceremony. This mild stimulant, infused from pounded roots and once drunk in parts of Papua New Guinea and most of the rest of the Pacific Islands, is never consumed in an entirely informal way in Fiji, but must always be marked by certain utterances and practices that distinguish its drinking as a special and meaningful activity. A bowl is normally presented to a particular person, often the most senior man within a group of visitors, who thus represents them as well as himself, or someone who has provided one with help or a consequential gift. The offering and acceptance each entail brief speeches delivered in a low and steady tone unlike that of natural speeches, and they include various stock phrases (as well as elaboration appropriate to the occasion) emphasizing relatedness or unity, mutual respect, and future good health. The kava is referred to as "the water of the land" or "the chiefly kava," thus linking it, even if there are no chiefs present, with chiefly ways of doing things, with customs of respect. Whoever is receiving the offering will drink first; the subsequent order reflects the principles of seniority and gender mentioned above, but in a negotiated and flexible rather than a rigid way. People clap before taking a cup and often also after others have drunk, when some may also call out, "Empty!" Draining one's cup is a social accomplishment that consolidates relationships or seals some more particular arrangement (actually, after drinking for hours, finishing a cup becomes also something of a merely physical accomplishment).

Another notable arena in which respect is conspicuous is that of normal movements within houses. These are rectangular with doors at one end and about halfway along one or both sides. The end entrance is said to be "low," and in Korolevu, houses are aligned roughly with the river, so that lower doors are downstream toward the lower part of the valley. Within the house, those who are senior in rank, age, and gender sit in the "higher" part, farther from the entrance, and may enter or leave by an upper door, while younger men, children, and most women sit nearer the low door. There is thus a kind of translation of the vertical, which is equated with the various dimensions of status difference, into the horizontal, such that it is disrespectful for a younger man or woman to move above his or her superiors. If one has to get something from that part of the house or reach up, one asks permission and then sits down on the floor and claps when the action is completed. People also say, "Tulou," which means "pardon," if they must get up next to somebody or otherwise pass "over" them. Respect thus pervades everyday action and movement. It becomes such a natural part of behavior that even when a foreigner like myself returns to the urban scene, the manner in which people clump arbitrarily about rooms and sit up in chairs rather than cross-legged on mats is vulgar and disconcerting, until one has readapted.

Respect, kinship, and sharing are thus the core of the Fijian perception of their traditional way, their customs, their culture. This is, of course, an ideological construct: when the Fijians convey a collective self-image to foreigners they do not, at least at first, say much about clan rivalries over matters such as chiefly succession and land or other disputes arising from the communal system or its interaction with commerce, which imperil the fabric of *loloma* and kinship. It is also often said that people are losing respect for the traditional hierarchy and the chiefs, though this lament appears also in documents twenty, fifty, or one hundred years old, so, like standards of morality and literacy in government schools, this is perhaps one of those things that has always been declining. I am less concerned here with the discrepancies between the Fijian ethos and its difficulties in practice than with the fact that all this has nothing to do with the outsiders' recognition of tradition and modernity as manifested in material things, such as thatched versus corrugated iron roofs, which in Samoa, too, have a variable incidence (tin there frequently being incorporated into traditional architectural forms) (figs. 49–53).

The Fijians are concerned above all with practices, while Europeans take objects as markers. For the Fijians, whether a village house is a *bure* or not makes no difference to the way one behaves within it, so a kava ceremony is no less a work of respect if a plastic bowl rather than its pottery or carved wooden precursor is used, or if the stuff is served in enamel bowls instead of coconut shell cups (fig. 54). Of course traditional housebuilding, like barkcloth making and other crafts, has folkloric significance—hence the pictures on the cover of the telephone directory and of Korolevu itself on the Fijian ten-dollar note. But this is far less significant culturally than the tenets about village values, which apply with the same force whether one is in villages with electricity near towns or in hamlets of the hills and outlying islands. Urban life is regarded as being quite different, but this is because Fijians in town are said to abandon the ways of the land and their kinship obligations, adopting instead the way of money and "the customs of foreigners." The conspicuous presence of imported things and the developed character of places like Suva and Lautoka are, of course, recognized, but they are secondary to the shift in orientation of townspeople's alleged behavior (which is exaggerated and stereotyped in discussions of this kind).

One perception thus demands that authentic cultures do not surrender their crafts and visually measures the corrosion of tradition in the incidence of material things that happen to have been produced in factories; the other privileges the application of a set of ethics and is indifferent to the substitution of borrowed for made objects.

Sunday night, very late. We have been at the next village upriver, since mid-afternoon drinking kava; the talk was partly about the prices of various cash crops and partly about a young woman who has just eloped to another village ("We knew she was going to the feast, we did not know she would go for good."

The old man is not angry; rather he seems to find this definitive social step remarkable, almost to be secretly admired). Soon after dark a kind of lay Catholic service takes place. I am more accustomed to Methodist ritual and am astonished by how much more participation this involves, everyone's personal prayer interdigitated with a collective refrain. The kava bowl remains in the center of the room. Much later, we eat and then depart. I take leave of my "grandfather."

"Tutura, mari sa la bale."

"Ia, sa vina. Kia tale na siga . . . "

(Another day . . .)

Outside, the moonless night's darkness has an intensity unimaginable in Electricityland. Our horses are tethered outside the village fence. My "father" fits the bridle and throws a thick sack across the horse's back.

"Vodo," he says, and mounts his own mare, capricious with a new foal. Our horses splash awkwardly through a bouldery rapid; we will cross the river three times in less than a mile. The stars are brilliant, almost harsh, but do not illuminate the land. Below the high edges of the mountains the blackness absorbs slopes, trees, stones (at primary school I was rebuked for talking of "light black" and "dark black," but now I am certain that the distinction is subjectively valid). Only the horses see the path.

I have emphasized that sharing through the fabric of kinship, hospitality, and respect is fundamental in Fijian perceptions of Fijian culture. These values are not, however, those of timeless tradition. Investigation discloses that many features of society and culture were very different earlier, especially in parts such as Korolevu, in the mountainous interior. Some of the most essentially traditional practices and ways of thinking now observable either originated in the colonial period (1874–1970) or were transformed by it.

A widely believed myth of Fijian history suggests that the British preserved Fijian village society, its communal character, and its traditional hierarchies. It is true that the colonial administration effectively precluded the alienation of Fijian land, and it would be perverse to question the basically positive nature of this policy. One only has to look at the contrasting dispossession of the indigenous people of Australia and New Zealand by other British settlers, and Tahiti and New Caledonia under the French, to realize that by the standards of its time, the British regime in Fiji was unusually sensitive to the rights of its colonized subjects (if markedly less so to those of the indentured Indian laborers).

While this singular and justly celebrated feature of the history must be acknowledged, it is not the case that the British left Fijians to their own devices in the countryside; while they continued to live in villages, there was a great deal of imposed change reflecting the political, social, and moral agendas of the colo-

49–50. Tin and thatch houses, Noikoro District, central Fiji, 1988.

51–53. Samoan *fale* (houses) around the capital, Apia, Western Samoa, 1996. The open oval form of the traditional structure is adapted with a tin roof and sometimes turned into a rectangle.

54. Drinking kava, Noikoro District, central Fiji, 1988: plastic bowl, tin house.

nial state. It is thus misleading to speak of "preservation." A majority of modern villages are in different locations than those occupied earlier: in reaction to rebellious activities, particularly in the same valley as Korolevu, the government forced most tribes to abandon their old hillforts for larger settlements that were more accessible to inspection. Subsequently, even these newly established villages were occasionally broken up or relocated with a view to quelling dissent.

Between the 1890s and 1920s the administration also made an extraordinary range of stipulations that purported to improve sanitation and the health of the native population. These influenced the division of labor (certain tasks being prohibited for women) and must have entirely changed the appearances of many villages. Toilets had to be constructed, pigs were to be kept in pens at a specified distance from the village, and food plants could not be grown around houses but were to be planted only in discrete gardens. Although it is clear that officials misunderstood the causes of the depopulation that these measures were supposed to alleviate, some of the rules probably were of benefit. But there were many others that merely imposed British standards—there were great efforts to end the residential segregation of men and women and to provide every newly married couple with their own house. These had to contain a specified number of sleeping mats and beds raised off the floor. Some of these regulations, which were backed up with fines in cash or labor, were accommodated without ever being exactly obeyed: even now many Fijian *bure* contain

Western-style wooden beds, but these are usually used for keeping clothes and other articles on top of, while a family sleeps beside them in a row on the floor.

The regulations had a direct impact on the appearance of houses, since rules were made about the floor, the number of doors, the nature of the walls, and so on: it was thought that Fijians would not build themselves adequate dwellings unless they were forced to. The result is that today's "traditional" house has many features, such as a floor made of split bamboo, that derive from the interference of white men. The process tended also to reduce preexisting diversity in Fijian house types: just as the language of the small chiefly island of Bau became the national "Fijian" language, and just as the colonial administration forced all Fijian clans and tribes to register their land on the basis of a model of tenure roughly derived from Bau (and which was quite at odds with some districts' customary practice), the house types of eastern Fiji supplanted the distinctive circular houses that at an earlier date were commonly found in the west. There has thus been a trend towards homogenization in Fijian cultures, though this has actually taken place very unevenly: to some extent it entailed merely the voluntary acceptance of other groups' customs, but it also required more repression than is now realized. Around the turn of the century, hundreds of Fijians were fined or jailed every year for extraordinarily trivial offences; their freedom of movement in particular was severely restricted. All of this created the placid villages that travelers now see as remnants of old Fijian culture.

What of the main elements of the Fijian way? The ethic of sharing is probably now emphasized so much because the administration attempted to squash it: mutual giving was misconstrued as "begging" and thought to stifle initiative and preclude the development of any spirit of economic enterprise or competition among Fijians. Requesting anything of more than a certain value was thus a punishable offence, and as the two most distinguished anthropologists to work in Fiji, A. M. Hocart and Marshall Sahlins, observed in 1912 and 1962 respectively (in the words of the former), "the best part of the law is that it cannot be enforced" (1912).

Proscriptions and resistance to them were thus perpetuated over decades (in conversation, Fijian officials have echoed complaints made by district officers about the villagers' unwillingness to pay provincial taxes since the 1870s; Jone, an acquaintance in the administration, shakes his head sadly, "They don't understand that it's all for their own benefit"). The consequence was thus that Fijian culture developed a reactive or oppositional character, making a virtue of some of the features the British attempted to stamp out.

For the same reasons, the stress on mutual support and solidarity among kin has a greater force now than it ever could have possessed formerly. A "communal system" will never be a symbol of identity in the absence of dichotomized and threatening individualism. The current strength of the ideology is connected not so much with reacting to the British as with another cultural project—that of collective Fijian self-definition in contradistinction to the ways of Indians and foreigners. Proud assertions about Fijian hospitality are often linked with the observation that "among you foreigners this is impossible. If you see a stranger walking past, you shut your door." The notion that things are shared or given is not an isolated idea but the correlate of a proposition that Indians pursue "the path of money," are thought to be ruthlessly individualistic, and are believed not to engage in any wider cooperation with relatives. I was occasionally told something like this: "You see how it is with us. If someone is building a house, many others will come and help. Later, we have a feast; we eat and work together. Among the Indians this doesn't happen. It's every man for himself." These stereotypes, often articulated in a more dogmatic way by Fijians involved in business or town life than those who are actually continuously embedded in the sharing relations alluded to, have contributed in a regrettable way to the separateness of the races and some of the attitudes behind support for the military coups in 1987. The notions of respect and the centrality of chieftainship also figure here; in a recent autobiography, an Alliance politician blamed the difficult situation partly upon the inability of the Indians to understand or respect the system of traditional chiefly leadership (Vakatora 1988).

The position of the chief was also something that changed: in the earlier polities, the reciprocal obligations of traditional leaders were strong, but the administration institutionalized chiefly privileges, such as entitlements to produce, and overlooked the complementary process of redistribution. Other significant figures, such as traditional shamanic priests, were rendered illegitimate and marginalized by both missionaries and the government: the latter actively campaigned against cult activities because these acquired a millennial and "seditious" character in the late nineteenth century (Fijian Christianity still has a syncretistic dimension, and cults, often related to social grievances, have broken out in many parts of the country thoughout this century). The deportation to small and remote islands of some "fanatical" priests was only the most extreme expression of a campaign that saw hundreds of men and women fined, jailed, and flogged. In the absence of the priests, the chiefs became more central than they ever had been before.

On the other hand, the drinking of kava was "democratized"—although consumed in spirit houses among other contexts in the precontact system, the drink seems mainly to have been monopolized by the chiefly elite; the everyday ceremony that is now paradigmatic of the Fijian ethos is thus also an outcome of changes since last century. It would be wrong to infer from all this that contemporary rural Fijian life is not traditional; now customs conceived as such really do regulate social life, and, in fact, it is much more traditional than it could have been before.

Statements about early life in western Fiji depend on scrappy and sometimes unreliable observations in the accounts of foreigners, such as colonial officials, and upon oral traditions, which convey a great deal, but never exactly a simple depiction of former activities. There is thus much that one does not know, especially because nineteenth-century descriptions mostly deal with, and are biased toward, the eastern Fijians whose chiefs later collaborated with Britain in the colonial project mentioned above.

Ethnographic fieldwork also generates a kind of partial knowledge. Anthropologists often write as though the specific facts they mention only derive from a larger scheme—a structure of beliefs or social relations—that is comprehended as a totality. It is not acknowledged that notions about this "system," which, of course, only really exists in particular events and images, derive from the practical details and the anthropologist's perception of them. Gaps in the fieldworkers' knowledge and practical misunderstandings are only mentioned in ethnographic books insofar as they are subsequently filled or rectified. There are often references to early confusions that are later dispelled on the basis of a fuller perception of indigenous ways of thinking. Of course, one does work things out as one proceeds, but this is really a literary strategy that conveys the impression that, in the end, the anthropologist's knowledge encompasses the social world of the people studied. But as in any other project, there are really scraps and loose ends.

A man from another village is telling you a myth. He is interrupted and later goes away. You never see him again and are left with half a story. Something you do is regarded as utterly hilarious for reasons that never quite become clear. An "aunt" begins to tell you about a scandal but gets distracted. Then someone else shows up in whose presence it cannot be discussed. Because the topic is sensitive, you do not want to ask her about it directly, and you hope that at some stage she will bring it up again by herself. This does not happen, and you consider broaching the subject despite its awkwardness. You procrastinate and the right moment fails to arise. Later you decide that you don't care if you never know why that man is so malicious in your house.

I am sitting on a mat with a woman of about eighteen. I am reading some mail and she is scribbling on the back of a discarded envelope. Then she prints quite neatly in English: "Fucking is just interesting." In idle moments over subsequent weeks I wonder what she meant. Was "just" intended to convey "merely," so that the sentence would be analogous to "His action was just self-interested"? But this is a form of words that diminishes whatever is referred to, and one does not reduce something to being *only* interesting, in the way that some superficial book could be only entertaining. And isn't it a very peculiar claim to make about sex anyway? Especially since this (unmarried) woman is an upright Seventh-day Adventist; I suspect that unlike many others of her age, she wouldn't know. Yet no written message can be utterly random. I can't ask her to elucidate directly because she doesn't trust me—she once caught me watching her undress (this is sometimes nearly unavoidable in one-room houses, but I should have looked the other way). So what categorically resists my comprehension in this place of different people is not a long speech or an elliptical aside in a dialect in which I am at best semifluent, but four words written clearly in my own language.

Ethnic stereotypes have been referred to in discussions of the causes and justifications of the Fijian military takeover, but the relationships that particular people sustain with others across the boundaries also motivate action, restraint, and judgment.

Fijian marriage feasts often bring hundreds of visitors and last for several days; the immediate period of intensive preparation may be two or three weeks. In the midst of one such hectic change in the village pulse I was surprised to see a gaunt man in his late forties.

"Who is that Indian?" I asked.

"You mean Ricky?" It was as though I had been corrected, his personal name substituted for an inappropriate generic. It turned out that his wife was a Fijian woman from the village. She was my "sister," and he was thus my "cousin." I could also address him by a more specific term meaning literally "occupant of the house."

Whenever large feasts took place he was apparently in the habit of coming to the village, and he would help by bringing large quantities of bread from bakeries in town or otherwise through making his truck available. A distinction is always made between true owners of the land (*taukei*) and those whose origins are elsewhere, but this activity of contributing to ceremonies is central to belonging: it was one of the bases of my own acceptance by the people and the adoption at various stages in the past of Fijians from other districts.

"He is a good man," I was told. At the same time I found out that several other women from the district had married Indians. No Fijian men, however, had taken Indian wives.

That was in late September. In the middle of October, Ricky drove his truck into a telephone pole beside the highway near Sigatoka. Precisely how the accident occurred and the nature of his injuries were discussed several times as we drank kava. The immediate family of Ricky's wife visited the hospital at Lautoka. One day I was sitting with my "mother" as she scrubbed wild yams for lunch. She paused and gazed across the tranquil space of the village at nothing in particular.

"Isa, Ricky!" she said and resumed her work. "Isa" is an expression of empathy and often regret. This was a very ordinary allusion to misfortune and our common vulnerability.

Two weeks later we heard that he was dead.

8

The Inversion
of Tradition

Constructions of tradition, which entail both claims about identity, nationalism, or ethnicity, and renderings of history, have become a central topic for anthropological and historical research. In the histories of rural Europe, the British Empire, contemporary Quebec, insular Oceania, and in many fourth world and minority movements, "inventions," "reinventions," or "objectifications" of tradition, culture, and community are now being identified and explored. In the Pacific, this proliferation of work on tradition and custom shows no sign of faltering,[1] and assumptions have clearly become more sophisticated. For instance, while some Pacific scholars, and some of the contributors to the influential collection edited by Hobsbawm and Ranger (1983), often saw invention as proportionate with inauthenticity,[2] it is now emphasized that created identities are not somehow contrived and insincere; culture is instead inevitably "tailored and embellished in the process of transmission," and that process is "dynamic, creative—and real" (Linnekin 1991:161; cf. Jolly 1992c).[3] Following Wagner (1981), the artifice of invention has thus been naturalized.

While this shift marks a positive step, the debates might be productively extended in two further ways. It is still broadly presumed that objectifications of culture are likely to be affirmed and upheld by the peoples concerned;[4] in contrast, this chapter draws attention to ambivalent and negative attitudes to reified customary regimes. Secondly, despite the interests in colonial history that mark current work in historical anthropology, reifications of tradition have frequently been seen as cultural phenomena that stand, essentially, on their own. It's not that historical interactions with other populations, and particularly colonial experiences, are denied or undiscussed; the problem is rather that these have not been effectively integrated analytically. This chapter insists that self-representation never takes place in isolation and is frequently oppositional or reactive: the idea of a community cannot exist in the absence of some externality or difference, and identities and traditions are often not simply different, but frequently constituted in opposition to others. Hence, what is important is not so much the categorical fact that difference provides a foil for identity, but the actual histories of accommodation or confrontation that shape particular understandings of others, and thus determine what specific practices, manners, or local ethics are rendered explicit and made to carry the burden of local identity. There is no abstract sense in which certain features of a society or culture are important and will therefore be prominent in objectifications of that society or culture;[5] rather, the process of choosing emblematic activities, dispositions, or material artifacts is indissociable from a history of encounters and what is at issue in those particular encounters.

Hence, the aim here is not to review the diverse developments in the literature on tradition and identity, but to draw these terms into a broader analysis of cultural objectification;[6] I stress that this is often a reactive process and seek also to draw attention to a neglected dimension of the reifications of custom, indigenous ways, and tradition that have now been examined in such diverse contexts—from pagan enclaves in the otherwise Christian nations of the Solomon Islands and Vanuatu to minority assertions in Australia, New Zealand, and Hawaii. Despite the diversity of lines of interpretation, it has almost always been tacitly assumed that the people concerned have a positive attitude toward the reification of indigenous tradition or custom that they present. That is, because emphasis has been placed upon the role of such constructions in the affirmation or assertion of local identity, negative and ambivalent attitudes toward the customary or the traditional have remained largely invisible. For instance, Handler suggests that:

> to meet the challenge of an outsider's denial of national existence, nationalists must claim and specify the nation's possessions: they must delineate and if possible secure a bounded territory, and they must construct an account of the unique culture and history that attaches to and emanates from the people who occupy it (1985, 211).

The central idea that has informed many specific studies in the Pacific is similar: that political contest and affirmation have required an elaboration of identity. I do not dispute the correctness or the importance of this departure point, but it seems crucial also to recognize political contest within a national (or tribal) population, which is manifest not only in the process of selecting aspects of past heritage or present custom that are privileged in the construction of ethnic identity, but which may also involve more radical rejections of what is local and traditional. Once the scope for such valorizations has been recognized, their political and cultural significance seems considerable, both in apparently routine circumstances and in the politico-religious movements that have been of such interest to Pacific anthropologists and historians. My main point, then, is a very simple one: if a set of meanings is objectified and named as the custom of the place, or, for example, "the Samoan way," it is possible to take a variety of stances toward any such reification.

Much of the literature on tradition has, naturally enough, explored perceptions of the past, as well as the significance of history for present identities. These questions are of less significance for the present analysis than the fact that formulations of contemporary identity are generally at issue; sometimes the intrinsic worth of local sociality, rather than its primordial or historical distinctiveness, is stressed. Placing constructions of custom, tradition, and local identity together may elide distinctions important in other contexts, but I suggest that it is fruitful insofar as the broader dynamics of such objectifications are exposed.

This chapter aims to sketch out some of these dynamics by ranging widely, and inevitably somewhat superficially, across examples from Oceanic history; though I have described particular cases in greater detail elsewhere (chapters 2 and 9), the aim here is rather to establish the generality of the processes and suggest something of their potential permutations. I argue that reactive objectification is a fundamental cultural process that proceeded in precolonial indigenous societies, facilitating mutual differentiation, but that it was transformed after contact with Europeans and underwent further development as the character of colonial encounters changed. I explore the ways in which the recognition of both others and selves made particular practices or customs emblematic; different encounters produced different referents for what was characteristic of a place or a people. The dynamic was thus at once particularizing and totalizing, in the sense that novel notions of whole ways of life or customary regimes were engendered, yet these entities were epitomized by certain customs or ethics, sometimes in the domain of economic or exchange practices, sometimes in sexuality and gender relations. I conclude by suggesting that the fact that these generalized constructions of customary ways can be inverted or negatively valorized as well as affirmed may have broader ramifications for the way anthropologists think about culture.

Objectification and Opposition

Posing these questions entails an interest in the investigation of culture that diverges from most received perspectives in cultural anthropology, in the sense that interpretation has until recently emphasized the position and resonance of particular meanings within totalities, rather than processes of explication provoked by cross-cultural contact and contest. That is, despite their great diversity, ways of talking about culture in anthropology have proceeded by relating particular metaphors enacted in ritual, mythic idioms, forms of behavior, notions of relatedness, to some more general set of values, dispositions, key symbols, or structures. While these various forms of cultural analysis have clearly proved fertile in a number of ways, there is one form of difference that these theoretical differences have not refracted, one distinction that has been generally elided. In adducing a set of key tropes or structures, an interpreter perforce refers to diverse statements, acts, images, and narratives; cultural forms that have a certain implicit generality are analytically linked to enunciated propositions and intentional acts. There is a tendency, then, to suppress the difference between practices and ideas that are simply done or thought, which simply take place, and ideas or acts that are set up as definite entities to be spoken of, reflected upon, and manipulated by people in the situation under consideration. The former—like any action or statement—always express, even if idiosyncratically, broader concerns, meanings, and social relations, but are not themselves regarded as symbolic entities or acts emblematic of a particular form of sociality. Practices that are explicitly singled out by people and taken to express or distinguish their way of life do not necessarily have greater social effect, in some abstract calculus, than tacit constructions of agency and personhood or the deep structures of alliance and hierarchy, but they clearly do have quite different potential uses and implications.[7]

In particular, objectified practices and social totalities can be seen to be manifest in each other. An aspect of behavior, a dialect, a literary style, or a way of dealing with relatives may be taken to be emblematic of a way of life, a kind of locally distinctive sociality, or the being of a people—a tribe, a migrant group, a colonized population, a class, the embattled peasantry of a region, or a gay subculture. In any of these contexts, the community that is imagined is not simply conceived of in its empirical complexity; its singularity and distinctiveness is understood, rather, through particular resonant practices and characteristics. There is thus a dialectical process whereby the group and the particular practices are redefined as they come to connote each other.

Objectification must thus be understood as a diacritical and indeed oppositional process: a variety of dominant and dominated groups reify the attributes both of others and themselves in a self-fashioning process (cf. Inden 1990, 2–3 and passim). A concept of place, of here, of us, is thus likely to be what Reinhart Koselleck calls an "asymmetrical counterconcept." With respect to individual names and forms of address, Koselleck points out that certain terms coincide

with one's own self-recognition (mother/son), while others are applied dis-
paragingly by one party to the other (old bag/layabout); in the domain of collective names, there is a comparable field of classifications distinguishing "we" and
"they" applied unequally by one party to the other that "function to deny the
reciprocity of mutual recognition" (1985, 159, 160).[8] Koselleck's discussion of
the semantics of oppositions of this kind focuses on well-known and fundamental instances from European history—Hellene/barbarian and Christian/pagan
(see also Hartog 1988; Hall 1989)—but what is said is highly suggestive for
formulations of identity on a more localized scale in colonial contexts:

> Concepts employable in a particularly antithetical manner have a marked
> tendency to reshape the various relations and distinctions among groups,
> to some degree violating those concerned, and in proportion to this viola-
> tion rendering them capable of political action (162).

This draws attention to the cultural and ideological instability produced in
particular encounters: a violating term of address (such as "primitive") is, if
its significance is recognized by the party referred to, liable to be seized upon
and inverted, or otherwise responded to, in a way that produces a new self-
recognition and alternative construction of we-they distinctions.

If conceptions of identity and tradition are part of a broader field of oppositional naming and categorization, the question that emerges is not How are
traditions invented? but instead *Against what* is this tradition invented? Or, in
general, How does the dynamic of reactive objectification proceed? In some
contexts, the ways in which foreigners or colonizers are reified in indigenous
vision may be influenced much more by existing local schemes than the visitors
themselves, if their presence and intrusions have been transitory; this tends to
be true of early European contact in Oceania. Where colonialism has had a more
sustained and repressive impact, indigenous peoples may come to couch their
identity and resistance in terms made available by the dominant: they celebrate
and affirm what colonialist discourse and practice subordinates and denigrates
(in Koselleck's terms, they invert the values attached to the asymmetrical dual-
isms of the dominant [cf. Keesing 1989, 25–30]).[9] Prolonged and profound
contact may not pervasively alter a culture, but it is likely to produce a neotraditional discourse and rhetoric salient in certain practical domains that is organized primarily in novel and oppositional terms.

These points will be expressed more concretely through examples; I will then
proceed to show that the traditions or ways of life thus objectified are not uniformly affirmed: while the enduring value of the culture of the place may be
asserted in the countercolonial practice of the dominant indigenous groups, this
traditionalist discourse may itself be reactively opposed from within neotradi-

tional society. As has been evident in European cultural critique at least since Montaigne, the facts of difference permit a relativistic and critical explication of one's own culture that can take the form of a rejection of tradition. Such repudiations consist, however, not in absolute negations that deny the construction of identity in particular terms, but instead invert the values attached to that identity through a kind of negative self-fashioning, valorizing what is other and foreign rather than what is associated with one's place.

Contact and Externality: The Preconditions for Objectification

My primary interest here is in objectifications consequent upon colonial contact. While it seems quite appropriate to make the colonial process central to interpretative efforts in the history and anthropology of the Pacific, it is also necessary to recognize the uneven and heterogeneous character of colonial entanglement and avoid the suggestion that cultural dynamism arising from intersocial contact only occurred after European contact. To the contrary, it is clear that there was a great deal of local and long-distance exchange in Oceanic prehistory, and it is tempting to suggest that the striking fact of Melanesian cultural and linguistic diversity reflects some process of willful local differentiation and particularization. It is quite apparent that in certain areas neighboring groups tend to develop and project values and practices that are mutually antithetical; for instance, while the Baining in the interior of New Britain were often represented by travel writers merely as the sort of extreme primitives you would expect to find deep in the jungle (e.g., Klémensen 1965, 142–90), their lack of ceremonial exchange, bridewealth, ranking, relatively formal leadership, and various other attributes might be seen as an oppositional response to the political complexity and elaborate shell money economy of the groups now known as Tolai, who encroached upon and threatened the Baining. The same may be said of the Siwai of Bougainville—one of the founding examples for the anthropological characterization of the Melanesian "big-man," but striking also for their inversion of their Buin neighbors' centralization and hierarchy (Spriggs in press).

If argument about such processes in prehistory can never be more than highly speculative, reactive objectification can perhaps be identified more clearly in the case of the relationships between Fiji, Tonga, and Samoa. For at least the two centuries prior to Cook's visits to Tonga in the 1770s, chiefly elites within these island groups exchanged spouses, various trade items, valuables, and skills such as canoe building (for a characterization of these hierarchical relations as an interisland prestige-goods system see, for example, Kirch 1984, 237–42). While ethnohistoric documentation of the precise nature of early rela-

tions is insecure, Tongan influence appears manifest in features of Fijian political relationships as well as many material culture items, and there is no doubt
that warriors, craft specialists, and others traveled back and forth (Clunie 1986).
In this context, notions developed of *fa'a Samoa, fa'a Tonga,* and *vakaviti*—the
Samoan, Tongan, and Fijian ways. Despite (or because of) the numerous cultural similarities between the three groups, particular practices mediated the
expression of difference, and in the case of tattooing, the origin myths explicitly
represent distinctions as a result of the inversion of the other:

> Fijians account humorously for the Tongan practice of tattooing being
> confined to the men instead of the women. They say that the Tongan who
> first reported the custom to his countrymen, being anxious to state it cor-
> rectly, repeated in a sing-song tone, as he went along, "Tattoo the women,
> but not the men; tattoo the women, but not the men." By ill luck he struck
> his foot violently against a stump in the path, and, in the confusion which
> followed, reversed the order of his message, singing, for the rest of his
> journey, "Tattoo the men, but not the women." (Williams 1858, 1:160).

Needless to say, various inversions of this story were told by Samoans and
Tongans (Rivers 1914, 2:437). My point here is not that a reactive response
actually produced the Fijian practice of female tattooing or the Tongan and
Samoan practice of male tattooing; this is not impossible, but the historic causa-
tion of the pattern of variation is not accessible and might be explained in other
ways. It does seem, however, that the myths make the opposition of Tongan and
Fijian practices explicit, and thus make them available as emblems for ethnic
difference.

The Samoan historian Malama Meleisea has reacted sharply against the proposition (enunciated by Marxist sociologists) that constructs such as the "Samoan
way" are merely reactive products of the colonial period (1987, 16). He is justified, in the sense that the term *fa'a Samoa* was used precolonially in this context
of regional definition, as he is in rejecting the broader implication that modern
identities are inauthentic fabrications:

> Because the Samoans conceived of *fa'a Samoa* as a framework for action
> based upon the social structure of the *'aiga* [descent group] and the *nu'u*
> [polity] and the authority of *matai* [titleholders] and *fono* [councils], new
> practices, ideas and goods could be accepted and incorporated into it so that
> either the system remained unchanged in its essentials, or else was not
> perceived to have changed fundamentally (17).

It is appropriate to stress the incorporative character of local cultures, but the
last two statements—which have quite different implications, elided by the sim-

plicity of "or else"—tendentiously pass over the fact that whatever salience and content ideas like *fa'a Samoa* had in the eighteenth century are clearly very different from their meanings now: a way of phrasing and enacting identity in the interests of differentiating oneself (a Samoan) from others who are Fijians or Tongans perforce has quite different emphases to the expression of difference from whites who might be German colonists in the late nineteenth century or American tourists in the late twentieth. This is not to say that there have not been basic and important continuities in certain Samoan cultural structures, values, and dispositions but that the ways in which these are expressed and rhetorically mobilized have shifted. The refiguring of content is apparent even in a passage Meleisea quotes from the missionary John Williams to establish that *fa'a Samoa* was a relevant concept in the 1830s:

> The wives of the Tahitian teachers [Williams] had left in 1830 tried to teach the Samoan women to cover their breasts with cloth but . . . They liked the cloth very well to put around their middles but they could not induce them to cover their persons of which they are exceedingly proud especially their breasts which are generally very large. They are continually wishing the teachers wives to lay aside their garments & "faasamoa" do as the Samoan ladies do, gird a shaggy mat around their loins . . . anoint themselves beautifully with scented oil, tinge themselves with turmeric, put a string of blue beads around their neck & then faariaria [*fa'alialia*] walk about to show themselves. You will have, say they, all the Manaia, the handsome young men of the town loving you then (1987, 16–7, quoting Williams [1984, 117]).

It is clear here that what was at issue in the encounter with the eastern Polynesian missionaries were the codes of dress and overt sexual restraint upon which the teachers and white missionaries had bestowed the burden of the difference between heathen and Christian. In this context, *fa'a Samoa* was not about Fijian tattooing or the permutations of Tongan and Samoan hierarchical etiquette. It was plainly about forms of dress and adornment and the licence that those forms now appeared to signify. In the same way, the embeddedness of Samoan conduct in the corporate bodies of kin group and polity, and its deference to titular authority and traditional councils, could never have figured as explicit representations of Samoan custom in the precontact period simply because a social world that appeared not to be structured by kinship, reciprocity, and hierarchy was not readily available or visible. Nor would a sense of the contingency of these forms of sociality have been prompted by the brief encounters with whites of the early nineteenth century; the manifest forms of hierarchy apparent in dress and authority on naval vessels (and to a lesser extent others) would, to the contrary, have encouraged the assumption that whites were ranked. Even if the Samoans recognized that there were fundamental differences between European customs and their own, these were obviously not important at the time of Williams's visits: local people did not tell the Tahitians to be *fa'a Samoa* by holding their own *fono* or installing their own *matai*. These shifts make it necessary to qualify Meleisea's legitimate rejection of the idea that tradition and identity are merely recent epiphenomena of colonialism: objectification and cultural juxtaposition did occur quite independently of colonialism, but their development over the colonial and postcolonial periods involved qualitative changes and distinct arenas of differentiation.

This was in part because differences between islanders and Europeans were far starker than differences between one Polynesian or Melanesian island and the next and thus prompted a more complex and totalizing recognition of indigenous ways as a whole, distinct from other possible wholes. Islanders encountered others not merely through being visited, but also by traveling, which was provided by the earliest explorers and traders: on Cook's voyages islanders such as Tupaia visited other parts of indigenous Oceania (often assisting as interpreters and with barter arrangements), and while many of those who ventured into the temperate climates of Europe and North America died before returning, some, such as Omai, who caused such excitement in London, went and returned; once trade developed, many others acted as crew and visited not only other islands (on which they occasionally deserted), but also places of white settlement, such as Sydney, and Asian ports, such as Canton and Manila (Maude 1968, 135). These travels engendered consciousness both of broader conceptions of similarity and specific difference among Pacific islanders, and more categorical difference with whites. While postmodernists have suddenly decided that we need to talk about cosmopolitanism and globalization, even in the eighteenth century many islanders had stepped outside their own societies and obtained vantage points upon their customary practices: experience enabled them to perceive their own cultures comparatively.

Later, in the western Pacific, the ramifications of indentured labor (conducted from the 1850s on) were widespread. Though some areas were virtually overlooked by recruiters, thousands of men and a much smaller number of women from various parts of Vanuatu (then the New Hebrides), the Solomons, and Papua New Guinea, among other places, worked on plantations within their own island groups, in Fiji, and in north Queensland. This experience provided a sharp contrast between the sense of "traditional" life at home and the experience of colonial relationships, wage work, and so on on the plantations; it also permitted a new sense of supratribal fraternal male identity amongst (say) Malaitans or islanders generally, who would previously have seen themselves primarily in more localized terms (Keesing 1986; Jolly 1982, 1987; Otto 1992a). Plantations were crucial sites for the formation of neotraditional culture, as they were for the emergence of pidgin languages that became crucial vehicles of nationalist discourse in the linguistically heterogeneous countries of the southwestern Pacific. Although indentured labor was never of such significance elsewhere in Oceania, various forms of labor migration and circular migration have similarly provided islanders with direct experience of other societies.

In the earlier phases of contact, in the late eighteenth and early nineteenth centuries, travel and overseas work was engaged in sporadically by individuals; but such contact as took place nevertheless prompted certain oppositional constructions of existing and introduced ways. As the Samoan example shows, these were often juxtaposed in the encounter with Christian missionaries, who were frequently indigenous teachers rather than whites. If earlier encounters tended to be structured by preexisting terms in indigenous culture, later nineteenth-century colonial relationships engendered a more deeply "neotraditional" culture, which was made on plantations and in opposition to the tangible domination of plantation experience.

Historical Phases, Shifting Emblems

Through these different movements of colonial history, objectifications of custom and tradition assumed different forms and had different significance. As Jean Comaroff has noted in quite a different context, "Tshidi tended to perceive the structural contradictions of their predicament in terms of an opposition between an idealized and objectivized *setswana*, 'traditional Tswana ways,' and *sekgoa*, 'white culture.' The referents of these reciprocally defining categories, however, had shifted since their specification in the nineteenth century" (1985, 192). Similarly, in the Pacific, the key symbols that were emblematic of indigenous practice were altered over time, and dramatic economic changes were conducive to an increasing emphasis on the juxtaposition of whole modes of life. The oppositional element apparent in the neotraditional identities associated with plantation work and formal colonial domination was not, however, novel; even in early cultural confrontations, European perceptions of the discrepancy between civility and barbarity were resisted, inverted, and played upon; islanders seem to have registered foreign perceptions of what was horrifying and paraded these practices in a taunting manner. For example, Bruny D'Entrecasteaux's voyage in search of La Pérouse followed Cook in visiting both Tonga and New Caledonia and magnified the invidious ethnographic contrasts already noted between these populations. It was not suggested in evolutionary terms that the people of New Caledonia were more primitive than the inhabitants of the central Pacific, but unbeknownst to Cook, they were revealed to be cannibals. The "fact" of their cannibalism was attested to by an artifact, an "instrument which they call *nbouet*" that was used to cut up those killed in battle:

> One of them demonstrated its use on a man belonging to our ship, who lay down on his back at the other's request. He first represented a battle . . . he shewed us that they began by opening the belly of the vanquished with the *nbouet* . . . He shewed us that they then cut off the organs of generation, which fall to the lot of the victor . . . It is difficult to depict the ferocious avidity with which he expressed to us that the flesh of the unfortunate victim was devoured by them after they had broiled it on the coals (Labillardière 1800b, 2:224–5).

It is evident here and in other cases that these were *performances of cannibalism* that responded to the sailors' manifest preoccupation with the topic, and they intentionally and effectively produced shock (Cook 1955–74, 1:236–7, 2:818–9; Earle 1838, 205; see Obeyesekere 1992b). Although islanders at this stage had a very limited knowledge of European interests in and perceptions of Oceania and its inhabitants, and Europeans were at least equally ignorant of islanders and their perceptions of contact, one key trope of the European discourse of savagism had been disclosed to them, and since this was one that empowered savagery at the same time as it placed it outside European sociality, it's not surprising that the ferocity of the cannibal was so rapidly seized upon and inverted by savages themselves. A late revival of cannibalism in the Marquesas, decontextualized from early ritual contexts, can similarly be interpreted as a reactive display, but the balance of power was very different in the 1860s and 1870s; unlike the confident mockery of eighteenth-century islanders, this flaunting of savagery seems instead a gestural protest at a moment of despair in one of the most destructive of Pacific colonial experiences (Dening 1980, 287).[10]

The movement entailed in these performances typifies the *explication* that the notion of cultural invention conveys only inadequately. The Maori, among other islanders, may well have practiced anthropophagy prior to European contact and no doubt represented this in various ways; but they were not cannibals. The topos of cannibalism and the idea of the cannibal as a species of human being emerged from Columbus's encounter with the Caribs and cannot be extricated from European expansion and its attendant negatives of savagism (cf. Hulme 1986, 14–7).[11] Hence, something already present becomes explicit or is made explicit in new terms that alter its content, valorization, and ramifications. The process that needs to be looked at, then, entails articulation rather than invention. Being able to articulate something entails the use of language, but in colonial circumstances the notion of competence within a single language game is inappropriate; instead, a multiplicity of insecure contexts for cross-cultural speech was created. Commands of language were often partial and secondary, but the articulation of novel claims was both possible and necessary, and what was enunciated had at least limited effects within the home communities of both colonizers and colonized, as well as in the peculiar and transitory situation of interaction.

These situations of course became less transient; while the visits of mariners in the late eighteenth and early nineteenth centuries were usually brief (even if contact with deserters was more continuous), the establishment of mission stations, consulates, trading bases, and (in the cases of territories once annexed) colonial administrations resulted in a permanent intrusion. Most of these things happened in an uneven way over the period from the mid–nineteenth to the early twentieth century in most parts of the Pacific; the details of these histories need not be entered into here. What is of interest are the ramifications of the presence of external forces that sought to transform or at least modify indigenous religion, domesticity, exchange, and production, and (in the case of colonial administrations) to make out of the flux of indigenous history visible societies or polities that could be mapped and regulated.

To refer to the transformation that is often now most significant in indigenous historical imaginings, conversion to Christianity was frequently a drawn-out process, entailing a good deal of badgering on the part of missionaries and shifting perceptions amongst indigenous authority figures. What they had to think about repudiating was not indigenous religion, as an anthropologist might have construed it, but the particular array of practices and beliefs that the encounter had made constitutive of heathenism. (Needless to say, when Christianity finally was adopted, this usually took place because of a new congruence with indigenous strategies and imagined futures, rather than because the missionary agenda was accepted in any simple sense.) In the field of gender relations in particular, disjunctions between indigenous practice and what missionaries (or administrators) saw as natural, moral, or fitting produced flashpoints in which the capacity of the latter to intrude and impose was directly tested against the assertion of local autonomy. In Fiji, the widows or female servants of chiefs, and in Aneityum (in southern Vanuatu) all widows, were strangled on the deaths of their husbands; this, like *sati* in India and cognate practices elsewhere,[12] prompted peculiar horror in European minds, not least because the deed was frequently performed by female kin and because the women themselves often protested against intervention to save their lives (Wallis 1851, 67–9, 254; Spriggs 1981; Jolly 1991). Widow strangling capitalized (whether consciously or not) on what was not only horrifying but also nearly unintelligible for the missionaries: the willfulness of those they wanted to construe as victims of heathenism and idolatry. In Fiji there were numerous cases when missionaries and more particularly their wives attempted to prevent stranglings from taking place, and there was clearly a great deal more than this particular practice at issue. Shortly after the Methodists Hunt and Lyth arrived in Somosomo (north-eastern Fiji), in 1839, it transpired that the king's son Ra Mbithi[13] had been lost on a canoe voyage:

> The ill news caused terrible excitement in the town, and, according to custom, several women were at once set apart to be strangled. The mission-aries began their work by pleading for the lives of these wretched victims. The utmost they could effect was to get the execution delayed, until the schooner should have gone to search for the young chief . . . The vessel returned, but not with any more favourable news. Now a greater number of women were condemned, and again the missionaries pleaded hard that they might be spared; but the old king was angry with the strangers for presuming to interfere with the affairs of his people, and indignant at the thought of his favourite son dying without the customary honours . . . Sixteen women were forthwith strangled in honour of the young chief and his companions, and the bodies of the principal women were buried within a few yards of the door of the missionaries' house (Calvert 1884, 252–3).

When Fijians later adopted Christianity, widow strangling and a variety of other practices that had been emblematic of heathenism, as well as behavioral markers such as long hair, were abandoned. The *lotu Wesele,* or Methodist Church, which had all along been interpreted in indigenous terms (Sahlins 1985, 37–40), was received and rapidly ceased to be represented as something antithetical to Fijian custom: from an early point, the interwoven character of the ways of the land and of the church were manifest. Methodism was thus rapidly indigenized, and the distinction between paganism[14] and Christianity ceased to map the contest of the Fijian-missionary encounter or the rivalry between native Christians and heathens; it was historicized to mark the Fijian transition from the epoch of darkness to that of light. The contrast between Fijian and white culture in religious terms was thus superseded, but other dimensions of the colonial encounter continued to engender juxtaposed reifica-tions of indigenous and foreign ways. From the 1860s onward, questions of the extent to which Fijians engaged in plantation labor and cash cropping were hotly contested in administrative, settler, and indigenous circles, especially after ces-sion to the Crown in 1874, and the apparent threat of capitalist modernity to the traditional polity stimulated much elaboration of what indigenous society and customs consisted of.

This work of imagination was not an autonomous indigenous effort, but a process that involved both British colonial administrators and Fijians, or particularly the Fijian men, mostly of chiefly status, who were actively involved in the bureaucracy of indirect rule that was rapidly established in the 1870s. Like many British colonial administrations, especially those where government was seen to proceed through some form of indirect rule or otherwise delicate social management, the state in Fiji voraciously sought ethnographic, geographic, and demographic knowledge, and the mass of information was rigorously set out, minuted, and filed. If Bali was a theater state, the Crown Colony of Fiji was an archive state, or rather one in which order was theatrically evoked through rituals of itemization and hierarchical transmission. The work of documentation and regulation proceeded in many specific domains: as Peter France (1969) has described, native social organization and corporate landholding were codified, with considerable difficulty and with much violence to local variation; as I have outlined elsewhere (1990c), inquiries into health and sanitation amongst Fijians permitted an elaborate mapping of customs thought to be associated with a lack of stamina and high mortality. Though the connections made between general well-being and particular practices, such as aspects of the division of labor and offerings to chiefs, were extraordinarily nebulous, these efforts produced an image of a communal social order in which responsibilities to kin and to the chiefly hierarchy stifled individual effort. There was much debate within the administration about the desirability of imposing changes that would break up communal village society in the interest of promoting native commerce and industry, but the direction of policy was in favor of the conservation of tradition.

Though the images of Fijian society produced through the government's surveys and inquiries might be regarded merely as mystifications, the reformulated conceptions of custom rapidly came to be shared by many Fijians, and it would be wrong to understate their contribution to the process of objectification in the first place. As Bernard Cohn has stressed:

> Central to the process of objectification have been the hundreds of situations that Indians over the past two hundred years have experienced in which rights to property, their social relations, their rituals, were called into question or had to be explained . . . [in particular] the census . . . touched practically everyone in India. It asked questions about major aspects of Indian life, family, religion, language, literacy, caste, occupation, marriage, even of disease and infirmities. Through the asking of questions and the compiling of information in categories which the British rulers could utilize for governing, it provided an arena for Indians to ask questions about themselves (1987, 230).

Similarly, the Fijian process is best understood not as crude fabrication or invention (pace Clammer 1973), but as an imaginative process in which Fijians creatively refashioned the relationships that they had the opportunity to articulate. But while wholly negative views of this moment of collaborative objectification need to be avoided, it must also be recalled that the situation of dialogue was constituted in a field of power relationships in which certain Fijians were far more capable of responding to questions than others; in general, chiefs and senior men were authorized speakers while younger men and traditional priests were not. It is thus no surprise that customs of rank and chiefly respect were codified, as were "rules" restricting the movement of women, while a variety of cult activities, usually practiced by younger people and particularly warriors, were stigmatized and delegitimized (Kaplan 1989). In general, the proximity of particular groups to colonial authorities and the particular legitimacy the administration bestowed on chiefs made it possible for relationships that had previously been fluid or reciprocal to be transformed into fixed and hierarchical ones in reinvented Fijian custom. Objectification, though not a matter of mystification or political manipulation, is irreducibly political.

From the late nineteenth century onward, there was extensive debate in Fijian forums such as chiefly and provincial councils, as well as in British administrative circles, about the degree and nature of Fijian involvement in commerce and the ways in which indigenous customs were thought to inhibit such involvement. Ironically, the polarized notions of distinct paths of custom and commerce became highly energized rhetorically, but they often glossed over actual interpenetration and some compatibility between the neotraditional kinship economy and certain forms of cash cropping. The early phase of the reification of the communal order is apparent from the objectification of the practice of *kerekere*, a "custom" that figures extensively in literature on economic development in rural Fiji and more generally in anthropological studies.[15] The former tended to represent *kerekere* as a form of begging among kin that depleted any wealth accumulated by more enterprising individuals; the latter, which is exemplified by Sahlins's *Moala*, emphasized that *kerekere* was not like begging at all, but amounted to a mechanism permitting the soliciting of goods, services, resources, use rights, and so on. More significantly, it was contextualized as "the prevailing form of economic transaction among kinsmen as individuals"; *kerekere* expressed an "essential kinship ethic," and it worked at once to produce material equality, donors gaining in prestige what they lost in goods or labor (Sahlins 1962, 203).

These accounts, like the wider characterization of Fijian society as a kinship order exemplified by reciprocity, redistribution, and such practices as *kerekere* are in no sense untrue to Fijian practice. What was passed over, however, was the changing significance of *kerekere* in Fijian rhetoric. Localized give-and-take no doubt always proceeded, but *kerekere* assumed quite a new significance during the investigations into the Fijian customary order that were conducted over the first decades of colonial rule. The commissioners investigating the decline of the native population charged themselves with specifying exactly what Fijian society consisted of, and followed others in emphasizing the "system" of chiefly requisitions (*lala*) and *kerekere:*

> After *lala*—or perhaps before it—*kerekere* (the mutual appropriation of property) is the principal feature of the communal system (Government of Fiji 1896, 45).

What was one practice among many thus came to be identified as a central and emblematic institution within a wider "communal" order. In this influential report and in many subsequent regulations and provincial council resolutions the suppression or abolition of *kerekere* was recommended. Subsequently, the inhibiting force of this custom upon enterprise was reiterated not only in administrative and scholarly reports, but even in the summary ethnographies that preface tourist guides. In this case again, what was previously present came to be articulated and represented as a badge of Fijian tradition. Later in the twentieth century, the emphasis in what is constitutive of "the Fijian way" seems to shift from *kerekere* to large-scale customary ceremonies (*solevu*), particularly those conducted at the time of betrothal and marriage and at various other life-crisis events. Today, in the parts of rural Fiji marked by strong and continuing commitment to "the way of the land," these require substantial amounts of garden produce, cattle, cash, and labor. These are the occasions when dedication to Fijian custom is most conspicuously displayed, but in local accounts, the manner of the land is also manifested in more quotidian ways: by hospitality, frequent reciprocity among kin and coresidents, and an array of respect usages regulating movement within houses, especially in relation to persons who are more senior in terms of age, rank, or gender (for example, it is quite wrong to stand up and reach over a more senior person for a hanging object or to light a lamp without seeking permission and respectfully clapping subsequently). Male kava drinking, which can take up an enormous amount of time, is a ritualized activity that embodies the commitment to sociality and the observance of respect.

It is not necessary to go into great detail about this idealized but nevertheless enacted version of Fijian customary life (but see also chapters 7 and 9 here, and Thomas 1991, 189–200; Toren 1984, 1989). Suffice to say that the social attributes are the inverse of those attributed to Fiji-Indians and that in this instance, the oppositional character of cultural objectification alluded to above enters into interethnic rivalry in a conspicuous manner. Of greater interest here is the instability that cultural explication makes possible, which arises from a transformation of the equation between communalism and what would now be called underdevelopment; though rural Fijians constantly affirm the moral superiority of the Fijian way over the customs of Indians and those of white foreigners, they also lament that Fijians are "poor," and in intra-Fijian debate, this negative side of the equation often receives the greater emphasis.

The Inversion of Tradition

From the 1870s onward, the local representation of the Fijian way privileged communalism, a hierarchical social order entailing respect and chieftainship, and a ceremonial life manifested particularly in kava drinking. Given that this was upheld as virtuous, yet also seen as a disabling and constraining customary system that inhibited social advancement and commercial success, the fact of articulation always permitted a rejection of what was customary in favor of its antithesis: this is what can be described as the negation of tradition. It must be recalled that, in practice, the modified forms of subsistence and exchange-oriented production, and farming for taxes or cash were not, in fact, necessarily utterly incompatible or mutually corrosive; but they tended to be represented as such, and when Fijians did not become wealthy, it is unsurprising that the dichotomized structure of neotraditional culture consistently generated ambivalence with respect to tradition, and occasional outright rejection.

Hence there was a continuum between indigenously organized agricultural cooperatives and movements that the administration regarded as millennial and seditious. The most famous was Apolosi R. Nawai's Viti Kabani (Fiji Company) which sought in the First World War period to displace white middlemen and more effectively market native produce; it also, however, had a distinctly anti-chiefly and anti-British agenda (Macnaught 1979). In opposition to the traditionalist affirmation of custom, movements of this kind can be seen to embody an indigenous modernism that repudiated the custom-bound past and various forms of obligation and constraint that epitomized it. One of the clearest instances of this is the Bula Tale Movement of the early 1960s, discussed in chapter 2, that involved a sort of secession from Fijian custom on the part of four villages on the western island of Viti Levu. To reiterate, the movement's program of reform inverted very precisely all of the key symbols of Fijian tradition. Marriages were not arranged and were not to be large communal events structured around kava presentations and ceremonial exchange: "When a couple wished to marry it is their doing, and only their parents should be there." Similarly, major mortuary ceremonies were abandoned, and the use of whales' teeth in honorific presentations and transactions was rejected. Kava drinking in general was abolished, as were rank and precedence in eating: "When I eat, my wife and children must also eat." Equality, not hierarchy, was the rule, according to an article in the *Fiji Times*, 12 August 1961 (see appendix).[16] In addition, Western medicine was embraced; while twenty-seven years later in a nearby area I found the commitment to the use of traditional remedies to be almost dogmatic, childbirth only took place in hospitals if complications were anticipated.

While the Bula Tale is perhaps unusual in its categorical rejection of the Fijian way, more selective negations of tradition are apparent in many contexts. Certain breakaway churches and cooperative movements either permitted restricted kava drinking in certain formal contexts or altered the practice so that everyone drank at once, rather than in rank order (Spate 1960, 175). Given the centrality of this ritual in both nineteenth-century polities and the neotraditional chiefly regime of the colonial period, these apparently slight modifications had resounding implications. District officers' reports from early this century refer often to abstention from kava drinking, and this may register an earlier form of this ambivalence with respect to tradition.

Given that the Methodist Church was very closely identified with the traditional hierarchy, it is not surprising that some of this dissent was also expressed in changing religious affiliation, which throughout the South Pacific has provided a major context for political conflict throughout the Christian period. As the material discussed in chapter 2 indicated, Adventism seems "preadapted" for an oppositional role by the doctrinal emphasis upon health, which leads to an equation between kava and the alcoholic beverages prohibited in American and Australian branches of the church; hence Fijian adherents repudiated not only the traditional ritual drink and the enacted deference to hierarchy, but also pork, which was an important component of customary feasts. Because Adventists also celebrate the Sabbath on Saturdays, there is a conspicuous behavioral cleavage between their social routines and those of Methodists and Catholics; this was (and still is) extremely divisive in small villages that tend to be rigorously Sabbatarian. Hence, defection to Adventism provided a powerful way for disaffected factions within particular villages to express their rejection of the rest of the community.[17]

Elsewhere in the Pacific, Adventism similarly tends to be a "modernist" church in contrast to other congregations such as Catholics, Lutherans, Anglicans, and so on. A survey revealed that Adventists in the western Solomons were far more positive about extractive development in their province, and tourism, than near neighbors affiliated with other churches (Sonia Juvik pers. comm.). Within Fiji, new fundamentalist churches that are attracting many urban Fijians often have a negative or qualified attitude to "the way of the land."[18] In the case of the Assemblies of God, this is indicated in dress by the fact that trousers are preferred to the Fijian *sulu*, a sarong-like garment, introduced by the missionaries, that has become the standard local male garment and (being marked as Fijian rather than foreign) the appropriate wear for ceremonial contexts, despite its bright color and apparently casual appearance. In rural areas, Assemblies adherents often live outside villages (the paradigmatic locations of customary sociality) and engage in individualized cash cropping, avoiding the communal economy. There is thus some coincidence between the specific form of individualism that these denominations champion in Western countries and what could be seen as a historically necessary reaction to the codification of indigenous society primarily in collective and communal terms.

This cultural dynamic is not peculiar to Fiji. A wide-ranging review of phases of traditionalism and modernism in the diverse histories of Oceanic societies would obviously require much more space than is available here, but I will refer to one case that manifests a similar oppositional dialectic of cultural objectification and another that illustrates some further aspects of these dynamics. The Paliau Movement in Manus (in the Admiralty Islands, Papua New Guinea), is a well-documented but otherwise not atypical Melanesian politico-religious movement of the kind that has often been misleadingly reduced to a "cargo cult." While preoccupations with European wealth and manufactured articles were often conspicuous in certain phases of these movements, they also had political agendas and pragmatic projects of social reform that have been distorted and diminished by such labeling (Keesing 1978; Kaplan 1990b, 1995). In a recent analysis, Ton Otto shows that the objectification of tradition was a central element: "The radical changes pursued by Paliau and his followers were structured according to a logic of antithetical transformation thereby creating an opposition to the colonial culture as well as to their own tradition" (1992a, 427). Otto notes that the contract labor experience gave men a knowledge of other indigenous cultures and white society that permitted cultural dichotomization of the kind referred to earlier. Moreover, the health, wealth, and power of whites, as opposed to natives, led to negative perceptions of local culture, which was totalized as something received from the ancestors and presumed somehow to be responsible for native poverty and backwardness: "Thus, indigenous cultures were generalized, related to the past, and critically assessed in one conceptual move" (Otto 1992a, 430). Given the importance of the external vantage point for social critique, it is significant that the leader of the movement, Paliau (born ca. 1910–1992?), worked as a contract laborer and then as a native constable before and during the Second World War. As in other parts of the Pacific, the experience of the war catalyzed much prior discontent with colonial dominance (see

White and Lindstrom 1989): islanders (whether in actual theaters of battle or in contact with bases and other support facilities) were exposed to Western wealth and strength on a scale far greater than anything they had previously seen; they had extensive dealings with American soldiers, who seemed generous and did not observe the colonial etiquette and status differentiation characteristic of relations between the British or Australians and Papua New Guineans; and the presence of black Americans, which was interpreted in various ways by is-landers during the war, suggested that black people were not intrinsically dis-sociated from wealth or the various powerful machines introduced during the war effort.

The broader encounter with Europeans and Americans made it clear that colonial dominance, as experienced up until then, was not the inevitable or necessary shape of relationships between islanders and developed societies; in many regions the ramifications included both secular and millennial reform movements. Paliau's was better organized and more successful than many oth-ers, but the details of its history are not relevant here. Otto's analysis of the reform program instituted by Paliau after his postwar return to Manus stresses that the message embodied in the "Long story of God," a historical charter-myth drawing both on indigenous forms and biblical narrative, was structured by negations applied to "the colonial system from the native point of view. The negations of Paliau's political program are threefold: it is anti-tradition, anti-mission, and anti-government." Otto notes, however, that

> there is a distinct disparity between the negation of tradition and the other two negations. The "way of the native" was valued as inherently negative. The only way to attain equal footing with the white man was to abolish tradition completely. This meant breaking the chains of the past but also implied the end of the leadership of the older generation. Paliau's quest for emancipation was not just from the white people but also from indigenous leaders, whose dominance was based on the institutions of the past . . . The negations of government and mission are of a different order. Unlike tradition these institutions were not seen as inherently bad. What was wrong with them was their use by white people who, led by their selfish-ness, maintained an unjust inequality . . . Paliau's negation concerned the white man's corruption of both mission and government aimed at deceiv-ing the natives and depriving them of the real benefits of these innovations (1992a, 444).

The Paliau Movement thus resembles some Fijian movements and no doubt others in the sense that tradition was blamed for the poverty and backwardness of indigenous people. Progress necessitated not only concrete economic projects, such as the pooling of resources and involvement in cash cropping, but also new forms of social organization and leadership that displaced traditional institutions; but more generally, in each case, institutions that were emblematic of the traditional order, such as bridewealth payments and major feasts, were rejected. It is evident that these shifts and revaluations amount to something other than a gradual process of acculturation: instead, they attest to a willful strategy, an exploitation of novel cultural and political possibilities.

The operation of inversion that proceeds here has a counterpart in the history of European dichotomized counterconcepts. In his exploration of the semantics of the Hellene/barbarian distinction, Koselleck noted that the standard antithesis of civility and crudity that these terms carried could be reversed,

> forming an underlying and continually reemerging tradition which was cultivated in particular by the Cynics. "Barbarian" here served as a positive contrast to a cultivated existence and its consequences. Features charged with utopianism were twined around these simple, genuine beings who were close to nature and removed from civilization: the antithesis was turned on its side, its terms were changed, and it was put back into use. The characteristic asymmetry was thus maintained within the same experiential space, except that the counterconcept now performed the function of critique and self-criticism (1985, 170–1).

In general, primitivism is a negation of the civility or modernity on the part of those who are "civilized" or "modern." In tribal societies a similar dialectic can proceed whereby modernism amounts to a negation of traditionalism on the part of those inhabiting "traditional" societies. In custom and *kastom* movements, the indigenous "we"—figured through communalism, kinship, rootedness to place, and the like—is affirmed, and their construction of the ways of whites may characterize foreigners primarily through their transience and their lack of solidarity, mutual care, reciprocity, respect, and so on. This asymmetrical representation resembles that of the non-Cynical Greek in the sense that the other is represented primarily as a lack (of the civility of the *polis*); it is this affirmation that the literature on custom and identity has generally focused upon. But indigenous constructions can also negate the "we" and valorize the other, in the fashion of the Cynic, though obviously for quite different reasons. In the present, traditionalism in peripheral societies corresponds to Western modernism in the sense that in each case the values specific to the place are affirmed; "we" are on a higher plane than "them" in terms of technological refinement and sophistication from the point of view of the West, and in terms of morality, social ethics, and tradition from the perspective of the periphery. In a formal sense, there is also a correspondence between Western primitivism and indigenous modernisms. Endogenous values are rejected in favor of what is taken to be the condition of the other: a natural, located life, from the perspective of the jaded urban dweller, and modernity, individualism, and wealth, from the perspective of the tribal person or peasant. Cultural critique, enabled by the example of the other, proceeds through a kind of negative self-fashioning, and in each case permits the enunciation of a project of reform.[19]

Of course, there is no unitary field of discourse within which all of these identities are constructed. Traditionalism in peripheral societies does not affirm the same thing that Western primitivism has presumed to be the essence of those cultures. Nor does it merely assert the value of what oppressive colonizing discourses denigrated. The process of mutual recognition has always been much more partial and uneven, and colonized populations are not so unimaginative or unoriginal as to draw only upon colonizers' constructions of their own sociality. Rather, as in the case of Fiji, there was a complex process whereby institutions that were already present were revalued and reinterpreted in a manner that depended upon the efforts of both whites and Fijians. In contexts where local culture has resisted white intrusion most effectively, and where indigenous dynamism retains its own relative autonomy, there will clearly be much greater continuity and flexibility in what is represented as traditional; and the importance of oppositional objectification may be limited to certain contexts of cultural and political rhetoric.[20] Where contact has been more destructive, as has often been the case for indigenous minorities within settler-colonial nation-states (Australia, New Zealand, New Caledonia, and Hawaii in the Pacific), resistant discourse may be structured by the discourse of the dominant to a much greater extent.

Conclusion: A Succession of Explications

Perhaps because the idea of inquiry privileges the disclosure of things that are not already visible, anthropology has long been oriented toward implicit or tacit meanings, toward deep structures that are only exposed through interpretative work and virtuosity. Explicit meaning, as something already on the surface, was uninteresting analytically. A correlate of the interest in practice that became significant in the late 1970s and 1980s was recognition of the fact that structuralist interpretations, among others, tended to treat actors as dupes who merely passively reproduced or enunciated cultural codes. As one critic in another discipline put it, "Barthes's failure, in *Système de la Mode*, to consult either fashion designers or fashion wearers, as a check to his analysis, vitiates and discredits all the generalizations he proposes . . . though the bracketing out of competence as a criterion can be taken as symptomatic of the structuralist strategy" (Bryson 1983, 72). In anthropology, as well as in other forms of cultural inquiry and history, it indeed seems that "the screening out of practical and operational determination within cultural life" is the reverse of what analysis should be effecting (73).

Though "practice" has since become a trendy word, it is not clear that the undoing of totalizing models of implicit cultures has proceeded as far as it might. The processes of oppositional reification and inversion discussed here suggest a different way of talking about particular cultural expressions and their meaning. A fact such as tattooing, reciprocity, or a perception of sexual "licence" may certainly still be explained or interpreted in a variety of ways, but from the perspective of practice, positional meanings might be displaced by an emphasis on the process of explication and reinvention. Hence, an allusion to a point of sexual ethics doesn't seem meaningful because there is an ethical grammar but because it is emblematic of some objectified tradition that is differentiated—or rather, that some people are actively differentiating from others and affirming or negating.

We take it for granted that innovation in modern art, literature, and music often proceeds through the rejection of previous styles and traditions and often draws on foreign and exotic models in fashioning new projects for the present and the future. But a theorist of ethnicity can state as an axiom that "the preservation and the continuity of tradition is enjoined on its carriers" (Nash 1989, 14). Tradition is not just a burden that must be carried, but also a thing that can be acted upon or deployed to diverse ends. If we transpose our common sense about change in art to other peoples' reifications of custom, sociality, and the past, it is evident that tradition can be an objectification of the heritage one has but wants to be rid of; as a resource, it is as necessary to progressivist projects of nonconformity as it is to those of cultural affirmation and preservation that, naturally enough, have attracted more anthropological attention and sympathy thus far.

Of course, the domains of self-conscious cultural production in Europe and America have more often than not privileged innovation, and it would perhaps be ethnocentric to regard the production of difference from a received array as a compulsion present in particular other cultures or cultures in general. Given, however, that there are structural oppositions between elders and youth in many societies and generational struggles about cultural value and authority, it becomes increasingly clear that the objectification of old ways, the inversion of tradition, may be almost a ubiquitous feature of ordinary change, and one that establishes how larger transformations arise from individual conflicts and individual biographies. If it would indeed be unjustifiable to universalize any will to change, an interest in the explication of culture seems called for by the circumstances of colonial and postcolonial histories: the pervasive facts of cultural contact make reform and reformulation a persistently available and immediate strategy for dealing both with what is inadequate in intersocial relations and what seems unsatisfactory or backward in one's own situation. Using the other as a foil for internal reflection and revolution has never been exclusively a Western privilege—and in that sense the naturalization of invention emphasized in recent scholarship might preclude some ethnocentric claims about the unique capacities of Western civilization. It would be wrong, though, to see objectification as merely something cultures have always done to each other in the course of inventing and refashioning themselves. The truisms would disguise the continuing ramifications of colonial asymmetries in which many of the contradictions and contradictory possibilities of nationalist, modernist, and minority discourses may be traced to the fact that they invert, rather than transcend, the identities and narratives created by colonialists and nation-states. They also, however, at once reproduce and negate traditionalist narratives, which means that "postcolonial" histories are marked by local precolonial or noncolonial relations, as well as those emanating from Europe.

9

Contrasts:
Marriage and Identity
in Western Fiji

You see how people get married here, how much work it involves. The mats, the drums, the animals, it's murder! If it's a woman, that's all right, you just go and eat. But if you've got a young man, you have to start raising cattle. With you foreigners, it's easy. You have a small party and that's it. It's better that way, here it is just too much.—Noikoro woman, aged about 45

You know how the Indians get married, Niko? The man goes to the woman's father and says, "Here's a thousand dollars. How about it?" He says, "That's not much." Then when the man offers fifteen hundred, he says "Ummm." Then when the man offers two thousand, he says, "All right." Different customs, say!—Noikoro man, aged about 40

When I began fieldwork in western Fiji in mid-1988, there were two matters that concerned me particularly: exchange and identity. The first, of course, had long been a hallmark of Melanesian anthropology; with respect to the second, which had become topical more recently, my interest arose from the marginality of western Viti Levu in the colonial and postcolonial Fijian nation, a condition that had often been alluded to in scholarly discussions of issues such as ethnicity and uneven development. If western Fijians had a strong consciousness of the differences between themselves and the people of the east whose chiefs had long dominated the bureaucracy and the state, how did they understand their customs and their history?

My assumptions about both of these issues were confounded. While, in contrast to earlier formalist interpretations, recent studies of prestations based on Melanesian cases had emphasized the cultural complexity of noncommodity transactions and their intransigence in the face of principles derived from Western political economy, I discovered that Noikoro people described the central feature of large-scale marriage presentations as "the price of the bride," using the same word that referred to the price of tinned fish, cash crops, or radios. They thus seemed to assert precisely what many anthropologists denied through analysis: an identity between a ceremonial gift and the transactions of the market. Even if the informants' statements were not taken at face value, this kind of claim could only distract me from the Melanesianists' interest in mapping exotic prestation forms that had been magically isolated from the world economy. Secondly, I found that antipathy toward eastern chiefly dominance had been exaggerated by writers themselves unsympathetic to the elite and had less significant ramifications for local identities and perceptions of the past than I had anticipated; although a degree of political disaffection was indeed widespread, localized allegiances and more generalized Fijian ethnicity both had the effect of muting any western Fijian identity defined primarily in the opposition to eastern Fiji and the chiefly establishment.

I had also, in prospect, taken these topics of exchange and identity to be essentially separate; in retrospect, and to the contrary, it seemed that western Fijian perceptions of marriage and reciprocity could not be understood without reference to identity; conversely, though it was not at all surprising that people engaged in cash cropping should make analogies between commodity and non-commodity transactions, the rhetoric around exchange provided an illuminating perspective upon the singular antinomies of "the way of the land" in rural Fiji. If my initial questions were discrete and inappropriate, this essay attempts to rationalize their convergence.

Noikoro

Noikoro people live in the upper part of the Sigatoka Valley, at the top end of a dusty eighty kilometer road that leads to the coastal market town named after the river and the valley. The village of Korolevu is occupied by about three hundred people; there are nine other Noikoro villages, mostly smaller and mostly some distance from the road. The people practice various forms of horticulture, collecting, fishing, and cash cropping. Peanuts and watermelons, and particularly corn and kava, are grown for sale. The latter is also drunk in an everyday but nevertheless ritualized manner by the men and to a limited extent by the women of the village. Although visitors remark upon the traditional character of the place—half the houses are thatched *bure* or *were vaviji*[1]—Noikoro people have interacted directly with non-Fijian outsiders, mostly notably British colonial officials, for more than a century; in fact, virtually all the present village sites postdate pacification in 1876. Christianity was adopted and to some extent imposed at about the same time, but has long since been integrated into the "way of the land": church and *vanua* are said to be interwoven like the strips of pandanus in a mat. Korolevu is similar to many other more isolated Fijian villages, except perhaps in the sense that religious affiliation is unusually diverse: just half the families belong to what is virtually the state denomination, Methodism, the others being Seventh-day Adventists, Catholics, members of the Assemblies of God, and Jehovah's Witnesses. Many other villages are closer to towns and to wage work and are supplied with electricity and frequent transport. Noikoro is no less connected with the cash economy, but for its people, the "path of money" seems more difficult.

Kinship tangibly dominates everyday life: immediate patrilineal groups are of supreme importance in the structuring of everyday associations in work, meals, and childcare. Those belonging to the households of close classificatory brothers are constantly gardening with each other, sharing a bowl of kava, or feeding each others' kids. Their houses are situated within an area of the village, and when feasts, ceremonial exchanges, and such things as church collections occur, they are the groups that jointly contribute. The same is true at a different level of the more inclusive clans known after the old mens' spirit houses as *beto*. Membership of these groups is usually spread across several villages, between which there is a great deal of mobility—people travel back and forth to help plant, to build a house, to contribute a presentation, or to drink kava—the last being a necessary rather than a contingent feature of visiting, unless one observes the *tabu* that define Adventist or Assemblies adherence.

Marriage

Noikoro people distinguish between marriages proceeding in the proper way, according to the custom of the land, and those that amount to elopement (*vitubataki*), which is identified with foreigners' customs. In a proper marriage, the choice of spouse and the timing of a complex sequence of prestations are decided communally, while elopement is registered with surprise, a spontaneous act on the part of the couple. The distinction is more ideologically significant than practically evident, since "elopement" is sometimes tacitly agreed to by the woman's kin, and should always eventually be followed by a compressed single-event version of the prestations that constitute a formal marriage.

Since my discussion here turns upon the ways in which marriage ceremonies are discussed, rather than on the structure or cultural logic of the prestations, I will only provide a cursory account of the sequence of ritualized transactions and attendant activities.[2] The man and the woman would always be cross-cousins or could be considered as such. A proposal would be initiated informally, sometimes by a gift of cash from the man directly to the woman; the husband's side would make an initial offering of *tabua* (whales' teeth), which would prompt some formal deliberation among the prospective wife's kin. Because of the difficulty of refusing whales' teeth, which are the "heaviest," or most respected and chiefly, of exchange valuables (Hooper 1982), and because informal agreement would usually have already been secured, acceptance and betrothal would normally follow. The actual actors in these transactions are generally not the man and the woman's father, but senior classificatory relatives, such as the father's elder brothers. This reflects the way in which, all along, the transactions are between two clans[3] rather than the two immediate families.

The whales' teeth may then "rest" for some time, as the male side makes preparations, since it is crucial that they have a sufficient number of cattle,[4] as well as a few pigs and various other resources, to provide for two substantial ceremonies and feasts that may be well attended. Although contributions come from several quarters, the animals must mainly be provided by the man's own extended family, as they are expensive items and other clan members have their own needs. One man stressed that "the animals are difficult. If you haven't got them, you don't get married." Though the notion that preparation for marriage is an expensive, taxing, and laborious business can hardly be said to be specific to Fiji, it was a particularly conspicuous theme in discussions of the matter.

There are in fact three further ceremonies, but the first, the *vavanua,* is hosted by the wife's people; if they live some distance away, this requires the hire of a couple of trucks and a stay of two or three days. At the *vavanua* the male side presents perhaps twenty whales' teeth, some locally woven pandanus mats, some drums of kerosene, and some purchased fabric. The bought articles are all subsumed to the category of *iyau ni vanua,* valuables of the land for exchange, and formerly consisted of articles such as pots and barkcloth that particular districts produced (cf. Thomas 1991, chap. 2). There is often also a presentation of cash, generally assembled from contributions of a few dollars each from young unmarried men and women. An older man explained that this event confirmed the betrothal: "It is the same as when you foreigners give a ring: the woman cannot then desire anyone else."

The next stage is the *dresivola,* which is constructed around the legal requirement that a couple fill in a form stating their intention to marry at least three weeks before the wedding. The wife's people visit the husband's village in large numbers, bringing only a few whales' teeth to express their respect, while notionally each married man on the husband's side will contribute one whale's tooth and two drums of kerosene, and each woman about four mats. These are never presented by individuals, but rather pooled together in several stages and then presented to the woman's side in a solemn ceremony in which the whales' teeth that encompass the whole offering pass between senior men who make speeches thanking God, referring to the history of relations between the groups, deprecating their own offerings, and honoring the other side (figs. 55–59).

Transactions of this type occur also at the actual wedding, which should follow two or three months later. For several weeks before this, the generally relaxed pace of village life is entirely transformed as preparations are made. Temporary structures are erected for sleeping and eating (though there is much more of the latter than the former), and trips are made up to the mountain plantations to prepare the very considerable volume of kava that will be drunk and also be sold to cover the costs of other supplies. Women often need to stay up all night to finish mats; other valuables such as cooking pots and barkcloth may also be produced, depending on the groups involved. As the ceremony, the *solevu*, approaches, the village will begin to fill up with visitors who come to assist, but who also impose an additional burden, as they need to be fed and accommodated.

Activities intensify once the wife's people arrive. Large numbers of people stay up all night drinking kava, dancing, and playing guitar music; older transvestite female clowns parody the strutting and fighting of men (cf. for other parts of Oceania, Huntsman and Hooper 1975, 415; Hereniko 1995); some pay relatively little attention to the formal ceremonies, which are not always staged in precisely the same manner. In one instance the wedding took place the morning after the party arrived; in the afternoon there was the *tevutevu* (unfolding), which involves provisioning the couple's house with a very considerable number of mats, pillows, beautiful locally made pillowcases, purchased mosquito nets, and kitchen articles, furniture, and so on. Many of the more expensive items came from the wife's side. Later on the same day, the main presentation from the husband's group (into which I had been adopted) took place. This consisted of three cattle (presented slaughtered), over a hundred drums of kerosene, about forty whales' teeth, over a hundred mats, and about thirty glazed cooking pots from the nearby village of Nakoro. It was this that—as several young and old men pointed out to me—constituted *na isau ni yalewa*, the price of the woman. It was also explained to me in other contexts that "we (or they) buy the woman."[5] It was so easy to nod in acknowledgment as this was explained to me, as if we were talking about something straightforward like the cash that was received for kava in the market. But a statement as simple as that would not need to have been repeated so often.

Why Talk about Buying?

If I had heard people equate the prestation with the purchase of the woman only in conversation directed at me, I would have supposed that the comparison was a "translation" into the idiom of money for my own benefit, rather than a notion that had any broader salience in indigenous discourse. The sense that its significance might be partial or perspectival was reinforced by the fact that this construction appeared to be only a male view. Women never equated the presentation with a price, either in ordinary conversation or in the casual interviews I participated in. In fact, in the earlier stages of my fieldwork they refrained from volunteering accounts of the ceremonies at all, leaving me with the sense that they might well disagree with the male view but would not express an alternate perspective. Subsequently, however, I did have extended conversations about the histories of particular marriages and about the logic of the ceremony. Women tended to refer to the quantity of valuables and say something like, "In Fiji, a woman is a sacred thing!"[6] or "The woman stays; the valuables go back with her people." To a large extent, these propositions and those of men are in fact complementary; the value of the woman is the cause of the wealth, which is substituted for her. Men do not explicitly acknowledge the supreme worth of women, which is displaced onto whales' teeth, and it is not surprising that women do not employ an idiom that suggests that they are like things that change hands in the market.

A greater discrepancy between the ideas of men and women is apparent in the social and practical consequences of exchange. Once the ceremony has been concluded, men are apt to say simply but emphatically, "For them, it is finished," or "For us, it is finished," depending on whether they are in the wife-taking or wife-receiving group. These terse observations imply that the woman will work and stay no more with her natal group; now "everything to do with her" is in the hands of her husband's people. These rhetorical propositions perhaps relate more directly to the efficacy of prestations just concluded than future arrangements, but the wife is in fact usually incorporated in an un-qualified way. One indicator of this is the fact that if there is a difference in religious affiliation—which is by no means uncommon—then the wife must change. If the husband is an Adventist, this entails a dramatic shift of behavior: one day the woman can eat pork, shellfish, and eels and smoke or drink kava; subsequently, these are all proscribed.[7]

It is manifestly also the case that virtually the whole of the woman's productive effort becomes oriented to her place of marriage, both in everyday gardening and in the production of valuables. Women only begin to weave mats after marriage, so they never produce *iyau*—exchange wealth—for their natal group. This fact is, of course, crucial to the deeper logic of the circulation of value and persons in this kind of regionally extensive restricted exchange system (see Thomas 1991, chap. 2), but here I am more concerned with perceptions and their historical context than the level of more fundamental but implicit relationships. The

55–59. Intraclan prestations of mats, cattle, and other goods in the lead-up to a major marriage. Noikoro District, central Fiji, 1988.

generality that women only work for their clan of marriage requires some quali-fication. Where women have married into groups a considerable distance from their place of birth, this is true nearly absolutely, but in cases of intravillage or intradistrict marriage, women—and especially those who are older and tougher-minded—are not infrequently seen in their brothers' houses, helping out with one of the long and tedious tasks associated with the cultivation of cash crops, or simply sustaining the relationship through cooking, eating, and talking.

Another sense in which the primarily male notion that women are definitively transferred to their husband's village is contested emerges in women's percep-tion of where they belong. On several occasions I asked women I had not previously met where they were from ("where is your village?" being a standard item of such smalltalk) and received the slightly aggrieved or indignant re-sponse "Here! Korolevu!" even though they had in some cases been living elsewhere for many years.

To a considerable extent, then, the claim of Noikoro men that the right to expect a woman to contribute fully is "purchased" is substantiated in an erasure of her natal group's claims upon her in particular. Although an examination of casual giving and sharing would qualify this statement, in the ceremonial con-texts that are uppermost in Fijians' perceptions, it would be unthinkable for a woman to work in some way for her own people, rather than her group of marriage. But from an anthropologist's perspective the notion that the move-ment of the woman amounts to an act of buying is most unsatisfactory when one considers the wider set of relationships a particular marriage sets off and reproduces. The father, for example, must make a feast (the *sebua*) for his wife's people when the first child is born; at a later stage *iyau* will be taken when the children are formally presented to the mother's group. In other words, the burden of relationships that a woman would otherwise sustain with her own group are transferred to the next generation, when her sons and daughters are *vasu* to their mother's brother (the *koko*).[8] The position of the "sacred" sister's son is well known in Fijian and Tongan ethnography, but in Noikoro, it lacks the feature that captivated the imagination of Hocart and the missionary ethnogra-phers (Hocart 1923; Williams 1858)—the *vasu* (who can be either male or fe-male) is not entitled to appropriate property from the mother's natal house or group. Instead, there are obligations, particularly to sustain a generalized social link: visiting for pleasure, drinking plenty of kava if male, helping out with whatever work needs to be done, and making specific contributions to fundrais-ing activities such as building new churches. The seriousness of the bond is visible in mortuary feasts, when a sequence of *tabua* and other valuables pass from the clan of the dead person to the people to whom he or she was *vasu*.

There is thus a discrepancy between a very complex pattern of expectations and reciprocities set in train by a marriage and the claim that the crucial feature of the event is a transaction that closes off expectations and "finishes things," so far as one group is concerned. The insistence upon this rhetorical claim, and upon the definitive notion of purchase itself, might be readily explicated if these statements were only made by the wife-taking side, since that group would obviously seek to emphasize the extent to which their affines' claims over the woman were at an end, but this is not the case.

The paradox turns upon the notion of price, which might be dismissed as a foreign accretion essentially alien to Noikoro understandings; but that would, in the first place, presume an identity between the Fijian and some standard Western conceptions of what price is. In this context an extremely simple observation, made very frequently during *solevu*, is crucial: the work of a big marriage or any other ceremony is very difficult. In observations and asides in the midst of cutting firewood, butchering cattle, making mats, and getting together the drums of kerosene that are to be presented, the amount of work is often referred to. Such remarks may be made in relation to the whole event, which is certainly a great practical accomplishment rather than something that transpires automatically, but they are often also uttered specifically in relation to the property that constitutes the woman's "price." The cattle and kerosene are said to be difficult because of the monetary value they represent: the former may be worth (if sold) between two hundred and five hundred dollars each, and new full drums of kerosene cost about twelve dollars each.[9] Though whales' teeth cost less individually (sixty to one hundred dollars for large teeth, which are the only ones acceptable in important ceremonies), they are seen to supersede in importance and difficulty the other components of the prestation; they are said to be "weighty," and they are in fact physically heavy. These are propositions about the morality of price. In the usual market situation, a price may be too high or unexpectedly low; this may imply unfairness or an intention to extort on the part of whoever imposes an inappropriate figure. But usually the difficulty or ease of putting together whatever happens to be the price of a thing is irrelevant to moral calculation. Whether a purchaser can buy something outright or needs to make sacrifices and take out loans is irrelevant to the justice of the price; in Noikoro, however, the fact of difficulty is central. The singular feature of the *solevu* is the transformation of ordinary relaxed village life into feverish, virtually round-the-clock work, and it is evident that if the pace were not different, if the work were not excessive, the commitment to the project would be lacking. So although there are certain quantitative notions about how much should be presented—say, two drums of kerosene per man and four mats per woman—the figures are not chosen to accumulate a given total but because the amount may be difficult and barely feasible.

References to the cash value of the goods contributed are also significant. This is to emphasize that those who have made the *solevu* have a commitment to the way of the land rather than the market. The ambiguous nature of cattle is relevant also: for many people they are primarily animals that should be killed only for important occasions "in the way of the land," but they can obviously also be sold, and many rural Fijians who pursue "the path of money" do so by cattle farming. Others will sell their beasts when compelled to do so, or they will represent occasional sales as forced rather than as routine elements of their domestic economy. Further elaboration of these values, and of the meaning attributed to marriage ceremonies in western Fiji, depends on some elaboration of the broader constitution of neotraditional village culture.

Alternate Paths? Postulated Dilemmas in Rural Fiji

As others have noted, custom and tradition are frequently juxtaposed to other terms, which are often construed as mutually exclusive or mutually corrosive "ways" or social orientations. Among resistant pagans, the strongest opposition is between *kastom* and *skul* ("church" in Vanuatu; see Jolly 1982, 1992a) or the *lotu* (in some other contexts); elsewhere, the key juxtaposition may be between tradition and *bisnis* (Foster 1992). Similarly, the dichotomy between tradition and commerce is central to both ideological debate at the national level in Fiji and to the rural perception of the social world. The opposition has strong ethnic associations and is constituted at various levels: between Fijians and foreigners; between Fijians and Fiji-Indians; between the village, which is closely associated in contemporary nationalist ideology with Fijian roots and authenticity, and the place of the market—town. The village is a place of rules, of respect observances, of kinship, and of sharing; town is a money place, a place of difficulty, a place where food cannot simply be extracted from the ground. The Fijian notion of customary ways differs from the ideology of *kastom* found in Vanuatu and the Solomons (see Keesing and Tonkinson 1982): Christianity, and especially the Christianity of the Methodist and Catholic Churches, are part of the Fijian way, not an intrusion that displaces it or exists in tension with it. The point of similarity with other western Pacific cases is, however, that a view of the world has developed that is highly dichotomized: practices that may actually be closely interconnected, such as ceremonies and cash cropping, are represented as manifestations of alternative courses, implying entirely different moral and social perspectives. Fiji-Indians are believed to be completely dedicated to the pursuit of commerce, and thus preoccupied with money to the detriment of kinship and wider social obligations (a view explicit in the entirely inaccurate account of Indian marriage quoted at the beginning of this paper). "With us, if someone is building a house, we all join and work, later we eat together. With the Indians this is not possible; with them it is every man for himself." The same contrasts might be made between the customs of Fijians and those of *vavalagi* (foreigners).[10] Clearly a white ethnographer is likely to be particularly exposed to such discourse, given that the differences between his or her way of life and local ethics are a matter of considerable interest to the host people, but in this case it would be incorrect to infer that the money/custom contrast lacks salience in debate within the indigenous society, as the writings of Fijian anthropologists (e.g., Ravuvu 1988) make clear.

The dichotomy between customary practice and self-motivated activity recurs in contexts where the latter does not specifically or necessarily involve economic gain. It is no surprise that there is a gap between the representation of "elopement" as a spontaneous and willful action on the part of *individuals* and the actualities of nonformal marriage. There are occasionally consultations and attempts on the part of a prospective husband's clan to get a certain couple together with assurances that prestations can take place at some later date. On one such occasion, there seemed to be uncertainty on the bride's side, and her people did not, in fact, arrive at the husband's part of the village as expected; instead, a message was sent indicating that a marriage could only take place if the proper sequence of gifts was made. The rebuff was shrugged off and kava drunk late into the night; the only disconsolate person seemed to be the would-be husband himself.

The complexities of this kind of interpenetration between the "customary" and what transpires practically make it evident that the opposition is not really between "traditional" practice and individualistic departures from it; what is known of earlier Fijian social life suggests considerable fluidity and instability, rather than the sovereignty of custom. The "way of the land" is highly reified as a reference point for practice, as is apparent in several ways from marriage ceremonies. Both men and women are often very specific in describing ceremonies about what quantities of *iyau* and *tabua* should be presented at a particular point, but when occasions of the type were actually witnessed, it was clear that most people did not have a precise idea of the number of mats or drums given, or cattle killed; in fact they sometimes asked me questions I was about to ask them. There is thus the implication that the whole procedure adheres to some prescriptive model, but all that is important in the event is the appearance of abundance. There is also a good deal of discussion in these contexts about what is and what is not "the custom."

All this arises from the distinctly neotraditional character of rural Fijian society. The singular feature of policy in the colonial period, which had no counterpart in the Solomons, Papua New Guinea, or Vanuatu, was the extraordinary extent to which Fijian society was the subject of anthropological characterization and analysis in administrative circles, and the diagnoses informed—or misinformed—land policy, sanitation, and economic development projects (France 1969; Thomas 1990c). Much of this discourse, from the 1880s and 1890s on, was preoccupied with postulated tensions between communalism and individualism, especially insofar as the former was thought to inhibit the advancement of commerce amongst Fijians (for influential reports see Spate 1959, Belshaw 1964). Though the polarity may now be anthropologically discredited, it is alive and well in the Fijian debates that have "concerned every aspect of the relationship between culture and economic organization" (Rutz 1987, 557). This emerges not only in the Fijian press and official publications but also often in conversation: a chief enthusiastic about development once referred to the Fijian impulse to be hospitable and share everything with kin, adding, "This is what we have to break." My claim here is not that villagers' perceptions of the world are derived in any simple sense from what has since become known as a dual-sector model in the sociology of development, but that these views have converged with rural Fijians' experiences and contacts with Fiji-Indians in towns and their project to fashion their own oppositional identity partly on the basis of exchange practices.

Ceremonial practice is hence understood as a "communal obligation" that is both very necessary for the perpetuation of clan sociality and a heavy burden, a constraint that makes advancement in the path of money very difficult. In fact, the obstructions to development are diverse and stem as much from wider difficulties of marketing and distribution as from the organization of horticultural production (Ravuvu 1988); there is no doubt that ceremonies actually require and stimulate cash cropping, rather than hinder it (cf. Rutz 1978, which includes references to a very extensive literature). What is important, though, is the cultural fact that Fijian ways are not constituted intrinsically, but through sacrifice—through a commitment that must detract from one's capacity to make money and otherwise get on in the wider world. A secondary school textbook presents the "dilemma" of "the cost of kinship"; a young man chooses to go back to his village to attend a funeral rather than stay in town to sit his exams (Benson 1977, 57–8). The proportionate and mutually corrosive character of advancement and tradition were made apparent, also, on occasions when I heard people remark on the fine appearance of piles of valuables and Fijian poverty almost in the same breath.

Gifts of cattle and beef are highly expressive in these ceremonies, not simply because some claim that cattle should be reserved for customary feasts, but precisely because it is also possible to sell them: what is stretched out on the grass as the whales' teeth pass from one clan to another is not simply special food, but a signal of dedication to the land, as opposed to the sacrifice of tradi-tion for the market.

This must also be why "price" is the appropriate reduction of a complex series of gifts. In many instances neotraditional societies celebrate tribal or kinship economies by emphasizing the differences between a system notionally suf-fused with solidarity and generosity, and one of uncaring and impersonal trans-actions. Such contrasts are also, of course, found in Western literature on transi-tions between traditional and modern worlds, especially where the past or the others are romanticized—and the romanticizations of educated indigenous ideologues draw as much on such European categories as on the actualities of the "traditional" societies (cf. Keesing 1989). The Fijians whom I have written about here do elaborate similar contrasts and frequently point out that they will not let someone walk past their house without calling them in to drink tea or eat. "In your country," they would say, "this is not possible: you keep your doors shut." It would have to be acknowledged that this is not merely a mystification—there are real differences, which Fijians who have traveled for work or war service have directly witnessed—but some other ethnic characterizations seem less grounded in actualities and more invidious in their effects: Fijians also differentiate themselves by emphasizing that their rituals are works of respect, that respect pervades their behavior, and that customs of respect are absent from Fiji-Indian society, as well as from the society of white foreigners.

The representation of marriage is more complex and paradoxical: Fijians do not suggest that their presentations exemplify a kind of transaction radically opposed to those conducted in the market, but instead assert that they are the same, and moreover allude to the cash values of the exchange items. The crucial consequence of this identification is the observation that valuables are convert-ible into things that might be bought or sold; in many instances, the specific items might be directed to the market rather than to a ceremony; the alternatives that preoccupy Fijians are therefore not abstract options but are tangibly and concretely embodied in the things before us. Though there are other ways in which polarized social alternatives might be represented, this particular practice is highly poignant precisely because a common standard of value is alluded to: it opens up what Robert Musil, in *The Man without Qualities* (1953), called a sense of possibility—things could just as easily be some other way. While a sense of contingency may often be destabilizing, producing a shifting boundary between *doxa* and heterodoxy (to use Bourdieu's terms), in this case the sense of alterna-tives reinforces and parades a practical commitment to one way of life rather than another that seems to encroach upon it.

The choices for Fijians are projected onto a larger cultural canvas through contrasts with foreigners, whose approach to marriage is considered to be casual, unrestrained, and selfish, and with Fiji-Indians, who are thought to be preoccupied with commercial gain. These propositions clearly define Fijians positively in relation to others, but the same discriminations are made between Fijians who hold fast to the way of the land and those who have "picked up the customs of foreigners," to use the disparaging words of one older man. Urban workers and some commercial farmers who live away from villages are seen as followers of the path of money, and this is often reflected in religious affiliation: first-generation converts to Seventh-day Adventism and other fundamentalist churches such as the Assemblies of God are often individualists and modernists who (to varying degrees) reject communalism and village life (see chaps. 2 and 8). Adherents of both of these denominations are less often seen at ceremonies, but they are noticeably active in cattle ranching and other forms of commercial farming; both are perforce oriented away from customary procedures because kava is proscribed and Assemblies people sometimes criticize aspects of custom such as "arranged marriage," which of course can only be identified as such once an individualistic Western alternative is postulated. Again, actualities of behavior are not reducible to the polarized attributions: many "independent" Fijian farmers actually sustain close involvement with kin (Overton 1988), particularly through their contributions to feasts, while some of those who neglect their obligations continue to reside in villages.

Of course, there are many potential divisions within Fijian villages, and they arise for instance from land or chiefly succession disputes, from clan rivalries, or from different views concerning religion and politics. The juxtaposition of the way of the land and the path of money is not the only ideological issue, but it is notable that differences over religion, for example tend to reflect the tension that is postulated between hierarchical communalism and individualism. The centrality of these contrasts for Fijian identity has been illustrated by the extensive debate following the 1987 military coups, which has not privileged the constitutional issues that are apparently more fundamental from the perspective of outsiders, but has focused instead on the long-standing issue of increasing the involvement of Fijians in business. Though many of the impediments are by no means peculiar to Fiji, there is a strong perception in the country (among some Indians and whites as well as Fijians themselves) that a natural antipathy has to be overcome.

Exchange and Identity

To some extent, the constructions of identity considered here might be thought to arise from the essential character of Melanesian societies. As the anthropological literature on the region has reiterated, despite a multitude of theoretical shifts since Malinowski, gift giving and complex exchange cycles are the substance of sociality; even in recent accounts that avoid or deconstruct the assumptions that have made "societies" visible (Strathern 1988; Battaglia 1990), it is apparent that flows of persons, aspects of persons, and things reflexively create value and significance in each other. If reciprocity and ceremonial exchange are in fact so crucial, it would be surprising if they did not assume some centrality in neotraditional representations of the indigenous as opposed to the foreign. Indeed, as Foster (1992) notes, broad contrasts between custom and *bisnis* that fashion identities through reference to exchange practices are central in many western Pacific societies.

However, there are also cases where distinctions between custom and "church" or "government" are more significant (Otto 1992b) and contexts in which the issue of local distinctiveness with respect to other Melanesians may be more prominent than oppositions between Melanesian and white culture (Neumann 1992b). This signals the need to ground the content of oppositional representations in colonial encounters and postcolonial circumstances in which particular social and cultural alternatives are at stake. Reciprocity, hierarchy, and engagement in ceremony are not rendered diagnostic of the Fijian way because these are fundamental attributes of Fijian culture (even though all three certainly are); more generally, customary exchange is not made central to Melanesian tradition because exchange was the substance of traditional sociality (even though it was, as it largely remains, pervasively and fundamentally important). Rather, these institutionalized practices are rendered central in rhetoric about identity because of histories and conflicts of the kind that elsewhere render pagan ritual central in opposition to Christianity. The prior attributes of societies could obviously be represented in diverse ways: certain colonial experiences engender juxtapositions that privilege particular elements.

In Fiji, contrasts would obviously not be made between the way of the land and Christianity because the latter was long ago assimilated to indigenous culture; choices do not have to be made between persisting with valued rituals and church adherence. On the other hand, perceived tensions between a desirable customary communalism, which is linked with hierarchy and respect usages, and engagement in commerce have so preoccupied administrators and many others in Fiji that identity is understood, above all, in these social, economic, and moral terms. The attachment to other ethnic groups of the inversions of one's own attributes is manifest in the fateful imagining of Fiji-Indians as commercial individuals who virtually lack culture. Though an ironic reversal of the conventional constructions of India as hierarchical, customary, and mystical (see Inden 1990), this stereotype emerges from a project to fashion self and other that resembles Orientalist discourse in its dynamic of oppositional reification—

though it hardly needs to be added that Fijians have a very different location in the global cultural economy to the theorists, civil servants, and area studies experts who continue to represent the Middle East and Asia for Europeans and Americans. It is, of course, this marginality that accounts for the connections between their contrasts and the juxtaposition of wealth and poverty, even though the question of ethnicity and anti-Indian feeling has always been more visible to Western eyes.

Epilogue:
From Contrast to
Relation

The process of oppositional objectification discussed in the last part of this book is engaged in by scholars as well as people in general. Their characterizations may be more nuanced than those of nationalists or those at play in ethnic jokes, but cultural analysts tend nevertheless to evoke entities and totalities that can be juxtaposed. In Oceanic anthropology, Margaret Mead's Samoa, which figured sexual freedom in contrast to American constraint, is perhaps the most florid example, and the easiest to identify and disavow. For many Samoans, an inversion of those terms would seem more appropriate: their world is dominated by custom, respect, restraint, and obligation, while *palagi* are individualists who act anyhow.

As anthropology has become increasingly antiessentialist, it is perhaps less likely that broad-brush contrasts of the kind central to Mead's rhetoric will continue to be advanced. Yet there are many other contexts in which charged oppositions between peoples and cultures are deployed. Indigenous nationalists will no doubt continue to have reasons for affirming the distinctness of their sociality and vaunting its collectivity, spirituality, and groundedness in opposition to the seeming atomism, rationalism, and rootlessness of Western modernity. And academics who conduct their work in empathy with the struggles of such people can only abet these visions through large oppositions between the European and the native. If the colonial process almost by definition turned upon a primary contradiction between the cultures of the colonizers and the colonized, I would insist that the contradiction can only be undone by a rhetoric that respects the differences on both sides, that acknowledges the tremendous significance of that binary relation while refusing to fetishize it.

This is one of the reasons why I have drawn material together in this book that might seem to occupy fundamentally different fields. It might appear that the chapters in the second section are essentially essays in European cultural history, and elite cultural history at that. They trace shifts in intellectuals', travelers', and scientists' perceptions; they deal with literate culture and with publications. They seem concerned with a different world from that discussed in the subsequent section, which explored indigenous perceptions of identity, elite and non-elite, in Oceania. My interest in framing these discussions together was in part simply to make the point that despite the sustained character of colonialism in the Pacific, there were many senses in which outsiders' and locals' perceptions occupied and still occupy radically different spaces. Despite the centuries of violence, the generally more subtle permeation of Christianity and commoditization, and the current damage of poverty, the consciousnesses of Oceanic peoples are not for the most part aptly described as "colonized."

However, I also wanted to discuss the differences between European and indigenous imaginings in Oceania while refusing to let either term solidify into anything as fixed or constant as a worldview. The plethora of debate and confusion about Pacific peoples during and subsequent to the early voyages should preclude the characterization, so frequently evoked, of "the Western idea of . . . ," or "the colonial image of . . . " It is true, of course, that white travelers, writers, and others frequently reiterated denigrating or romanticizing stereotypes. But they used them in different ways to different purposes, and moreover, they often used related notions to denigrate or affirm European people, practices, and institutions. The logic of this discourse was not predominantly a facile self-other opposition, but as frequently, a rupturing self-other analogy. And the same is true of indigenous rhetoric, in which arguments about modernity and money are frequently used to criticize and empower different parties *within* indigenous society—witness Sailosi and the Bula Tale—rather than to simply assert native values against those of the colonial order.

If there were, to be sure, identifiable coherences in evangelical missionary projects, efforts of exploration, and administrators' ideologies, these distinct visions do not add up to a Western knowledge that produced Western images of Pacific places and cultures. The West is only an artifact of its advocates' and opponents' rhetoric, and the more the real provincial plurality that is disguised by the universalist term can be acknowledged, and the more indigenous culture is evoked in its specificity rather than as a generalized nonmodern condition, the more the various European colonizing efforts can be supposed to have been superseded.

Oppositional objectifications no doubt always start with truth and end in stereotype. Hence even the crudest "nativist" or New Age visions of a radical difference between primal spirituality and alienated modernity rest upon a legitimate and proper recognition of the indissociable connections of land, culture, and person in indigenous communities and the displacements and contingencies of life and meaning that follow from the sovereignty of ever more open markets. But it needs to be recalled that indigenous people were and are voyagers too; that displacement attendant upon war as well as migration could sever people's connections to land; and that spirituality was often a highly charged and contested matter, rather than a set of purely affirmative connections. And, on the other hand, European societies are full of people with highly particular, even genealogical, attachments to place, and not only because modernity is so rarely unaccompanied by a reflexive nostalgia for rural community.

This is where, again, Epeli Hau'ofa's account of "the sea of islands" is inspiring. The pattern of communication and interaction he evokes—for which there is a good deal of archaeological and ethnohistorical evidence—would lend little support to any Pacific nationalism that claimed an originally distinct history or pure tradition. Practices, languages, art forms, and so on are locally various and in many cases highly distinctive, yet at the same time, they reflect long histories of exchange and relatedness. Again and again, Pacific culture and practice manifests a continual process of interaction and borrowing, whether in the area of New Guinea, the Torres Strait, northern Australia, eastern Indonesia, or the clusters of related archipelagoes further east. No island is an island.

It might be suggested that voyaging has always been the privilege of an elite. A voyaging aesthetic could be seen less as an indigenous value than as a recoding of the long-standing European interest in travel, which has always wavered between risk and reaffirmation, between an effort that is genuinely outward-looking and one that is self-congratulatory. In many parts of Oceania, it would need to be conceded that in the past, trade and voyaging were undertaken mainly by chiefly people, or at least by higher-status men, while most rarely ventured beyond the places in which they belonged. Globally, it is certainly true that the vast majority of people lead lives that belie the fashionable, if not new, notions of displacement and diaspora. But if these ideas are apt anywhere, they do reflect Pacific realities: the dispersal of Polynesians, in particular, beyond their island homes is astonishing.

In a deeper sense, however, Pacific cosmologies and socialities have always been constituted by migrations. Origin stories sometimes postulate locally autochthonous ancestors, it is true, but more typically they relate extensive voyages, successive sites of residence, and further movements—or interactions between people of the place and people of the sea. Identities are constituted through a dialectic between attachment to place and alliances and movements. Sociality, paradoxically, could be said to be founded in extension. Home is not a unity but a divisible set of debts, attachments, and entitlements. These are not utopian ideas. I do not put them forward as a charter for an ideal reformation of cross-cultural relations in Oceania. Voyaging will always involve intrusion and injustice as well as gift giving and new knowledge. It will always foster stereotypes and misrepresentations as well as deeper appreciations of other people's stories and situations. The idea of the sea of islands is perhaps already empowering the Oceanic future; whether it continues to do so is a matter for the people of the place, rather than for a marginal observer and occasional visitor such as myself, to determine. What I can say, however, is that such an Oceanic paradigm, derived however loosely from indigenous practices and histories, promises to reveal a great deal more of the region than the exhausted forms of global knowledge grounded in nations and ethnicities. If the preconditions of that global knowledge most salient to this part of the world—the Enlightenment voyages of discovery—are again subject to discredit, as they were in the eighteenth century, there is, ironically, much to be discovered and rediscovered now. Tupaia's map may have been a lonely document for a long time, but the space of interaction it exemplified, between insiders' and outsiders' passions for voyaging and knowledge, is one that may be opening up again.

Appendix:
The Bula Tale
Movement

This reproduces a 1961 newspaper article concerning this movement that expresses particularly clearly the manner in which dissent and sociopolitical innovation depend upon the selective constitution and rejection of "Fijian customs."

New Way of Life in Four Villages

Four villages in Nadroga have formed a co-operative society under the leadership of Apimeleki Ramatau Mataka, a former clerk in the Medical Department. Among other things, they have done away with traditional Fijian customs and with orthodox Christianity.

Apimeleki told a *Fiji Times* reporter that the co-operative was a "government of its own" and all laws were made by the management committee. He criticized Fijian laws and said that most of them should be abolished. Apimeleki said that members of the co-operative society still believe in Jesus Christ, but they have stopped the "practice of worshipping."

The village church at the headquarters of the group, Emuri, has been converted into living quarters.

Other villages in the society are Togovere, Kabisi, and Vagadra. The use of the tabua and yaqona and feasts in connection with weddings and deaths have been abolished. Apimeleki said that some people had called him a Communist. "I am not ashamed of my actions," he said.

NAME CHANGED

The name of the co-operative society, which was previously Dranilami (Lamb's Blood), has been changed to Bula Tale [Live Again]. Apimeleki explained that when a couple wished to marry it is their doing, and only their parents should be there. When vows are exchanged they go home and live together. There is no feasting. Yaqona drinking and the presentation of the root in ceremonies have been abolished.

"I am the only man in the co-operative society who is allowed to touch yaqona, because I travel from place to place on business and sometimes have dealings with chiefs," he said.

"When a member is ill, we don't tinker with Fijian cures but send him or her to hospital for treatment," he added.

SOCIETY'S PRINCIPLE

The principle of the society, he said, was to live equally.

"What I eat, my wife and children must also eat. In the Fijian custom the man of the house eats first and eats the best of the food. Whatever is left over is eaten by his wife and children. The system employed in the member villages at present is that everyone eats together in a common dining house. The cooking is done by turn, and everyone eats the same sort of food."

CO-OPERATIVE STORES

"Nobody buys anything. We have co-operative society stores in each village and if any one requires anything like toilet gear etc, he just goes to the store and asks for it," Apimeleki said. When a lali is sounded at 6 am each day the men go out and clean up the villages. The villages' activities begin at 6 am and end at 9 pm, the official bedtime. The men work in the plantations during the day. The produce is sold at the society's various markets which are in the various centres in the north-west. Early this year they bought a lorry to cart the produce. Apimeleki said that the minimum return after produce is sold on Saturday is £50, but they have received as much as £89.

TWO PARTS

"The money is split into two parts in the first instance. One part goes to the bank and the second part is distributed equally among the four member villages," Apimeleki said. "This money is also used for emergencies like sickness."

He said he has stopped members of the society from taking part in communal work, like building bures in villages. "We contribute our share in money," he said. "That is one reason why I have been called a Communist. It does not worry me. All I am interested in is the success of my members."

Apimeleki has plans for the society's own school, dispensary and clinic. These, when they are built, will be open to the public as well, he said.

Fiji Times, 12 August 1961.

NOTES

Introduction: Tupaia's Map

1 This was an avowedly deconstructionist project rather than a "postcolonial" one, but the article certainly presumed the two claims of postcolonial theory that During refers to.

1 Partial Texts: Representation, Colonialism, and Agency in Pacific History

1 For critiques of postcolonialism see During (1992), Suleri (1992), and Thomas (1994) among others.

2 See also the book (Connolly and Anderson 1987).

3 Clifford has also commented briefly on the Joe Leahy films: "It remains uncertain whether Joe Leahy is a Melanesian capitalist or a capitalist Melanesian" (1992, 102).

4 Maude however placed more emphasis than Davidson upon ethnohistory and oral tradition (see Maude 1971, 9–11).

5 Donald Denoon (1986) has drawn attention to the cognate problem of "isolationism" in Australian history.

6 For a brief account of Davidson's work see H. E. Maude 1973. Although various kinds of consultancy work continue to be carried out, it is difficult to imagine any report by an expatriate being as important now as Spate's 1959 review of the Fijian economy (Spate 1959).

7 Dorothy Shineberg (1967, chap. 12) provided a good account of the succession of different commodities received for sandalwood, but did not attempt to contextualize these desires in indigenous Melanesian perceptions.

8 Expressed particularly in *The Interpretation of Cultures* (1973) and *Local Knowledge* (1983); it is notable that historians almost always refer to one of three or four key essays in Geertz's earlier volume, rather than to the wider range of his work.

9 The extent to which any particular text is informed or constrained by the theoretical bor-

rowing is of course variable. In his fine book on Pohnpei, David Hanlon (1988, xv, xxi–xxii) refers to Geertz but in fact devotes relatively little space to cultural interpretation.

10   This point was made in certain reviews of Howe's *Where the Waves Fall* (Ralston 1983; Hempenstall 1984). For examples of recent work oriented more toward conflict during the colonial period see Hempenstall and Rutherford 1984 and Kelly 1990 and 1991.

11   For a completely new appraisal of the Tuka see Kaplan 1995.

12   As Edward Said has written, somewhat ambiguously, "There is nothing particularly controversial or reprehensible about such domestications of the exotic . . . what is more important . . . is the limited vocabulary and imagery that impose themselves as a consequence [for Orientalist discourse in the European West]" (1978, 60, 67).

2   Alejandro Mayta in Fiji: Narrations about Millenarianism, Colonialism, Postcolonial Politics, and Custom

1   This has been especially contentious since the military coup in 1987, when an interim administration attempted to impose strict observance by decree. Shifting government opinion and pressure from the churches themselves later led to this being relaxed, but an intransigent faction within the Methodist Church then set up roadblocks in an attempt to restrict movement and preclude any commercial activities on Sundays; the defiant attitude of certain prominent church leaders and their numerous supporters came close to creating a crisis of state authority. The decree was initially directed mainly against Fiji-Indians, but the subsequent dispute was essentially intra-Fijian and did magnify old tensions between Adventists and others.

2   Little research has been done with Adventists in the Pacific to date; the most sustained study is that of Hviding (1995). This fails to substantiate the notion that they are money people with no culture.

3   Dissent was not, however, restricted to that period: more localized protests and "revivals" of non-Christian religious practices have appeared sporadically in many parts of Fiji since, and earlier manifestations of syncretistic and inspirational religion may be regarded to some extent as historically continuous with contemporary urban Pentecostal churches.

4   On that point, this essay inverts the novel by sustaining through the contrivances of scholarship the claim that this is history and leaves it to critics to circle it off as mere fiction.

5   As was noted in the previous chapter, this was one of the textbook cases for comparative cult studies (notably Worsley 1957, Burridge 1969), although the "cargo" element allegedly characteristic of many Pacific movements was virtually absent. For reappraisal see Kaplan 1990b, 1995.

6   Colo North Provincial Council Minutes, 15 April 1896, National Archives of Fiji; the archival sources cited in this chapter are in this repository unless otherwise indicated.

7   These were *turaga ni koro, buli,* and *roko tui* respectively.

8   Joske later changed his name to Brewster because of fears concerning anti-German sentiment. He was the author of a book of reminiscences and ethnography (Brewster 1922) concerning the "hill tribes" with whom he worked; this is one of few accessible sources for the anthropology and history of the area (but see also de Marzan 1987).

9   Colo North Provincial Council Minutes, 20 May 1897; CSO 1460/1898; letter from A. B. Brewster (Joske) to Spence, 26 April 1918, Fiji Museum, document 24 (bbb); Brewster 1922: 253–4.

10   Many elements of the colonial project—descriptive specification through censuses, codification of customs, village regulation and consolidation—were motivated by a symbolic effort to make Fijian society as a totality visible (for elaboration see Thomas 1990a).

11   CSO 1460/98.

12   CSO 4625/02.

13   CSO 2018/18, 6336/18; Willis to Small, 25 March 1918, F/1/18.

14   Transcribed in Sauvakarua, Navatusila District, in 1988.

15   Most of the Fijian words quoted in this article are in standard Fijian (derived from the Bauan dialect). Viji is a western interior equivalent of Viti (Fiji).

16   The Fijian term is actually ordinal: "the Seventh church."

17   It is not clear whether the food taboos and prohibitions on drinking and smoking that distinguished Adventism were also adopted.

18   CSO 6336/18.

19   Ibid.

20   Ibid.

21   See, for example, Colo North Provincial Council Minutes for 1902, 5837/1902 and 5471/1902, in which particular emphasis is placed by the witness and prosecution alike on putting "down the names of people."

22   *Fiji Times* (hereafter *FT*), 27 March 1918.

23   *FT*, 28 March 1918.

24   On the extensive use of Fijian words in English discourse in the colony see Siegel 1987, esp. app. C.

25   *FT*, 27 March 1918.

26   *FT*, 10 April 1918.

27   For instance, the Catholic Fiji-language history referred to him as "edua na tamata ulu ca" (Na ekelesia katolika 1936, 302).

28   Harold Chambers to Small, 25 May 1918, F/1/1918.

29   6043/18.

30   Harold Chambers to Small, 25 May 1918.

31   A recent official Adventist history celebrated Pauliasi's role in obtaining conversions and noted that "the European missionaries . . . were quick to realise that the key to the spread of Seventh-day Adventism in Fiji was the indigenous worker" (Dixon [1985], 202). This was perhaps even more true than the writer realized. The spread of the SDA in Fiji can be traced through the religious statistics in the *Blue Books:* it was not mentioned at all before 1909 and between then and 1917 claimed between five and six hundred members and adherents. In 1918 the effect of the defections was that this rose to just under seventeen hundred; around two thousand were claimed between 1920 and 1930. Catholicism was also an option for those who aimed to express some kind of protest, and chiefs often complained about the activities of Catholic teachers or priests (e.g., 2973/1889). The connection with dissent related to millenial cult activities was often also manifest: "Samuela has gone over because he considers Roman Catholicism antagonistic to the Government and consequently so to his chief and because he has a grudge against the Wesleyans

for giving information in the recent Tuka prosecutions" (1011/1892). Although the government did not feel it could do much to prevent people changing denominations, missionaries required passes to move around, and in discontented areas such as Colo North these seem to have been generally denied (e.g., 1956/1892).

32 The word used in this context was *taukei*, owners of the land. This refers contextually to the occupants of an area as opposed to a group of visitors (and often the hosts versus the receivers of a feast), but since the political instability leading up to, and since, the 1987 coups, the term has been politicized as an ethnic category equivalent to "Fijian," especially in the nationalist rhetoric of the now fragmented Taukei Movement. Parallels between indigenous Fijians and other "native owners," such as the New Zealand Maori, have been made and disputed.

33 This paraphrases several statements. Apart from those made on the occasion discussed, similar statements were often reiterated in explanations of former activities at the *nanaga* ritual sites and in spirit houses.

34 *Beto;* elsewhere, *bito* or *bure kalou.*

35 *Fiji Times,* 12 August 1961. See Appendix: The Bula Tale Movement, below.

36 Ibid.

37 For further discussion of objectification see Cohn 1987 and chapter 8 below.

38 See especially Robertson and Tamanisau 1988, but for an important earlier discussion see Durutalo 1985, which contains extended discussion of various protests and the Nadroga movement. The remarks here reflect the 1988 situation and have not been updated.

39 Willis to Small, 25 March 1918, in F/1/18.

40 Dissent of some kind from the dominant chiefly-Methodist Fijian hierarchical order is reflected in present patterns of religious affiliation: according to the 1986 census, of 329,305 Fijians, 244,381 were Methodist, 45,385 were Catholic, 13,269 were Seventh-day Adventist, 12,814 were Assemblies of God, and 9,713 were "other Christian," which must include Jehovah's Witnesses and various local Pentecostal sects such as the Congregation of the Poor. It is certainly not to be assumed that all or even most non-Methodists are in some sense opposed to the chiefly system and the official constructions of Fijian custom, but substantial numbers of Assemblies people, Adventists, and "other Christians" could be expected to be following another path. There are also a few hundred Fijian Hindus and Muslims (Population Census 1986, Parliament of Fiji, Parliamentary Paper No. 4 of 1988, vol. 1:100).

3   Liberty and License:
New Zealand Societies in Cook Voyage Anthropology

1 He begins by indicating that two women join the older man, whom he meets first, and says that of these, the younger was singularly voluble. In the same diary entry, in accord with ship's noon-to-noon time, he explains that the whole family was encountered the next morning, "which consisted of the Man, his two wives, the young Woman before mentioned his daughter, a Boy of about 14 or 15 years of age and three small children." In fact, no young woman is "before mentioned" except the younger of the two wives, that is, the same woman with whom George identifies the girl who strikes the man (Cook 1955–74, 2:116–7).

2   There is a different account again in the log, in which Cook refers to "a Man his Wife a Middle aged woman sister to either yᵉ man or wife . . ." (1955–74, 2:117 n. 3).

3   Compare Anderson 1784–86, 128 and Anderson 1790, 2:453. Virtually all later popular editions of Cook's voyages are based on Anderson, but the wording here, and many of the plates used in first and subsequent editions of Anderson, are actually derived from Moore.

4   See the account of the spears known as *here,* which were used for hunting *kereru* (wood pigeons), in Hamilton 1896–1901, 214–5, quoting from Tamati Ranapiri. Examples may be seen in the Auckland Institute and Museum and in other New Zealand collections.

5   With respect to narratives of extraordinary violence during the Putumayo rubber boom, Taussig writes, "The importance of this colonial work of fabulation extends beyond the nightmarish quality of its contents. Its truly crucial feature lies in the way it creates an uncertain reality out of fiction, giving shape and voice to the formless form of the reality in which an unstable interplay of truth and illusion becomes a phantasmic social force" (1987, 121). It is the idea that certain encounters generate "an unstable interplay of truth and illusion" that I find especially salient; the New Zealand incidents clearly do not possess quite the same nightmarish terror as the rubber boom stories.

6   The salience of the category of the sublime to these encounters is discussed in greater detail by Jonathan Lamb (1991, 110 and passim).

7   Compare Cook 1777, 1:85–6. The close correspondence between the wording of parts of Cook's *Voyage* and sections of George's may be attributed to the fact that, during the protracted and abortive negotiations over who would write the official account of the voyage, Forster senior submitted a specimen based on Cook's manuscript to the Admiralty that covered the Dusky Bay incidents (cf. Forster 1778). It is possible that this is copied in BM Add. MS 27889 and was drawn upon by Cook in writing the narrative that was printed, though at the time of writing I have not had the opportunity to compare the manuscripts and publications systematically.

8   In George's *Voyage* the terms "savage" and "barbarian" are less carefully distinguished than in his father's *Observations.* I do not attempt here to reconstruct the actualities of Maori familial behavior in this period, but it is worth noting that another light is thrown on the incident by a woman of Queen Charlotte's Sound, "Ghowannahe" (Ko Wanahe?), who reported to participants in Cook's third voyage that "with respect to domestic policy . . . the fathers had the sole care of the boys as soon as they could walk, and that the girls were left wholly at their mother's disposal. She said, it was a crime for a mother to correct her son, after he was once taken under the protection of the father; and that it was always resented by the mother if the father interfered with the management of the daughters" (Rickman 1781, 65). I am grateful to Anne Salmond for drawing this passage to my attention.

9   The Germans are far more conspicuous in Forster's references in *Observations* than other groups such as Hottentots and Americans.

10 Gibbon, incidentally, was far less categorical on this point than the other writers cited, and his account was presumably more influential than theirs (1994, 1:239–43).

11 Millar refers specifically to the liberty of women and free intercourse between the sexes.

12 After "nations" is a footnote reading "See Hawkesworth's Compilation," meaning see the range of incidents reported from the voyages of Carteret, Wallis, and Byron, as well as Cook's first voyage, in Hawkesworth 1773.

8   Since one reader of this essay assumed that I aimed to base a general, integrated, non-structuralist cultural theory on Koselleck's work, it should perhaps be made explicit that I am not interested in "theory" of this kind at all; rather than pursuing such grand chimera I am interested merely in finding terms in cultural analysis that seem adequate for arguing about issues that seem politically and intellectually salient at the moment. My use of Koselleck is thus partial and strategic; in fact, his larger projects (such as the *Geschictliche Grundbegriffe* [Brunner, Conze, and Koselleck 1972–]) happen to be rather foreign to my own agendas.

9   In the literature on nationalism, Chatterjee's important analyses—which, together with other Subaltern Studies sources, have influenced Keesing's formulations—must be mentioned here: "The problematic in nationalist thought is exactly the reverse of that in Orientalism . . . There is consequently an inherent contradictoriness in nationalist thinking because it reasons within a framework of knowledge whose representational structure corresponds to the very structure of power that nationalist thought seeks to repudiate" (1984, 155–6; see also Chatterjee 1986).

10   Ivan Brady recently alerted me to this aspect of Marquesan cannibalism.

11   Of course, *anthropophagi* was not originally a neutral descriptive term, but in present usage, it may be contrasted with "cannibal," which is clearly more emotively laden.

12   See Inden (1990) on *sati*; the response of the Landers to widow suicide in west Africa is comparable (Hallett 1965, 64–6).

13   Rabici in conventional orthography.

14   Now known as *na lotuvakatevoro*, the devil's religion.

15   My earlier discussion of *kerekere* (Thomas 1992a) made more categorical claims that were criticized by Sahlins (1993), who drew attention to an important range of evidence that I had not taken into account.

16   My main source for this movement is the newspaper article in the appendix. Though the newspaper was probably primarily interested in the story's curiosity value and the source might therefore be considered inadequate, Mataka's quoted statement resonates too deeply with similar accounts and persisting Fijian preoccupations to be dismissed as a journalistic distortion. On the other hand, the allegation that the movement was "Communist" in character, which was also raised in the *Fiji Times*, was entirely spurious.

17   In any particular case of religious change, factors related to local rivalries are mixed up with larger ideological questions. Whatever the reasons for particular changes, which are often very difficult to reconstruct through field inquiries, Adventists do tend to be dissociated from tradition and more interested in commerce than non-Adventist Fijians, though the contrast is less conspicuous among second- and third-generation adherents, who of course did not actually take the conscious step of changing their denominational affiliation.

18   The fact that certain churches had a modernizing orientation was alluded to by Oskar Spate in a confidential memorandum for the British Colonial Office that was prepared at the same time as his influential and controversial report of 1959, which essentially advocated the dismantling of the neotraditional order (Spate 1959). In relation to the conservatism of the Methodist Church, Spate wrote, "There is much more constructive social realism and hope for the future among the Catholics, even perhaps the Seventh Day Adventists, than in the Church which is in effect the Establishment in Fiji" (1990,

112). I would expand on this and suggest that it is precisely their disconnection from the chiefly hierarchy and the tradition it represents that has made these other denominations attractive to discontented Fijians. Though in many instances families and groups who are now Catholic or Adventist may not be radically antitraditional, examination of the reasons why changes of affiliation are made nearly always establishes that some combination of local rivalries and broader ideological factors was at issue; specifically, abandoning Methodism almost always entailed at least hostility to particular chiefs, if not chiefs in general, and some antitraditional stance.

19   It might be added here that the non-Western examples I have used need not have been restricted to Pacific or other "tribal" or rural societies. Jun'ichiro Tanizaki's novels about the twenties and thirties in Japan (especially *The Makioka Sisters* [1957]) work over, with enormous subtlety, dilemmas between tradition and modernity, between a highly objectified construct of the West and an equally reified Japan, that are associated for instance with individualistic freedom on one side and constraint and formality on the other. As is often the case, the contrast between the West and tradition is reproduced internally between modernized and backward domains, in this instance Tokyo and Osaka. It is significant also that, as in the Pacific, the contexts in which foreign and domestic values are reified, and subsequently clash, are paradigmatically to do with sexual ethics and forms of marriage ("my tastes ran to the chic and up-to-date, and I imitated the Western style in everything . . . If I'd had enough money to do whatever I pleased, I might have gone to live in the West and married a Western woman; but my circumstances wouldn't permit that, and I married Naomi, a Japanese woman with a Western flavor" [1986, 58]); similarly the frustrated Kaname in *Some Prefer Nettles*, confined by the failure of a traditional marriage, finds sexual freedom in dealings not with a geisha, but with a Western-educated Eurasian prostitute (1955, 159–71). Presumably because its ambivalence about tradition was taken to be antinationalist, *The Makioka Sisters* was banned during the war.

20   Klaus Neumann's comparison of custom among the Tolai and Tami of Papua New Guinea illustrates this very clearly (Neumann 1992b).

9   Contrasts: Marriage and Identity in Western Fiji

1   *Bure* is standard Fijian (derived from the Bauan dialect); *were vaviji*, the expression in the Noikoro dialect. Most of the conversation through which the information presented here was obtained was in Noikoro.

2   For an account of marriage ceremonies in an area not far from Noikoro see Belshaw 1964; in general, this holds surprisingly well for the 1980s. Teckle (1986) provides valuable information drawn from the cognate (i.e., western Fijian) society of Vatulele; Ravuvu (1987) has provided detailed descriptions of ceremonies in the Wainimala Valley of the eastern interior of Viti Levu. These accounts may be compared with Quain's ethnography from the other large island of Vanua Levu (1948).

3   The groups referred to here as clans are the exogamous *beto* rather than the more inclusive units known as *mataqali*. *Beto* is also the word for the men's house formerly associated with the ancestor spirits of each group and is usually spelled *bito* in other western Fijian dialects. As Hocart (1952) and others have pointed out, *mataqali* is a polysemic

Battaglia, Debbora. 1990. *On the bones of the serpent: Person, memory, and mortality in Sabarl Island society.* Chicago: University of Chicago Press.

Bayly, C. A. 1989. *Imperial meridian: The British empire and the world, 1780–1830.* London: Longman.

Belshaw, C. S. 1964. *Under the ivi tree: Society and economic growth in rural Fiji.* London: Routledge and Kegan Paul.

Benson, C. 1977. *Richness in diversity: An English language book for form 6.* Suva: privately printed.

Bergendorff, Steen, Ulla Hasager, and Peter Henriques. 1988. Mythopraxis and history: On the interpretation of the Makahiki. *Journal of the Polynesian Society* 97:391–408.

Binney, Judith. 1986. Review of *Islands of History,* by Marshall Sahlins. *Journal of the Polynesian Society* 95:527–30.

Borofsky, Robert. 1987. *Making history: Pukapukan and anthropological constructions of knowledge.* Cambridge: Cambridge University Press.

Bourdieu, Pierre. 1977. *Outline of a theory of practice.* Cambridge: Cambridge University Press.

Brady, Ivan. 1985. Review of *Tuvalu. Journal of Pacific History, Bibliography, and Comment,* 52–4.

Brewster, A. B. 1922. *The hill tribes of Fiji.* London: Seeley, Service, and Co.

Brown, George. 1910. *Melanesians and Polynesians: Their life-histories described and compared.* London: Macmillan.

Brunner, Otto, Werner Conze, and Reinhart Koselleck. 1972– . *Geschichtliche Grundbegriffe: Historisches Lexikon zur politischsozialen Sprache in Deutschland.* Stuttgart: Ernst Klett Verlag.

Bryson, Norman. 1983. *Vision and painting: The logic of the gaze.* London: Macmillan.

——. 1989. Chardin and the text of still life. *Critical Inquiry* 15:227–52.

——. 1990. *Looking at the overlooked: Four essays on still life painting.* Cambridge, Mass.: Harvard University Press.

Buchan, John. 1910. *Prester John.* London: Nelson.

Burke, Edmund. 1987. *A philosophical enquiry into the origin of our ideas of the sublime and beautiful.* Ed. and intro. J. T. Boulton. Rev. ed., Oxford: Basil Blackwell.

Burney, Fanny. 1904–05. *Diary and letters of Madame D'Arblay (1778–1840).* 3 vols. Ed. Charlotte Barrett. London: Macmillan.

——. 1988. *Cecilia, or Memories of an heiress.* Ed. Peter Sabor and Margaret Anne Doody. Oxford: Oxford University Press.

Burridge, Kenelm. 1969. *New heaven, new earth: A study of millenarian activities.* Oxford: Basil Blackwell.

Calvert, James. 1884. *Missionary labours among the cannibals.* Published in one volume with *Fiji and the Fijians,* by Thomas Williams. London: Charles H. Kelly.

Cameron, Ian. 1987. *Lost paradise: The exploration of the Pacific.* London: Century Hutchinson.

Campbell, Ian C. 1989. *A history of the Pacific islands.* Berkeley and Los Angeles: University of California Press.

Capell, A. 1941. *A new Fijian dictionary.* Suva: Government Printer.

Cardinal, Roger, and John Elsner, eds. 1994. *The cultures of collecting.* London: Reaktion Books.

Carrier, James G. 1992. Approaches to articulation. In *History and tradition in Melanesian anthropology,* ed. James G. Carrier. Berkeley and Los Angeles: University of California Press.

Chatterjee, Partha. 1984. Gandhi and the critique of civil society. In *Subaltern studies III,* ed. Ranajit Guha. Delhi: Oxford University Press.

——. 1986. *Nationalist thought and the colonial world: A derivative discourse?* London: Zed Books.

Clammer, John. 1973. Colonialism and the perception of tradition in Fiji. In *Anthropology and the colonial encounter,* ed. Talal Asad. London: Ithaca Press.

Clendinnen, Inga. 1987. *Ambivalent conquests: Maya and Spaniard in Yucatan, 1517–1570.* Cambridge: Cambridge University Press.

——. 1991. *Aztecs: An interpretation.* Cambridge: Cambridge University Press.

Clifford, James. 1988. *The predicament of culture: Twentieth-century ethnography, literature, and art.* Cambridge, Mass.: Harvard University Press.

——. 1992. Traveling cultures. In *Cultural Studies,* ed. Lawrence Grossberg, Cary Nelson, and Paula Treichler. New York: Routledge.

Clunie, Fergus. 1986. *Yalo i Viti/Shades of Fiji: A Fiji Museum catalogue.* Suva: Fiji Museum.

Cohn, Bernard S. 1985. The command of language and the language of command. In *Subaltern Studies IV,* ed. Ranajit Guha. Delhi: Oxford University Press.

——. 1987. The census, social structure, and objectification in South Asia. In *An anthropologist among the historians and other essays.* Delhi: Oxford University Press.

Colley, Linda. 1992. *Britons: Forging the nation, 1707–1837.* New Haven, Conn.: Yale University Press.

Comaroff, Jean. 1985. *Body of power, spirit of resistance: The culture and history of a south African people.* Chicago: University of Chicago Press.

Comaroff, Jean, and John Comaroff. 1991. *Of revelation and revolution: Christianity, colonialism, and consciousness in South Africa.* Vol. 1. Chicago: University of Chicago Press.

Connolly, Bob, and Robin Anderson. 1987. *First contact: New Guinea's highlanders encounter the outside world.* Harmondsworth, England: Penguin Books.

Cook, James. 1777. *A voyage towards the South Pole, and round the world. Performed in His Majesty's ships the* Resolution *and* Adventure, *in the years 1772, 1773, 1774, 1775.* 2 vols. London: W. Strahan and T. Cadell.

——. 1955–74. *The journals of Captain James Cook on his voyages of discovery.* 4 vols. Ed. J. C. Beaglehole. Cambridge: Hakluyt Society/Cambridge University Press.

Cook, James, and James King. 1784. *A voyage to the Pacific Ocean.* London: G. Kearsley.

Copley, Stephen, ed. 1984. *Literature and the social order in eighteenth-century England.* London: Croom Helm.

Corris, Peter. 1973. *Passage, port, and plantation: A history of Solomon Islands labour migration, 1870–1914.* Melbourne: Melbourne University Press.

——. 1990a. *The cargo club.* Ringwood, Victoria: Penguin.

——. 1990b. *Naismith's dominion.* Sydney: Bantam.

Dabydeen, David. 1987. *Hogarth's blacks: Images of blacks in eighteenth-century English art.* Manchester: Manchester University Press.

Daniell, Thomas, and William Daniell. 1810. *A picturesque voyage to India, by way of China.* London: Longman.

Darnton, Robert. 1984. *The great cat massacre and other episodes in French cultural history.* New York: Basic Books.

David, Andrew. 1988. *The charts and coastal views of Captain Cook's voyages.* Vol. 1, *The voyage of the Endeavour, 1768–1771.* London: Hakluyt Society.

Davidson, J. W. 1966. Problems of Pacific history. *Journal of Pacific History* 1:5–21.

——. 1967. *Samoa mo Samoa.* Melbourne: Oxford University Press.

——. 1985. On having a culture: Nationalism and the preservation of Quebec's patrimoine. In *Objects and others: Essays on museums and material culture*, ed. George W. Stocking. Madison: University of Wisconsin Press.

Hanlon, David. 1988. *Upon a stone altar: A history of the island of Pohnpei to 1890*. Honolulu: University of Hawaii Press.

Hanson, Allan. 1989. The making of the Maori: Cultural invention and its logic. *American Anthropologist* 91:890–902.

Hartog, François. 1988. *The mirror of Herodotus: The representation of the other in the writing of history*. Berkeley and Los Angeles: University of California Press.

Hau'ofa, Epeli. 1993. Our sea of islands. In *A New Oceania: Rediscovering our sea of islands*, ed. Eric Waddell, Vijay Naidu, and Epeli Hau'ofa. Suva: University of the South Pacific and Beake House.

[Haweis, Thomas]. 1799. Preliminary discourse. In James Wilson, *A missionary voyage to the southern Pacific Ocean . . . in the ship Duff*. London: T. Chapman.

Hawkesworth, John. 1773. *An account of the voyages undertaken by the order of His present Majesty for making discoveries in the southern hemisphere*. London: W. Strahan and T. Cadell.

Hempenstall, Peter. 1984. Review of *Where the waves fall*, by K. R. Howe. *Journal of Pacific History, Bibliography, and Comment* 43–4.

Hempenstall, Peter, and Noel Rutherford. 1984. *Protest and dissent in the colonial Pacific*. Suva: University of the South Pacific.

Hereniko, Vilsoni. 1995. *Woven gods: Female clowns and power in Rotuma*. Honolulu: University of Hawaii Press.

Herzfeld, Michael. 1987. *Anthropology through the looking-glass: Critical ethnography in the margins of Europe*. Cambridge: Cambridge University Press.

——. 1991. *A place in history: Social and monumental time in a Cretan town*. Princeton, N.J.: Princeton University Press.

History of Prince Lee Boo, The. 1844. 19th ed. London: Grant and Griffith.

Hoare, Michael E. 1982. Introduction. In John Reinold Forster, *The Resolution journal of Johann Reinhold Forster*, ed. Michael E. Hoare. London: Hakluyt Society.

Hobsbawm, Eric, and Terence Ranger, eds. 1983. *The invention of tradition*. Cambridge: Cambridge University Press.

Hocart, A. M. 1923. The uterine nephew. *Man* 23:11–3.

——. 1952. *The northern states of Fiji*. London: Royal Anthropological Institute.

Hodges, William. 1785–88. *Select views in India*. London: the author.

Hooper, Antony, and Judith Huntsman, eds. 1985. *Transformations of Polynesian culture*. Auckland: Polynesian Society.

Hooper, S. J. P. 1982. A study of valuables in the chiefdom of Lau. Ph.D. diss., University of Cambridge.

Howe, K. R. 1977. The fate of the "savage" in Pacific historiography. *New Zealand Journal of History* 11:137–54.

——. 1984. *Where the waves fall: A new South Seas Islands history from the first settlement to colonial rule*. Honolulu: University of Hawaii Press.

Hulme, Peter. 1986. *Colonial encounters: Europe and the native Caribbean, 1492–1797*. London: Methuen.

Hume, D. 1882. *Essays, moral, political, and literary.* 2 vols. Ed. T. H. Green and T. H. Grose. London.

Hunt, Lynn, ed. 1989. *The new cultural history.* Berkeley and Los Angeles: University of California Press.

Huntsman, Judith, and Antony Hooper. 1975. Male and female in Tokelau culture. *Journal of the Polynesian Society* 84:415–30.

Hviding, Edward. 1995. *Guardians of Marovo lagoon: Practice, place, and politics in maritime Melanesia.* Honolulu: University of Hawaii Press.

Impey, Oliver, and Arthur MacGregor, eds. 1985. *The origins of museums: The cabinet of curiosities in sixteenth and seventeenth-century Europe.* Oxford: Clarendon Press.

Inden, Ronald. 1990. *Imagining India.* Oxford: Basil Blackwell.

Isaac, Rhys. 1983. *The transformation of Virginia, 1740–1790.* Chapel Hill: University of North Carolina Press.

Johnson, Samuel. 1751. A club of antiquaries. Essay no. 177. *The Rambler,* 26 November.

———. 1968. *Selected writings.* Ed. Patrick Cruttwell. Harmondsworth, England: Penguin.

Jolly, Margaret. 1982. Birds and banyans of South Pentecost: *Kastom* in anti-colonial struggle. In *Reinventing traditional culture: The politics of* kastom *in island Melanesia,* ed. Roger M. Keesing and Robert Tonkinson. Special issue, *Mankind* 13:338–56.

———. 1987. The forgotten women: A history of male migrant labour and gender relations in Vanuatu. *Oceania* 58:119–39.

———. 1991. "To save the girls for brighter and better lives": Presbyterian missions and women in the south of Vanuatu, 1848–1870. *Journal of Pacific History* 26:27–48.

———. 1992a. Custom and the way of the land: Past and present in Vanuatu and Fiji. In *The politics of tradition in the Pacific,* ed. Margaret Jolly and Nicholas Thomas. Special issue, *Oceania* 62:330–54.

———. 1992b. "Ill-natured comparisons": Racism and relativism in European representations of ni-Vanuatu from Cook's second voyage. *History and Anthropology* 5:331–64.

———. 1992c. Spectres of inauthenticity. *Contemporary Pacific* 4:49–72.

Jolly, Margaret, and Martha Macintyre. 1989. Introduction. In *Family and gender in the Pacific: Domestic contradictions and the colonial impact,* ed. Margaret Jolly and Martha Macintyre. Cambridge: Cambridge University Press.

Jolly, Margaret, and Mark Mosko, eds. 1995. *Transformations of hierarchy: Structure, history, and horizon in the Austronesian world.* Special issue, *History and Anthropology* 7. 1–410.

Jones, Owen. 1856. *The grammar of ornament.* London: Day and Son.

Joppien, Rudiger, and Bernard Smith. 1985–87. *The art of Captain Cook's voyages.* 3 vols. New Haven, Conn.: Yale University Press.

Kaeppler, Adrienne L., ed. 1978. *Cook voyage artifacts in Leningrad, Berne, and Florence museums.* Honolulu: Bishop Museum Press.

Kaplan, Martha. 1989. *Luve ni wai* as the British saw it: Constructions of custom and disorder in colonial Fiji. *Ethnohistory* 36:349–71.

———. 1990a. Christianity, people of the land, and chiefs in Fiji. In *The ethnography of Christianity in the Pacific,* ed. J. Barker. Lanham, Md.: University Press of America.

———. 1990b. Meaning, agency, and colonial history: Navosavakadua and the Tuka movement in Fiji. *American Ethnologist* 17:1–20.

Musil, Robert. 1953. *The man without qualities*. London: Secker and Warburg.

Na ekelesia katolika mai Viti. 1936. Lyons: Emmanuel Vitte.

Narokobi, Bernard. 1980. *The Melanesian way: Total cosmic vision of life*. Port Moresby: Institute of Papua New Guinea Studies.

Nash, Manning. 1989. *The cauldron of ethnicity in the modern world*. Chicago: University of Chicago Press.

Neale, Caroline. 1985. *Writing "independent" history: African historiography, 1960–1980*. Westport, Conn.: Greenwood Press.

Nelson, Hank. 1976. *Black, white, and gold: Goldmining in Papua New Guinea, 1878–1930*. Canberra: Australian National University Press.

Neumann, Klaus. 1992a. *Not the way it really was: Constructing the Tolai past*. Honolulu: University of Hawaii Press.

——. 1992b. Tradition and identity in Papua New Guinea: Some observations regarding Tami and Tolai. In *The politics of tradition in the Pacific*, ed. Margaret Jolly and Nicholas Thomas. Special issue, *Oceania* 62:295–316.

Nicolson, Malcolm. 1988. Medicine and racial politics: Changing images of the New Zealand Maori in the nineteenth century. In *Imperial medicine and indigenous societies*, ed. David Arnold. Manchester: Manchester University Press.

Obeysekere, G. 1992a. *The apotheosis of Captain Cook: European mythmaking in the Pacific*. Princeton: Princeton University Press.

——. 1992b. "British cannibals": Contemplation of an event in the death and resurrection of James Cook, explorer. *Critical Inquiry* 18:630–55.

Ortner, Sherry B. 1984. Theory in anthropology since the sixties. *Comparative Studies in Society and History* 26:126–66.

Osbeck, Peter. 1771. *Voyage to China and the East Indies*, trans. J. R. Forster. London: B. White.

Otto, Ton. 1992a. The Paliau movement in Manus and the objectification of tradition. In *Colonialism and culture*, ed. Nicholas Thomas. Special issue, *History and Anthropology* 5:427–54.

——. 1992b. The ways of *kastom:* Tradition as category and practice in a Manus village. In *The politics of tradition in the Pacific*, ed. Margaret Jolly and Nicholas Thomas. Special issue, *Oceania* 62:264–83.

——. 1996. After the "tidal wave": Bernard Narokobi and the creation of a Melanesian way. In *Narratives of nation in the South Pacific*, ed. N. Thomas and T. Otto. Chur, Switzerland, and Reading, England: Harwood Academic Publishers.

Overton, J. 1988. A Fijian peasantry: *Galala* and villagers. *Oceania* 58:193–211.

Parkinson, Sydney. 1784. *Journal of a voyage in the South Seas in H.M.S. Endeavour*. London: C. Dilly.

Pickering, P. 1986. A closet revolutionary. Review *The real life of Alejandro Mayta*, by Mario Vargas Llosa. *New Society*, 3 October, p. 30.

Pocock, J. G. A. 1975. *The Machiavellian moment: Florentine political thought and the Atlantic republican tradition*. Princeton, N.J.: Princeton University Press.

Pomian, Kryzstof. 1990. *Collectors and curiosities*. Cambridge: Polity Press.

Pratt, Mary Louise. 1992. *Imperial eyes: Travel writing and transculturation*. London: Routledge.

Price, Sally. 1989. *Primitive art in civilized places*. Chicago: University of Chicago Press.

Prichard, James Cowles. 1836–47. *Researches into the physical history of mankind.* 3d ed. 5 vols. London: Sherwood, Gilbert, and Piper.

Quain, B. 1948. *Fijian village.* Chicago: University of Chicago Press.

Quiros, de Pedro Fernandez. 1904–05. *The voyages of Pedro Fernandez de Quiros, 1595 to 1606,* ed. C. Markham. London: Hakluyt Society.

Ralston, C. 1983. Review of *Where the waves fall,* by K. R. Howe. *Pacific Studies* 9:155–60.

Raven, James. 1992. *Judging new wealth: Popular publishing and responses to commerce in England, 1750–1800.* Oxford: Clarendon Press.

Ravuvu, Asesela. 1987. *The Fijian ethos.* Suva: Institute for Pacific Studies.

———. 1988. *Development or dependence: The pattern of change in a Fijian village.* Suva: Institute for Pacific Studies.

Rey, H. A. 1954. *Curious George takes a job.* Boston: Houghton Mifflin.

Reynolds, Henry. 1981. *The other side of the frontier.* Ringwood, Victoria: Penguin.

———. 1987. *Frontier.* Sydney: Allen and Unwin.

Reynolds, Joshua. 1878. *The literary works of Sir Joshua Reynolds.* London: George Bell.

Rickman, John. 1781. *Journal of Captain Cook's last voyage.* London: E. Newbery.

Rienzi, J. L. Domeny de. 1836–37. *Océanie ou la cinquième partie du monde.* Paris: Didot.

Rivers, W. H. R. 1914. *The history of Melanesian society.* 2 vols. Cambridge: Cambridge University Press.

Robertson, Robert T., and Akosita Tamanisau. 1988. *Fiji: Shattered coups.* Leichhardt, N.S.W.: Pluto Press.

Robertson, William. 1777. *The history of America.* 2 vols. London: W. Strahan.

Robie, David. 1989. *Blood on their banner: Nationalist struggles in the South Pacific.* London: Zed Books.

Rokotuiviwa, P. 1985. The congregation of the poor: Fiji. In *New Religious movements in Melanesia,* ed. Carl Loeliger and Garry Trompf. Suva and Port Moresby: University of the South Pacific and University of Papua New Guinea.

Routledge, David. 1985a. *Matanitu: The struggle for power in early Fiji.* Suva: Institute of Pacific Studies.

———. 1985b. Pacific history as seen from the Pacific islands. *Pacific Studies* 8:81–99.

Ruskin, John. 1898. *Modern painters.* 5 vols. London: George Allen and Unwin.

Rutz, Henry. 1978. Ceremonial exchange and economic development in village Fiji. *Economic Development and Cultural Change* 26:777–805.

———. 1987. Capitalizing on culture: Moral ironies in urban Fiji. *Comparative Studies in Society and History* 29:532–57.

Sahlins, Marshall. 1962. *Moala: Culture and nature on a Fijian island.* Ann Arbor: University of Michigan Press.

———. 1963. Poor man, rich man, big-man, chief: Political types in Melanesia and Polynesia. *Comparative Studies in Society and History* 5:285–303.

———. 1981. *Historical metaphors and mythical realities: Structure in the early history of the Sandwich Islands kingdom.* Ann Arbor: University of Michigan Press.

———. 1985. *Islands of history.* Chicago: University of Chicago Press.

———. 1989. Captain Cook at Hawaii. *Journal of the Polynesian Society* 98:371–425.

———. 1993. Cery cery fuckabede. *American Ethnologist* 20:848–67.

——. 1989. Drinking cash: The purification of money through ceremonial exchange in Fiji. In *Money and the morality of exchange*, ed. Jonathan Parry and Maurice Bloch. Cambridge: Cambridge University Press.

——. 1990. *Making sense of hierarchy: Cognition as social process*. London: Athlone Press.

Vakatora, Tomasi. 1988. *From the mangrove swamps*. Suva: Institute of Pacific Studies.

Valentia, Viscount George Annesley. 1809. *Voyages and travels in India, Ceylon, the Red Sea, Abyssinia, and Egypt, in the years 1802 . . . 1806.* 3 vols. London: William Miller.

van Rymsdyk, John, and Andrew van Ramsdyk. 1791. *Museum Brittanicum: or, A display in thirty two plates, of antiquities and natural curiosities, in that noble and magnificent cabinet, the British Museum, after the original design from nature.* 2d ed. London: J. Moore.

van Wyk Smith, M. 1992. "The most wretched of the human race": The iconography of the Khoikhoin (Hottentots) 1500–1800. *History and Anthropology* 5:285–330.

Vargas Llosa, Mario. 1986. *The real life of Alejandro Mayta*. London: Faber and Faber.

Wagner, Roy. 1981. *The invention of culture*. Chicago: University of Chicago Press.

Wallis, Mary David. 1851. *Life in Feejee; or, Five years among the cannibals, by a lady*. Boston: W. Heath.

Webber, James. 1808. *Views in the south seas. From drawings by the late James Webber, draftsman on board the Resolution*, London: Boydell and Co.

Wendt, Albert, ed. 1980. *Lali: A Pacific anthology*. Suva: Institute for Pacific Studies.

——. 1995. *Nuanua: Pacific writing in English since 1980*. Auckland: Auckland University Press.

West, Francis James. 1961. *Political advancement in the South Pacific: A comparative study of colonial practice in Fiji, Tahiti, and American Samoa*. Melbourne: Oxford University Press.

White, Geoffrey M., and Lamont Lindstrom, eds. 1989. *The Pacific theater: Islands representations of World War II*. Honolulu: University of Hawaii Press.

White, Hayden. 1973. *Metahistory: The historical imagination in nineteenth-century Europe*. Baltimore: Johns Hopkins University Press.

Wilkes, Charles. 1845. *Narrative of the United States exploring expedition*. Philadelphia: Lea and Blanchard.

Williams, John. 1984. *The Samoan journals of John Williams, 1830 and 1832*. Ed. and intro. Richard Moyle. Canberra: Australian National University Press.

Williams, Thomas. 1858. *Fiji and the Fijians*. Ed. G. S. Rowe. 2 vols. London: A. Heylin.

Withey, Lynne. 1987. *Voyages of discovery: Captain Cook and the exploration of the Pacific*. New York: Morrow.

Worsley, Peter. 1957. *The trumpet shall sound: A study of "cargo" cults in Melanesia*. London: Paladin.

Wraxall, N. 1775. *Cursory remarks made in a tour through some of the northern parts of Europe*. London: T. Cadell.

Films Cited

Black Harvest. 1992. Bob Connolly and Robin Anderson. 90 min. Australia: Ronin Films.

Citizen Kane. 1941. Orson Welles. 119 min. USA: Mercury/RKO Radio Pictures.

Dances With Wolves. 1990. Kevin Costner. 224 min./180 min. USA: Majestic Film/TIG Productions (distributed by Orion Pictures).

First Contact. 1983. Bob Connolly and Robin Anderson. 54 mins. Australia: Ronin Films.

Joe Leahy's Neighbours. 1989. Bob Connolly and Robin Anderson. 90 min. Australia: Ronin Films.

Key Largo. 1948. John Huston. 101 min. USA: Warner Bros.

Notebook on Cities and Clothes [*Aufzeichnungen zu Kleidern und Staedten*]. 1989. Wim Wenders. 79 min. West Germany: Centre national d'art et de culture / Road movies filmproduktion.

Trobriand Cricket. 1979. Gary Kildea. 53 min. Australia: Ronin Films.

Categorization: of colonizers, 206; of indigenous societies, 81–86, 87, 92, 106, 113, 133–52, 190–91, 194–96, 199–201

Chambers, Harold, 58–59

Chieftainship: character of, in Fiji, 51, 52, 55, 175, 176, 182, 200–201; marker of Polynesia, in ethnological characterizations, 133–34, 152; in Oceania, 191; opposition to, in Fiji, 54, 55, 202, 205

Christianity, in Oceania, 50–51, 61, 62, 63, 149, 151, 154–55, 166, 177, 182, 193, 195, 197–98, 231, 203–4, 212, 220, 225, 227

Class, 42, 47, 65, 93, 109, 165–66

Classification systems. *See* Categorization

Clifford, James, 26

Climate: in Enlightenment thought, 82–83; in classifying societies, 82–83, 92

Cohn, Bernard, 199

Collecting, 23, 96–97, 100, 102, 105–9, 110–11, 113, 115–17, 125, 129, 131

Colley, Linda, 14, 94

Colonial government, 52, 54–55, 59, 61, 177, 180–83, 197–201, 222

Colonialism: anthropology and history of, 12–13, 36, 38–39, 43, 46–47, 48–49, 96, 153, 156, 163–64, 186, 190, 195, 208–9; in Fiji, 54–55, 172–183, 225; in Oceania, 32, 126, 128, 190–91, 194–209, 227

Colonial representation: theories of, 71–72, 133

Colonizers, culture of, 38–39, 41, 97, 177, 196–97, 180–81, 227

Colo West, 58, 59

Commerce: categorization of societies by, 148; eighteenth-century attitudes to, 87, 108–9, 148; indigenous engagement in, 37, 87–89, 101, 178, 182, 191, 194–205, 210–20, 232, 233; political context of, 108–9; and tradition, 220–26. *See also* Prestation; Trade

Communal obligation, 210–18, 220–24

Community, idea of, 186–87, 189, 222–23

Comparative anthropology: eighteenth-century conceptions, 82–85, 92

Conjugal relations: eighteenth century-

concepts of, 76–77, 79, 80–81, 87; Enlightenment concepts of, 72

Connolly, Bob, 23–27, 41

Contact, 11, 13, 36, 126–28, 135, 190, 193–97, 209; historiography of, 37–38, 41, 42, 49. *See also* Fatal impact thesis

Cook, James, 1, 37, 73, 75, 79, 87, 96, 101, 106, 137

Cook voyages, 72–83, 85–87, 89–92, 101, 105–6, 109–11, 118–25, 128, 135–38, 148–49, 194

Corris, Peter, 157–64, 166–67

Corrupting influence: of curiosity, 106–7, 114; of luxury, 109; of material goods, 101, 148

Creolization, 38. *See* Hybridity

Cross-cultural comparison, 12, 187–95, 202–9, 223–27. *See also* Categorization of indigenous societies

Cross-cultural history, writing of, 29–32, 39–42, 54

Cultural history, 33–34, 39, 42, 67, 186–92

Cultural practices: priority of, in Fijian culture, 176, 192; analysis of, 189, 230

Culture: codification of, 64, 67, 199, 204, 207; concept of, 38–39, 51–52, 67; construction of, 186–200; objectification of, 48, 64, 186–209 *passim*; rights to representation of, 10–11, 47–49, 129–32; unitary notions of, 40–42, 45

Curiosities, 111; artifacts as, 89, 97, 100, 101, 106–9, 111–21; islanders as, 1, 97, 100; and promiscuity, 115–16

Curiosity: 16, 100, 106–109, 113–114, 119, 121, 131; and travel, 106–9

Custom, 63, 64, 66, 187–206; categorization of societies by, 150, 152; exclusion from, 50–51; formation of, 186–205; interpretation of, 51–52, 84, 92, 151; recording of, 128, 199. *See also* Fiji: customs; Samoa: history and culture; Tonga: history and culture; Tradition: inversion of

Davidson, J. W., 30–32, 36

Davis, Tom, 5

Nicholas Thomas is Director of the Centre for Cross-Cultural Research at the Australian National University. He has conducted research in Fiji, the Marquesas, and Aotearoa New Zealand, and written widely on colonial culture, Pacific history and anthropology, and contemporary art. His books include *Entangled Objects* (Harvard, 1991), *Colonialism's Culture* (Polity and Princeton, 1994), and *Oceanic Art* (Thames and Hudson, 1995).

Library of Congress Cataloging-in-Publication Data
Thomas, Nicholas.
In Oceania : visions, artifacts, histories / Nicholas Thomas.
Includes bibliographical references and index.
ISBN 0-8223-2002-9 (acid-free paper).
ISBN 0-8223-1998-5 (pbk. : acid-free paper)
1.Ethnology—Oceania. 2.Material culture—Oceania.
3.Oceania—History. 4.Oceania—Social life and customs.
5.Oceania—Antiquities. I. Title.   GN662.T6   1997
306'.0995—dc21   96-54634 CIP